2023

上海虹桥国际中央商务区
发展报告

2023 Annual Report on Development of
Shanghai Hongqiao International CBD

上海虹桥国际中央商务区管理委员会　编

编审委员会

主　　任	钟晓咏
副 主 任	付乃恂　张　斌　胡志宏
	陈伟利　金国军
顾　　问	薛全荣　闵师林
成　　员	（按姓氏笔画排序）
	卫爱民　刘　飞　刘　涛　李毓纲　杨旭波　吴岳俊
	何泽岗　陈钟宇　赵　俊　贾开京　徐明生

编写工作组

主　　编	付乃恂
执 行 主 编	刘　涛
执行副主编	刘　骏
组 织 编 写	熊员文　段　瑾　万　杰　蔡斯绘
编 写 成 员	（按姓氏笔画排序）
	毛敬宽　朱小玲　宋吉祥　张　超　张可涵　张昆仑
	钮　涛　郑　汉　钱威丞　钱晨晨　徐　立　高婉莹
	曹　玫　谢安娜

序

2023年是全面贯彻落实党的二十大精神的开局之年。这一年，国家发展改革委印发《关于推动虹桥国际开放枢纽进一步提升能级的若干政策措施》（简称《若干政策措施》），这是继2021年《虹桥国际开放枢纽建设总体方案》（简称《总体方案》）落地之后的一次重大政策升级。上海市政府常务会议审议通过《高质量推进虹桥国际中央商务区建设三年行动计划（2023—2025）》《加快提升虹桥国际中央商务区服务企业"走出去"能级的若干措施》等文件，为上海虹桥国际中央商务区（简称商务区）建设发展充分授权赋能。

商务区深入贯彻党中央、国务院和市委市政府决策部署，紧扣一体化、高质量和国际化，进一步深化战略内涵认识研究，加强流量价值挖掘创造，推动总部经济能级提升，深化贸易功能内涵拓展，加强城市更新和基础设施支持，加快建设国家级进口贸易促进创新示范区、创建"丝路电商"合作先行区辐射引领区和打造本市生产性互联网服务平台集聚区，持续做大经济规模、做强核心功能、做高经济密度，巩固和放大多重国家战略叠加赋能优势，推动虹桥国际开放枢纽"一核两带"协同发展、相互赋能，不断提高商务区整体标识度和核心竞争力。

这一年，商务区准确把握自身定位和比较优势，紧盯经济倍增目标，高频度精准性"走出去"招商引资，深入实施虹桥国际商务伙伴计划，会同四区到北广深等地举办企业家圆桌会，开展"潮涌浦江 投资虹桥"等一系列高能级投资促进活动，推进商务区"走出去"功能平台实体化运作，做强国际经济组织集聚区，强化资源禀赋打造总部经济新格局，推动产业项目引领集聚，商务区经济发展呈现持续增长的良好态势。同时，加快推进城市配套建设，进一步完善区域交通体系，优化提升上海市"一带一路"综合服务中心、虹桥海外贸易中心、虹桥RCEP企业服务咨询站等功能平台，持续推动虹桥国际商务人才港、人力资源产业园虹桥园和虹桥国际中央法务区建设，强化优质公共服务供给，全方位提升服务长三角和联通国际能力。

商务区承载着多项国家战略，面对新的使命任务，商务区新时代发展必须用好国家战略赋予的政策地位、双向扇面的区位禀赋、综合枢纽带来的流量价值等优势，聚焦空间布局、功能平台、主导产业再提升再深化再优化，更好扬优势、拉长板、强特色，力争到2035年将商务区打造成为国家高水平对外开放的功能平台、长三角一体化高质量发展的排头兵、新发展阶段改革创新的试验田、高标准国际化中央商务区的标杆，努力在贯彻落实国家战略中当好践行改革开放排头兵、创新发展先行者。

本书的编撰，得到了上海社会科学院专业团队的支持。希望通过《2023上海虹桥国际中央商务区发展报告》这本书，让更多的人了解虹桥、关注虹桥、选择虹桥、热爱虹桥，与我们一起共创美好未来。

上海虹桥国际中央商务区管理委员会　党组书记　常务副主任

目　　录

序 I

第一章　经济高质量增长 001
 第一节　背景形势 001
 第二节　经济运行 003
 第三节　招商引资 007
 第四节　虹桥效应 011

第二章　国际化中央商务区 014
 第一节　深化战略内涵认识研究 014
 第二节　推进虹桥国际开放枢纽建设 022
 第三节　构建现代服务业集聚区 029
 第四节　提升总部经济能级 036
 第五节　赋能数字新经济 039
 第六节　打造一流城市品质 043

第三章　国际贸易中心新平台 048
 第一节　"丝路电商"合作先行区 048
 第二节　内外贸一体化 053
 第三节　助力企业"走出去" 056
 第四节　生产性互联网服务平台 060
 第五节　上海西片国际级消费集聚区 065

第四章	第六届中国国际进口博览会	070
	第一节　基本概况	070
	第二节　配套保障	081
	第三节　进博会溢出效应	085
	第四节　2023虹桥HUB大会	089

第五章	四大片区协同发展	094
	第一节　闵行片区	094
	第二节　长宁片区	101
	第三节　青浦片区	108
	第四节　嘉定片区	115

第六章	标志性CBD城市更新	122
	第一节　制定标志性CBD建设方案	122
	第二节　建立健全标志性CBD城市更新组织框架	127
	第三节　制定城市更新项目清单	130
	第四节　推进城市更新重点项目	133

第七章	精细化管理示范区	142
	第一节　建设和谐自然的品质城区	142
	第二节　提供高效便捷的交通服务	146
	第三节　推动绿色生态治理	152
	第四节　打造一街一景特色街道	157
	第五节　推进综合养护一体化	165

第八章	国际一流营商环境	169
	第一节　营商环境评估及体系构建	169
	第二节　跨区域的企业服务平台体系建设	175
	第三节　专业服务要素资源集聚与功能平台建设	178

第四节　企业产业链、生态圈构建及互动平台搭建 184

第五节　商务区人才高地核心区建设及人才服务提升 188

第六节　打造环境友好型宜商宜业商务区 193

附录 1　虹桥国际中央商务区大事记 203

附录 2　国家发展改革委《关于推动虹桥国际开放枢纽进一步提升能级的若干政策措施》 207

《2023 上海虹桥国际中央商务区发展报告》英译（节选） 211

第一章 经济高质量增长

第一节 背景形势

2023年是全面贯彻党的二十大精神的开局之年。习近平总书记在中共中央政治局会议上强调，实现新时代新征程的目标任务，要把全面深化改革作为推进中国式现代化的根本动力，作为稳大局、应变局、开新局的重要抓手，把准方向、守正创新、真抓实干，在新征程上谱写改革开放新篇章；要把发挥政策效力和激发经营主体活力结合起来，形成推动高质量发展的强大动力，推动经济实现质的有效提升和量的合理增长；要用好政策空间、找准发力方向，扎实推动经济高质量发展。

2023年，中国经济呈现企稳回升态势，回归常态化运行轨道，市场预期加快好转。消费和生产活动恢复正常，消费潜力逐步释放，服务业向好发展，增长动能持续增强，高质量发展的步伐稳健有力。数据显示，2023年前三季度受益于服务业的快速复苏，工业部门强劲发展、服务业增加值增速快于GDP总体增长，全球贸易触底反弹，中国经济彰显了超强的韧性。随着居民收入的改善，叠加政策支持和消费意愿的回升，消费对经济的拉动作用继续增强。创新动能持续赋能经济增长，绿色转型步伐加快将对我国经济发展注入新动力。尽管外部环境更趋复杂严峻，国内经济发展也面临压力，但我国经济长期向好的基本面没有改变，韧性强、潜力大、活力足的特点没有改变，支撑高质量发展的条件也没有改变。随着促进发展的积极因素累积增多，经济有望继续恢复向好。

2018年以来，已成功举办6届的中国国际进口博览会（简称进博会），依托中国大市场优势，发挥国际采购、投资促进、人文交流、开放合作平台功能，对加快构建新发展格局和推动世界经济发展作出了积极贡献。进博会将加快提升构建新发展格局的窗口功能，以中国新发展为世界提供新机遇；充分发挥推动高水平开放的平台作用，让中国大市场成为世界共享的大市场；更好提供全球共享的国际公共产品服务，助力推动构建开放型世界经济，让合作共赢惠及世界。

虹桥国际开放枢纽是中央推动长三角一体化发展的重大战略，也是我国对外开放战略的重要组成部分。作为虹桥国际开放枢纽"一核两带"发展格局的核心承载区，商务区在《总体方案》出台两年以来，"大商务"功能进一步提升，围绕做强优势产业、做大经济规模，商务区集聚一批国内外高能级企业、机构、平台，力争体现经济发展高密度、高质量、高产出、高效益。"大会展"功能进一步强化，充分发挥作为进博会永久举办地的平台优势和溢出效应，加快集聚国际国内高端展览会议，着力拓展会展产业内涵，推动"大会展"成为服务国内外企业抢占全球贸易制高点的战略支撑。"大交通"功能进一步夯实，商务区内外交通联结更加通畅，流量和要素聚合，以虹桥综合交通枢纽为核心的长三角主要城市群与国际交流更趋密切，综合运输一体化推进发展，"空铁联运"产品开通苏浙皖大部分城市。"大科创"功能进一步做实，商务区围绕优势产业，加快集聚市场化创新主体，科技创新策源能力持续增强，跨区域创新协作机制逐步形成，产业发展与科技创新耦合共生。

商务区正紧扣一体化、高质量和国际化，"引进来"和"走出去"两手抓，进一步打开发展和辐射的扇面，提高整体标识度和核心竞争力。加快"引进来"通道拓展，着力发挥世界级流量入口优势，放大进博会溢出效应，加快布局数字贸易、服务贸易新蓝海，建设高能级贸易主体首选地，吸引集聚更多国际贸易功能性机构落地，加快推进"丝路电商"合作先行区、国家服务贸易创新发展示范区创建，打造进出口商品集散地和进口贸易促进创新示范区。建立完善"走出去"的政策服务体系，做实支持企业国际化发展的虹桥海外贸易中心、虹桥国际商务人才港、虹桥国际中央法务区等一批综合性服务平台，加快发展生产性服务业，以专业综合的服务支撑，更好成为企业进军海外市场的重要通道和基地。强化大交通、大商务、大会展、大科创功能，发展高能级总部经济、高流量贸易经济、高端化服务经济、高层次会展经济，全力打造功能复合型国际化中央商务区和国际贸易中心新平台，更好服务构建新发展格局，为高水平制度型开放打好基础，形成部市协同、区域协同、市区协同的合力，促进改革举措早落地，更多总部型企业和高能级企业落户商务区，助力虹桥高质量发展。

第二节　经济运行

2023年，商务区按照市委市政府工作要求，紧扣一体化、高质量和国际化，持续做大经济规模、做强核心功能、做高经济密度，在政策制度创新、总部经济集聚、功能平台建设等方面实现新突破，不断巩固和放大多重国家战略叠加赋能优势，提高商务区整体标识度和核心竞争力，经济工作取得阶段性成效。

一、全力推动经济增长

2023年，商务区积极抓好总部经济能级提升，推动产业项目引领集聚，保持高频度走出去招商，全力扩大和促进消费，经济倍增目标取得阶段性成效。按自然口径计算，商务区1—12月实现税收收入473.32亿元，同比增长52.8%。

表1-1　2023年虹桥国际中央商务区自然口径税收收入　　　　　　单位：亿元

区　域	2021年	2022年	2023年	平均增幅（%）
商务区	342.47	309.84	473.32	17.6
闵行片区	64.67	68.29	100.15	24.4
长宁片区	131.83	96.43	188.35	19.5
青浦片区	100.67	103.32	124.52	11.2
嘉定片区	45.3	41.8	60.3	15.4

二、举办系列投资促进活动

2023年，商务区进一步深化"1+1+4+X"联合招商工作体系，深入实施商务伙伴计划，持续保持高频度、精准性走出去招商，靶向发力、招大引强，先后赴北广深等地开展约20场企业家圆桌会，组织举办"潮涌浦江　投资虹桥"投资促进大会和"虹桥财经汇""大虹桥企业家论坛"等一系列高能级投资促进活动。全年商务区实现固定资产投资额484.26亿元，外商投资合同金额33.05万亿美元，同比增长43.3%，外商投资实际到位金额4.77万亿美元。

表1-2 2023年虹桥国际中央商务区固定资产投资额　　　　单位：亿元

区　域	2021年	2022年	2023年	平均增幅（%）
商务区	511.55	497.46	484.26	-1.4
闵行片区	119.3	127.49	129.1	3.4
长宁片区	85.65	98.58	105.8	7.3
青浦片区	237.3	210.39	194.86	-5.8
嘉定片区	69.3	61	54.5	-6.2

三、激发消费新活力

2023年，商务区全力推进上海西片国际级消费集聚区建设，不断在挖掘消费热点、创新消费场景上下功夫，相继推出"元气虹桥　全球GO""五五购物节""虹桥数字黑科技嘉年华""四叶草55生活节""汽车嘉年华""虹桥天地嗨购节"等消费活动，培育消费新功能，激发消费新活力。五一期间，虹桥天地总销售额4 234万元，客流量超57万人次；蟠龙天地开业后总销售额超2 500万元，客流量超110万人次。暑期期间，虹桥天地总销售额近3亿元，客流量689万人次；蟠龙天地总销售额超1.3亿元，客流量400万人次。中秋国庆期间，虹桥天地总销售额4 188万元，客流量101万人次；蟠龙天地总销售额3 100万元、客流量133万人次。

1—12月，商务区实现社会消费品零售额651.23亿元，同比增长10.1%；商品销售额4 641.36亿元，同比增长8.2%。

表1-3 2023年虹桥国际中央商务区消费市场情况　　　　单位：亿元

区　域	社会消费品零售额				商品销售额			
	2021年	2022年	2023年	平均增幅（%）	2021年	2022年	2023年	平均增幅（%）
商务区	534.62	523.58	651.23	10.4	4 582.19	4 056.12	4 641.36	0.6
闵行片区	269.18	271.69	240.87	-5.4	1 770.92	1 519.3	1 764.09	-0.2

续 表

区 域	社会消费品零售额				商品销售额			
	2021年	2022年	2023年	平均增幅（%）	2021年	2022年	2023年	平均增幅（%）
长宁片区	83.6	73.3	164.05	40.1	2 004.3	1 869.2	2 004.55	0
青浦片区	87.54	101.69	148.41	30.2	428.72	428.72	548.42	13.1
嘉定片区	94.3	76.9	97.9	1.9	238.9	238.9	324.3	16.5

四、促进国际贸易创新发展

商务区以国家进口贸易促进创新示范区建设为契机，持续承接和放大进博会溢出效应，深化推进一批交易类、服务贸易类、贸易支撑类国际贸易中心功能平台，虹桥进口商品展示交易中心、新虹桥国际医学中心、虹桥海外贸易中心、虹桥国际会展产业园等能级持续提升。围绕会展经济、总部经济、服务经济等打造特色产业园区，高端医疗服务贸易、离岸贸易、数字贸易、跨境电商等新型贸易形态创新发展。

1—12月，完成货物进出口额759.34亿元，同比增长27.9%。其中货物进口额完成531.78亿元，同比增长27.7%；货物出口额完成227.56亿元，同比增长28.3%。

表1-4 2023年虹桥国际中央商务区进出口总额

区 域	2022年1—12月	2023年1—12月	同 比
商务区进口商品总额	416.59	531.78	27.7%
商务区出口商品总额	177.33	227.56	28.3%
商务区进出口商品总额	593.92	759.34	27.9%

五、推动产业发展壮大

商务区积极推动产业链、供应链、贸易链不断畅通，功能优势不断放大。东航、圆通、安踏等总部类企业业务规模得到恢复和增长，美的、天合光能、正大天晴、康德莱医械等一批重大项目形成产业引领，阳光电源、晶科绿能、锅圈等重点企业群不断壮大，成为推动区域发展重要动能。1—12月，规模以上信息传输、软件和信息技术服务业营业收入337.08亿元，同比增长29%；规模以上租赁和商务服务业营业收入615.52亿元，同比增长29.3%；规模以上科学研究和技术服务业营业收入75.53亿元，同比增长8.7%；规模以上工业总产值471.09亿元，同比增长2.6%。

六、加速集聚市场主体

商务区充分用好贸易型企业总部和民营企业总部政策，加大贸易型企业总部和民营总部、外资研发中心引进力度，加快打造长三角民营企业总部集聚区，经济活力不断迸发，市场主体加速集聚。1—12月，新增法人企业数10 490家（其中内资10 258家，外资232家），累计法人企业数64 050家（其中内资61 070家、外资2 980家）。

表1-5　2023年虹桥国际中央商务区法人企业数　　　　　　　　单位：户

区　域	2023年新增法人企业数			截至2023年底累计法人企业数		
	内资	外资	合计	内资	外资	合计
商务区	10 258	232	10 490	61 070	2 980	64 050
闵行片区	4 294	114	4 408	23 107	1 053	24 160
长宁片区	1 653	75	1 728	9 411	1 197	10 608
青浦片区	1 302	19	1 321	9 258	396	9 654
嘉定片区	3 009	24	3 033	19 294	334	19 628

第三节　招商引资

深入实施虹桥国际商务伙伴计划，强化"1+1+4+X"联合招商工作体系，持续保持高频度、精准性走出去招商，加快吸引和集聚各类总部企业高端商贸要素，打响"投资虹桥"品牌。

一、持续深化走出去招商

商务区充分发挥国际商务伙伴作用，凝聚四区合力"走出去"招大引强，赴成都、深圳、北京、厦门、泉州、海口、宁波、烟台、绍兴、广州、武汉主办了企业家圆桌会活动约20场，共同引进国内外优秀的链主企业、"锚"企业和各类总部企业。累计超300家企业参会，会后，各片区建立专人对接机制，持续做好项目跟踪和对接，其中近80家企业正在对接商洽或已开工、注册落地。

2023年3月31日，"'共享虹桥国际开放枢纽建设机遇'福建企业家圆桌会"在福州举办。会上，有关领导详细介绍了虹桥国际开放枢纽、长三角一体化、进博会等国家战略赋能，擘画未来虹桥发展蓝图，上海虹桥国际中央商务区管理委员会（简称管委会）相关职能部门作《共享虹桥机遇共创美好未来》主题推介。活动吸引了30余家企业参会，涵盖数字经济、国际贸易、高端制造等领域，与会企业家与商务区及闵行、青浦片区有关负责人进行热切交流，为福建的企业家开启了一扇投资兴业的机会之门。

6月15日，"长三角企业家圆桌会·宁波"顺利召开。商务区及长宁、嘉定片区和近30位宁波企业家相聚一堂，共同探讨合作机遇。在国家长三角一体化大战略布局中，虹桥与宁波的合作可以"互拉长板、互相赋能"，潜力巨大。会上，政府与企业进行了面对面交流，企业代表们对未来的合作充满信心，9家企业产生洽谈或投资意向。

8月25日，"长三角企业家圆桌会·绍兴"成功举办，吸引了来自生物医药、电子信息、智能制造等领域的20余位优秀企业家参会，管委会相关领导做了致辞和主题推介，闵行片区和嘉定片区进行投资环境介绍，到会企业家就所在产业、营商环境、政策扶持力度、国际化发展、遇到的瓶颈问题等与政府进行了面对面交流。

9月12日，"深圳企业家圆桌会"顺利举办。管委会相关同志围绕共享虹桥机遇作

图 1-1　深圳企业家圆桌会

主题分享。青浦、闵行片区分别介绍了各自片区的投资环境。圆桌会吸引了来自人工智能、航空、元宇宙、时尚消费、生命健康等不同领域30余位企业家参会，现场就产业发展情况、数字经济支持政策、人才政策等与政府进了沟通交流。

二、召开系列高能级投资促进活动

2023年3月9日，为促进商务区各片区协同发展，首期"虹桥财经汇"以"点虹成金　筑桥共赢"为主题，在虹桥国际中央商务区嘉定片区隆重举办。活动上，商务区管委会领导在致辞中表示，商务区在2022年克服新冠疫情影响，保持良好的发展活力，今年开局良好，经济的发展呈现强劲的韧劲。一大批长三角乃至全国的企业，将国际化的业务板块和研发中心落地在商务区。同时，以重点发展创新经济为主要特色的商务区嘉定片区集聚了一批具有创新活力的领军企业，区域内企业主体夯实，创新生态不断优化，人才服务不断升级，发展硕果累累。嘉定片区相关领导介绍了嘉定的"四城建设"以及新能源汽车产业集群、高端医疗芯片、在线新经济等领域取得的突破与进展；同时表示，商务区嘉定片区的定位是"开放北虹桥，创新领航地"，北虹桥把重大的机遇转化为区域的发展动能。合作才能共赢，共赢成就发展。嘉定是一座开放创新包容的城区，北虹桥更是一片正在崛起的投资创业的热土。在本次"虹桥财经汇"

第一章　经济高质量增长

第三节　招商引资

图1-2　首期"虹桥财经汇"

中,来自不同领域的专家、学者及机构高管齐聚,就数字化发展趋势、企业金融赋能、区域协同展望等发表了颇有深度的真知灼见;此外,来自北虹办、全斯美德、中国银行上海市分行等单位的嘉宾也分享了各自的观点与见解。

2023年5月25日,为全面展现商务区作为国家战略集中赋能区域的发展动能,并向海内外投资者发出盛情邀请,共享"大虹桥"发展机遇,商务区于长宁片区举办"潮涌浦江　投资虹桥"——2023虹桥国际中央商务区投资促进大会。上海市相关领导以及企业代表出席活动。活动上,管委会相关领导作商务区发展情况报告,长宁片区发布生命健康特色产业项目,上海市相关领导为虹桥"国际经济组织集聚区"揭牌并为新认定内资总部企业代表颁证,各片区重点产业项目进行集中签约,进一步做强经济规模、做强核心功能、做高经济密度。

图1-3　2023虹桥国际中央商务区投资促进大会

2023年10月12日，商务区于国家会展中心举办新一期"潮涌浦江　投资虹桥"暨"战略赋能新机遇　开放引领新高地"——2023虹桥国际中央商务区投资促进大会。上海市相关领导以及企业代表出席活动。管委会相关领导作"战略赋能新机遇、开放引领新高地"工作汇报，市政府相关部门就《若干政策措施》和《综合交通规划》进行政策解读和发布，嘉定片区发布"上虹桥"专项规划，市政府和商务区相关领导为商务区生产性互联网服务平台授牌，市政府相关领导为各片区重点产业项目进行集中签约见证。活动全面展现商务区在共享高质量发展机遇、助力长三角区域提升等方面的最新成就和下一步发展预期。

三、持续强化国际赋能，做大虹桥"朋友圈"

在做强国际经济组织服务集群方面，虹桥商务区加快政策优化和功能集聚，不断提升国际化视野，持续提升虹桥海外贸易中心能级，着力构建国际交流合作的工作网络，打造"类海外"营商环境，已吸引新加坡中华总商会、瑞士中心等37家国际贸易投资促进机构入驻虹桥海外贸易中心，联系超150个国家地区。

围绕国际专业服务、国际金融投资等领域，重新梳理形成2023年度虹桥国际商务伙伴及虹桥招商合作伙伴。虹桥国际商务伙伴主要的认定标准为国际知名的服务机构及国家级商协会组织，重在强化国际赋能和品牌引领，通过重点合作机构提升商务区国际专业服务能级；招商合作伙伴重在拓展招商渠道，围绕商务区产业定位寻找重点目标企业，做好对接、商洽和落地。2023年商务区进一步完善投资促进合作机制，共认定16家机构纳入虹桥国际商务伙伴，35家机构纳入虹桥招商合作伙伴，构建了宽领域、多层次、精准化的伙伴生态。

第四节 虹桥效应

一、讲好高水平开放、高质量发展的虹桥故事

聚焦重点活动。各大媒体围绕商务区重大活动、政策红利、发展动能等,对虹桥国际开放枢纽和商务区国家战略定位、蓝图、愿景,进行全面持续宣传,进一步扩大国际化商务区的影响力。《人民日报》、新华社、中央广播电视总台等中央媒体对虹桥持续关注,《解放日报》《文汇报》《新民晚报》、上海电视台、东方网等总计30余家主流媒体和网络新媒体予以大量报道。据初步统计,2023年,各大媒体报道商务区内容约355篇,其中《人民日报》报道23篇,新华社报道11篇,中央广播电视总台报道23篇,聚焦重点活动相关报道网络阅读点击量、播放量累计约3 010万次。

呈现虹桥高品质生活。结合商业活动、特色文旅资源、传统节庆窗口、交通设施完善,如"五五购物节"、数字高科技嘉年华、蟠龙天地开幕、端午七夕消费新场景新渠道、71路中运量西延伸开通等,展现虹桥美好生活,提振消费需求。

成为对外展示窗口。2023年,商务区海外社媒账号共发布519条内容,共有95条推文单条阅读量超10万次+,其中百万级推文2条。海媒账号阅读总量超4 017万次,转发、点赞及评论等互动数总人数超155万人次。

二、重大活动媒体争相报道

(一)2023年虹桥国际开放枢纽建设工作现场会、新闻发布会

两周年活动吸引了《人民日报》、新华社、中央电视台、中央人民广播电台、《光明日报》《中国日报》《国际金融报》《中国经济导报》、中国新闻网、《新华日报》、浙江网络广播电视台、《安徽日报》《解放日报》《文汇报》《新民晚报》、上海发布、《青年报》《劳动报》、上海广播电视台、上海人民广播电台、上观新闻、澎湃新闻、

图1-4 新华网客户端报道虹桥国际开放枢纽两周年

东方网、第一财经、界面新闻等30余家中央媒体、长三角省媒和本市媒体的广泛关注和报道。据不完全统计，相关报道网络阅读点击量已超过400万次。东方网关于两周年专栏报道，由中央网信办连续2日做全互联网推送并排名全网前三。中央电视台在现场会次日即作报道。

（二）2023虹桥国际中央商务区投资促进大会、2023虹桥国际中央商务区人才发展大会

2023虹桥国际中央商务区投资促进大会、2023虹桥国际中央商务区人才发展大会两次活动受到《人民日报》、新华社、中央广播电视总台等中央媒体关注报道。《解放日报》《文汇报》《新民晚报》及上海电视台、东方网等总计30余家主流媒体和网络新媒体予以大量媒体资源倾斜，东方网的会中图文直播实时浏览累计达22.5万人次。市级相关委办局、有关区等均作转发。

据初步统计，2023虹桥国际中央商务区投资促进大会、2023虹桥国际中央商务区人才发展大会相关报道网络阅读点击量、播放量分别约420万次、380万次。活动获得良好反响，得到社会各界特别是商务区企业、求职群体等多方关注。此外，通过前期

图1-5　2023虹桥国际中央商务区投资促进大会和人才发展大会广受媒体报道

宣传预热，在人才发展大会外场同步举办的"聚上海　创未来——2023虹桥人才招聘会"，累计吸引5 000余人来到现场应聘，各家企业累计收到简历3 000余份，意向录用700余人。

（三）精心策划虹桥HUB大会宣传报道

11月6日，第六届虹桥国际经济论坛虹桥国际开放枢纽建设分论坛暨2023虹桥HUB大会在国家会展中心（上海）召开。论坛的高质量举办，立刻引来各方关注，包括《人民日报》、央视"晚间新闻""新闻直播间"、新华社、中央广播电视总台、央视国际、中国新闻网、中国发展网、《中国日报》《国际金融报》《中国证券报》《中国经济导报》《经济日报》等多家中央媒体都对本次论坛以不同形式、不同角度进行了报道。

上海各大主流媒体也对论坛开展了广泛而深入的报道。《解放日报》《文汇报》《新民晚报》《青年报》《劳动报》、上海发布、上海电视台、上海教育电视台、东方卫视、上观新闻、澎湃新闻、东方网、第一财经、界面新闻等上海主流媒体纷纷报道了论坛的相关信息。第一财经和东方网设置了专题发布论坛的重要动态。据初步统计，截至11月10日，总计30余家媒体做广泛报道，其中中央媒体报道16篇、市级媒体报道40篇，相关报道网络阅读点击量、播放量已达1 134万次。

图1-G　央视《新闻直播间》报道第六届虹桥国际经济论坛

第二章　国际化中央商务区

第一节　深化战略内涵认识研究

2023年2月4日，上海市委书记陈吉宁调研商务区并作出重要指示，强调商务区承载了多项国家战略任务，要进一步深化对战略内涵的认识。2月10日，商务区明确"形成一个综合研究报告、编制一个三年行动方案、完成一项管理职能调整、制定五个配套政策文件"，即"1+1+1+5"工作体系。在市相关部门的指导推动下，商务区进一步聚焦主责主业，与闵行区政府顺利完成虹桥综合交通枢纽应急管理职能划转和相关机构人员转隶等工作；深化战略内涵认识研究、商务区建设三年行动计划、优化完善管理体制机制、提升服务企业"走出去"能级措施等主要成果已经市委市政府主要领导审阅，并于9月15日市政府常务会议审议通过。

汇聚多方合力，高位推动研究。商务区成立多方共同参与的深化战略内涵认识联合课题团队，共同商定重点研究方向，确定报告大纲，分工协作形成报告初稿并持续优化完善，先后三次向市领导汇报。过程中，商务区充分联动市级相关部门成立深化战略内涵认识研究推进专班，制定深化战略内涵认识研究专项工作清单和任务清单，逐项明确调研分工、时间节点、牵头单位和参与单位（包括分管领导、责任人和联络员）和具体成果形式，并严格按照"一周一联动、半月一汇报、一月一总结"计划安排，由商务区组织专题讨论会并报送研究开展情况。与此同时，商务区赴深圳前海、北京经开区等重要功能区实地考察学习改革创新经验，多次会同市级相关部门、四区政府、六个街镇和四个片区联合开展座谈研讨，广泛听取征集各方意见。此外，研究还充分吸收了复旦大学消费大数据和瑞安公司产业发展研究成果，以及仲量联行、毕马威等国际咨询巨头关于优化产业规划和布局、完善公共配套等方面建议，集思广益、集智攻关。

全面对标对表，深化内涵分解。根据陈吉宁书记调研商务区指示精神和市领导相关工作要求，商务区认真对照学习习近平总书记在历次中国国际进口博览会上讲话精神、《长江三角洲区域一体化发展规划纲要》《总体方案》对商务区的功能定位，以及上海"五个中心"建设和2035主体功能规划对商务区的要求，将"进一步深化对战略内涵的认识"细化分解为三大维度战略要求解读和四个方面战略内涵深化，集中围绕高水平对外开放、长三角高质量一体化发展、新发展阶段改革创新和高标准国际化中央商务区建设等内容作再认识再深化。在此基础上，结合落实国家战略要求和商务区自身发展需要，深化战略内涵认识研究从着力建设高水平对外开放的平台功能、着力打造长三角一体化发展的引擎功能、努力成为新发展阶段改革创新的试验田、努力建设面向未来的高标准国际化商务区等4个方面提出了12项重点举措，具体包括以海外发展中心为支撑体系的"走出去"功能平台、以进博会为代表的"引进来"功能平台、以高端资源配置能力为标志的国际贸易中心平台功能、以跨国公司全球布局影响力为象征的桥头堡功能、打造强劲活跃的新兴产业增长极、建设包容共享的长三角统一大市场、建设畅通内外的国际开放枢纽门户、实践"规建管服"全生命周期管理创新、建设最高标准的国际化营商服务环境、打造国际化标志性CBD核心区、共建特色鲜明的四个功能片区、持续提升国际化标准与品质等方面。

专栏2-1 ▶▶▶

商务区深化战略内涵认识四个层面的目标任务

面向2035年，商务区目标和任务主要体现在四个层面：国家高水平对外开放、长三角的高质量一体化发展、新发展阶段的改革创新、高标准国际化中央商务区建设。

（1）**国家高水平对外开放的功能平台**。彰显开放理念，服务以国内大循环为中心、国内国际双循环相互促进的新发展格局。全面推进以进博会为支撑的"引进来"功能平台建设，提升能级与辐射带动力。加快建设中国企业'走出去'一站式功能服务平台，放大国际企业"引进来"功能效应，提升资源要素的配置效率，推动商务区成为全球资源要素配置的节点枢纽和国际投资贸易的主阵地。

（2）长三角一体化高质量发展的排头兵。彰显协同理念，用好用足作为上海"一城两翼"空间格局之西翼核心地位，成为虹桥国际开放枢纽"一核"的链接支点，发挥对内集聚和对外辐射作用。推动一体化统一大市场和基础设施互联互通，打响长三角"一网通办"和"跨省通办"等服务品牌，推进跨区域协同开放和协同创新。

（3）新发展阶段改革创新的试验田。彰显改革理念，立足提升对外开放和服务长三角高质量一体化的水平，结合"引进来""走出去"，着重从市场经营环境建设、人才引进服务机制、开放经济信用建设等方面发力，全力打造市场化、法治化、国际化营商环境。加快探索跨区域协同发展机制，不断提升对外开放和区域协同水平。

（4）高标准国际化中央商务区的标杆。彰显国际理念，着力打造国际化商务区新标杆，以实施国家战略为牵引，建设功能复合的国际化中央商务区，推进国际休闲、国际体育、国际教育、国际医疗、国际文化、国际社区六大行动，提升商务区空间品质、魅力和影响力，带动上海相关区乃至长三角区域实现高质量发展。

配套成果转化，推进认识落地。结合调研成果，将商务区深化战略内涵认识研究4个方面12项重点举措，进一步细化梳理为配套贯彻落实的"一批平台和项目、一批建设指标、一批政策支撑"实施路径，从而夯实贯彻落实国家战略要求的四梁八柱。主要包括：打造一批高水平对外开放和长三角一体化发展的重点平台和项目，涉及6大类32项；标志性CBD、国际社区、生态休闲、服务设施、交通体系、城市运营等一批国际化建设指标（涵盖6个领域和21项检测指标）；聚焦贸易自由便利化、投资自由便利化、跨境资金流动自由、长三角一体化、人才支持、城市更新等六个类型，提出重点支撑的政策内容。与此同时，商务区还将其中具备条件、可操作性强的多个项目补充纳入、协调推进至《高质量推进虹桥国际中央商务区建设三年行动计划（2023—2025）》，切实推进深化战略内涵认识研究成果落地实施。

表 2-1 一批高水平对外开放和长三角一体化发展的重点平台和项目

序号	平台	项目	项目类型	序号	平台	项目	项目类型
1	"引进来"的高端贸易平台	国家会展中心	提升	4	长三角"一网通办"	长三角公共资源交易中心	提升
		长三角会议中心	新建			长三角技术转移与交易平台	提升
		综合保税区	提升			长三角知识产权保护与交易中心	提升
		国家跨境电商示范园区	提升			长三角跨区共享公共服务信息管理平台	提升
		数字资产交易中心	新建	5	长三角"科创协同"	长三角国家技术创新中心（虹桥分中心）	新建
		跨境电商全球集散分拨中心	新建			长三角区域合作大学	新建
2	"走出去"的专业服务平台	虹桥国际中央法务区	提升			长三角国际标准化平台	新建
		虹桥国际金融税务区	新建			长三角工业互联网公共技术服务平台	新建
		虹桥国际会计事务中心	新建			长三角科创金融中心	提升
		长三角人力资源示范产业园	新建	6	长三角"应用科技转化"	新虹桥国际医学中心	提升
		虹桥海外发展局	新建			虹桥国际在线新经济生态园	提升
		企业"走出去"安全中心	新建			北斗西虹桥产业基地	提升
		企业"走出去"数据中心	新建			徐泾数创社区	提升
		国际商务人才港	提升			数字经济产业园	新建
3	跨国企业事业型总部集聚平台	虹桥贸易总部园区	新建			临港嘉定科技城（金宝）	提升
		长三角"走出去"企业总部园区	新建				
		国际企业总部园区	新建				

表 2-2 一批建设指标

序号	6个领域	监测指标	单 位	2025 年	2030 年	2035 年
1	标志性 CBD	总部型企业/机构数量	家	300家左右	400家左右	500家左右
		国际航线数	条	4	7	10
		贸易服务平台	%	8	15	25
		税收坪效	元/平方米	3 000	5 000	7 000
		职住比	—	0.3	0.5	0.8
2	国际社区	新增国际社区数量	个	1	≥2	≥3
		外籍人口占常住人口比例	%	3	4	5
3	生态休闲	人均公园绿地面积	平方米	9.5	11.5	13.4
		主题开放空间数量	个	10	20	30
		400平方米以上绿地广场等公共开放空间5分钟步行可达覆盖率	%	90	93	95
		城市建设养护标准	—	所在区平均养护标准的1.5倍以上	整体超过本市中心城区养护标准	达到国际中央商务区相应养护标准
4	服务设施	市区级公共服务设施数量	个	4	7	10
		三甲医院数量	个	1	2	3
		高质量幼儿园、中小学数量（不含国际学校）	个	≥5	≥10	≥20
		卫生、养老、教育、文化体育等社区公共服务设施15分钟步行可达覆盖率	%	85	90	95
5	交通体系	公共交通站点600米用地覆盖率	%	50	70	90
		全路网密度	千米/平方千米	5.5	7	8
		慢行系统林荫覆盖率	%	30	50	80
		公共活动中心慢行立体交通覆盖率	%	50	70	100
6	城市运营	智慧化运营覆盖率	%	30	50	100
		绿色建筑星级运行标识认证面积	平方米	300	500	800

表 2-3 一批重点支撑政策内容

序号	政策类型	政 策 内 容
1	贸易自由便利化政策	推动进博会政策延展，将进博会期间展品税收支持、通关监管、资金结算、人员出入境等创新政策分批次延伸至以进口为主题的国际知名展会及"6+365天"常年展销平台
		建立进博会展品绿色通道，针对监管方式成熟的保健品、化妆品、乳制品、家居用品、二类医疗器械等进博展品，在办理相应进口许可证备案审批（或产品注册证）过程中，提高办证便利度，完善进博展品进入中国市场的绿色通道
		支持离岸贸易发展，优化离岸贸易外汇管理方式、加大财税支持力度等。支持数字贸易发展，推动数字证书、电子签名等国际互认，推动数据跨境流动，进一步完善国际互联网专用通道。落实医疗服务贸易支持政策，支持甲类大型医用设备配置，支持国外上市尚未国内获批的新药械在新虹桥国际医学中心先行先试，推动B保物流中心功能辐射新虹桥国际医学中心区域
2	投资自由便利化政策	试行"极简审批"投资制度。制定出台虹桥国际中央商务区放宽市场准入特别清单、外商投资准入负面清单，落实"非禁即入
		试行"准入即准营"，实施企业投资项目承诺制，制定发布虹桥商务区承诺制改革试点项目准入负面清单
3	跨境资金流动自由政策	商务区内符合条件的企业可以依法合规开立自由贸易账户。支持商务区内符合条件的跨国公司开展跨境资金集中运营管理，建立本外币一体化资金池。鼓励商业银行提供基于自由贸易账户的跨境金融服务便利，优化非自由贸易账户离岸贸易资金结算等相关工作。实施货物贸易和服务贸易外汇收支便利化措施，对符合条件的企业实行优化单证审核等便利化措施。鼓励金融机构在依法合规、风险可控、商业可持续的前提下，为商务区内企业和非居民提供跨境发债、跨境投资并购等服务。支持企业开展人民币跨境贸易融资和再融资业务。鼓励商业银行采用知识产权质押、预期收益质押等融资方式提供更多金融产品服务
4	长三角一体化政策	探索建立规则统一的制度体系。建立虹桥国际开放枢纽重点领域制度规则和重大政策沟通协调机制。全面实施全国市场准入负面清单，实行统一市场准入制度。加强标准领域合作，按照建立全国统一大市场要求探索建立区域一体化标准体系。探索建立各类要素跨区域自由流动制度。探索企业跨省转移涉及的商事登记冠名、生产许可证、企业营业执照、高新技术认定等相关政策。共建统一开放的人力资源市场。加强金融领域协同创新
		建立区域协同创新的合作机制。聚焦长三角优势产业领域，构建集聚企业主体、产业链条、创新链条的跨区域"合作网络"。探索跨区域"科创飞地""科创园区"合作机制和产业协同发展新模式。探索跨区域公共技术服务平台、创新合作平台、创新孵化中心、技术交易平台等的建设和运作管理模式。建立区域协同创新的保障机制

续表

序号	政策类型	政策内容
4	长三角一体化政策	探索一体化发展的共担共享机制。建立跨区域合作的各方利益保障机制，成立跨区域协商机构或组织，统筹协调成本共担和利益共享
5	人才支持政策	探索建立国际职业资格证书认可清单制度，率先建立会展、贸易等专业人才认定机制，允许取得境外相应职业资格或公认的国际专业组织认证的国际人才，经能力水平认定或有关部门备案后上岗
		加强国际人才落户、医疗、教育等支持政策。重点机构紧缺急需人才、紧缺急需技能人才、高等级技能人才直接引进落户；各类人才"居转户"缩短年限。争取在华永久居留人才享受市民待遇、外籍人才单独参加职工医疗保险等政策先行先试
6	城市更新政策	支持土地分割转让，符合规划分割等条件的，以带产业项目方式采用定向挂牌方式转让；支持"零增地"改扩建，在符合产业导向前提下，存量产业用地提高容积率和增加地下空间不再增收土地价款；探索工业上楼，鼓励工业用地和研发用地建设功能复合楼宇
		盘活存量闲置住房资源，推动存量商办空置空间向公益性设施及租赁性住房功能转型，释放存量空间价值

专栏2-2 ▶▶▶

高质量推进虹桥国际中央商务区建设三年行动计划（2023—2025）

商务区按照市领导的工作部署要求，与陈吉宁书记对商务区的一系列指示要求再对照，与总体方案、商务区"十四五"规划再对标，与战略内涵研究课题成果再梳理，聚焦关于加强流量价值挖掘创造、推动总部经济能级提升、深化贸易功能内涵拓展、加强城市更新和基础设施支持、打造国际一流营商环境等5个方面，梳理出30项工作任务，编制形成高质量推进商务区建设三年行动计划。同时，围绕未来三年发展目标，聚焦空间布局、功能平台、主导产业再提升再深化再优化，将已达成共识、具备可操作性的项目细化形成57条具体措施清单，倒排时间节点，挂图作战，项目化推进。力争到2025年，总部经济和现代服务业加速集聚，吸引集聚总部类企业560家以上，引进落地国际性经济组织50家以上，培育形成有影响力和竞争力的创新型企业1000家以上，基本建成虹桥国际开放枢纽核心承

第二章 国际化中央商务区

第一节 深化战略内涵认识研究

载区,全面确立中央商务区和国际贸易中心新平台功能框架和制度体系。

"三年行动计划"30项重点任务。具体分为五个方面:一是"加强流量价值挖掘创造"。强调打造世界级的流量入口,强化对内对外开放两个扇面的关键枢纽,延伸产业链条,拓展产业深度,把流量入口优势更好地转化为商务区发展胜势。围绕放大进博会溢出效应、构建上海国际会展之都核心承载区、打造西片国际级消费集聚区、促进跨境资金自由流动、加速科技成果跨区域转化方面提出了5项重点任务。二是"推动总部经济能级提升"。强调引进和培育更多符合区域战略定位的标志性、引领性、龙头性企业总部机构,依托跨国公司总部强大的网联功能和全球资源配置能力,推动和带动长三角企业创新升级和转型提升。围绕实施总部"虹聚"计划、提高企业境外投资便利化水平、设立"走出去"公共服务平台、全力推进新兴产业融合集群发展、搭建耦合共生协同创新平台方面提出了5项重点任务。三是"深化贸易功能内涵拓展"。强调围绕加快布局数字贸易、服务贸易新蓝海,建设高能级贸易主体首选地,吸引集聚更多国际贸易功能性机构落地,着力构建国际贸易中心新平台。围绕深化进口贸易促进创新示范区建设、高水平建设虹桥"丝路电商"辐射引领区、推进国际高标准经贸规则率先落地、积极参与国家服务贸易创新发展示范区创建、高质量打造上海"国际经济组织集聚区"、建设虹桥实物互联网示范枢纽、建立"虹桥开放指数"指标体系方面提出了7项重点任务。四是"加强城市更新和基础设施支持"。强调推动一流城市形态和一流城市品质相匹配,以城市更新为抓手,持续优化空间布局,升级软硬件设施,强化运营管理,推动商务区能级和品质提升。围绕进一步完善商务区规划实施评估、高品质打造标志性CBD、加快推进核心区整体开发建设、全面推进四片区开发建设和功能打造、提升商务区内多层次综合交通水平、推进租赁住房建设、补齐公共服务设施短板、提升城市空间品质、打造特色鲜明的高品质精细化管理示范区方面提出了9项重点任务。五是"打造国际一流营商环境"。强调强化优质公共服务供给,为各类市场主体投资兴业,打造贸易投资便利、资源要素齐全、政务服务高效、法治体系完善的国际一流营商环境。围绕打造营商环境"虹桥品牌"、建设商务区企业服务体系、集聚国际化专业服务要素、建设虹桥国际商务人才港方面提出了4项重点任务。

第二节　推进虹桥国际开放枢纽建设

虹桥国际开放枢纽是一种全新的开放形态。商务区作为虹桥国际开放枢纽核心功能承载区，全面对标对表虹桥国际开放枢纽建设总体方案，不断推动大商务、大会展、大交通、大科创"四大功能"深度融合，持续提升核心功能，建设国际化中央商务区取得新进展。对标高标准、高水平的国际规则制度体系，持续放大进博溢出效应，创新国际贸易，推动高端要素资源优化配置，开放优势充分彰显，构建国际贸易中心新平台取得新突破。强化制度政策创新，提高综合交通枢纽联通能力，推动长三角互联互通，关键基础支撑不断强化，提高综合枢纽门户功能取得新成效。

一、2023年虹桥国际开放枢纽建设工作现场会

3月1日，2023年虹桥国际开放枢纽建设工作现场会在国家会展中心举行，会议全面总结了《总体方案》出台两年来，"大虹桥"建设取得重要阶段性成果。虹桥国际开放枢纽"一核两带"7 000平方千米全域生产总值从2020年的2.3万亿元增长到2022年的2.69万亿元。现场会上，一批贸易平台、航空服务、区域合作项目签约。虹桥品汇与苏州、嘉兴、合肥分中心深化合作签约，上海机场集团与苏州、嘉兴、合肥深化航空合作签约，昆山市与海宁市"链接虹桥国际开放枢纽"战略合作签约。

会议指出，要更好发挥上海优势，与苏浙皖通力合作，推动虹桥国际开放枢纽建设不断走深走实。要助力区域科技协同创新，打造长三角科技创新共同体，共同推进高水平科技自立自强。加强基础研究协作，把握科技发展趋势和国家战略需求，聚合战略科技力量，搭建共性技术平台，全面提升开放共享水平和平台运行效率，支持长三角各地利用上海科研资源，在"卡脖子"领域联合开展重大科技项目攻关，力争尽快取得突破。优化科研服务供给，集聚全球创新要素，构建全链条科研服务体系，为长三角科技协同创新提供专业化的服务。要推进区域产业协同合作，着眼构建现代化产业体系，协同做好补链延链升链建链的大文章，合力提升区域产业能级，助力区域内产业数字化、智能化和绿色化改造升级，不断提升产业基础高级化和产业链现代化水平，推动在空间布局上形成产业生态，方便企业开展产业链供应链合作。要提升区

域开放整体能级，抓住"一带一路"建设深入实施等机遇，以上海自贸试验区成立10周年和国家实施自贸试验区提升战略为契机，加大先行先试和制度集成的力度，探索内外贸一体化发展的制度供给，为长三角企业统筹国内国际两个市场两种资源提供支撑。依托商务区商务、会展、交通功能融合优势，提高生产性服务业的分工细化和专业化水平，提升对生产过程的服务能级，加快发展商事仲裁、检验检测、会计审计、技术咨询等服务业，为长三角企业走出去提供更好支持。要放大进博会溢出效应，持续提升办会办展的国际化、专业化、品牌化水平。加快建设集展示推介、撮合交易、商贸洽谈、金融服务、技术交流等于一体的综合性平台，更好联动产业升级和消费升级，提升会展业附加值，共同把进博会打造成为推动国内国际双循环互相促进的重要纽带、参与全球价值分配的重要平台。

同时强调，要打造枢纽核心，高水平推动商务区建设。加强流量价值挖掘创造，更好把人流、物流、商流的价值转化为经济价值和创新价值，因地制宜延伸产业链条、拓展产业深度，把流量入口优势更好转化为发展胜势。推动总部经济能级提升，引进更多标志性、引领性的龙头企业，支持企业拓展研发、销售、贸易、结算等多元功能，实现向亚太或全球总部的升级。深化贸易功能内涵拓展，加快布局数字贸易、服务贸易新蓝海，吸引集聚更多国际贸易功能性机构落地，积极发展新型国际贸易，培育发展知识密集型服务贸易。加强城市更新和基础设施支持，围绕功能定位，持续优化空间布局、升级软硬件设施、强化运营管理，加大住房、教育、医疗等高品质生活服务供给，推动商务区能级和品质提升，更好把一流城市形态和一流城市品质匹配起来。

3月2日，为聚焦开放枢纽的核心区——商务区的建设成效，上海市政府举办新闻发布会。新闻发布会全面介绍了商务区坚持以多重国家战略为指引，致力服务构建双循环新发展格局，全方位加大对内对外双向开放力度，加快形成区域一体化的产业生态集群，促进高端要素资源跨区域集散。着眼服务长三角服务全国探索放大进博会溢出带动效应，共同打响"进口商品采购在虹桥"品牌，持续提升虹桥海外贸易中心全球化贸易投资服务功能，为长三角企业加快国际化发展拓展渠道；紧扣高质量，提升高端资源要素配置能级，坚持对标国际一流，加快提高商务区的整体标识度核心竞争力，加大吸引培育高能级总部机构力度，推动总部经济能级提升，加快集聚一批具有国际服务功能的专业服务机构，加快投资性公司和产业基金在商务区落地，高标准打造国际会展产业园；紧扣国际化，打造区域开放型经济新高地。为各类企业走出去提供专业服务支撑，全面推进虹桥进口贸易促进创新示范区建设，探索开展内外贸一体

图2-1 两周年工作现场会

化试点。依托自由贸易账户体系建设，加快布局和发展新型国际贸易。同步加快区域城市更新和基础设施支撑，全面提升公共服务国际化水平。

二、联动南北两带协同发展

商务区持续强化集聚辐射，高水平服务"一核两带"总体布局，积极为长三角城市的布局设点提供载体空间，利用政策优势进一步提高对外开放的层次水平。在产业联动方面，挂牌运作长三角民营企业总部集聚区和长三角民营企业总部服务中心，加快推进虹桥临空跨国公司（总部）科创园、南虹桥民营企业总部集聚区、虹桥新慧总部湾等总部基地，举办"长三角企业家圆桌会"系列活动。同时，"一核"与"两带"之间的产业联动日趋紧密，以"虹桥总部+腹地基地""虹桥贸易+腹地物流""虹桥商务+腹地休闲"等为特征的功能布局逐步成型。"中欧班列　上海号"从"大虹桥"始发，来自长三角地区的货源箱量占比达到86.9%，直接、间接服务长三角地区进出口企业2 000余家，有力助推长三角一体化发展。在资源流动方面，商务区持续强化高端人才集聚，商务区已成为近年来长三角跨城通勤量增长最明显的片区之一。同时，商务区各类公共服务资源加快辐射长三角，如新虹桥国际医学中心逐步实现资源和技术共享，面向长三角的企业商标受理窗口已正式对外提供服务。在项目驱动方面，商务区充分发挥综合交通枢纽门户功能，加快构建跨区域轨道交通网，持续加强航空运输服务能力。沪苏湖铁路、沪苏嘉城际线等一批跨区域重大交通项目实现开工；嘉闵线北延伸等跨省市项目前期工作加快推进。

江苏、浙江、安徽三地也高度重视、大力支持虹桥国际开放枢纽建设，认真落实《总体方案》，出台相关配套政策措施，加快推动开放枢纽协同建设发展。江苏省主动服务中央商务区能级提升，推动跨国公司加快集聚，空中客车、西门子、飞利浦、霍尼韦尔等一批外资项目密集落户北向拓展带。主动融入国际贸易中心建设，积极组织企业参展采购，成功举办相聚进博——苏州进口贸易促进大会等配套活动，持续提升"虹桥品汇 苏州港"品牌辐射能力，推动长三角自贸试验区联动发展。主动对接综合交通枢纽建设，推动铁路、公路、港口等互融互通。浙江省加快落地一批重点平台，先后推动印发数字贸易创新发展区和江海河空铁联运新平台两个专项建设方案，联手上海打造"重走一大路"红色旅游品牌，深化张江长三角科技城平湖园区建设，文商会旅、数字贸易、科技创新、江海河空铁联运等重点平台建设取得积极成效。加快落实一批重点任务，不折不扣落实国家《总体方案》明确的17项重点任务，全力推进落实浙江省《共建虹桥实施方案》明确的70条举措，其中33条举措已落地实施。加快建设一批重点项目，统筹推进总投资915亿元的15个重大项目建设，金山至平湖市域铁路、嘉兴机场、沪苏嘉城际铁路、上海至嘉兴海铁联运班列等一批重点项目签约启动、开工建设、开通运行。安徽省充分用好虹桥枢纽"汇"全球资源的机遇，积极组团参加进博会。充分用好虹桥枢纽"促"产业合作的优势，大力推进合肥国际金融后台服务基地建设，在上海松江建设产业创新中心，与闵行、苏州等地启动建设合作帮扶共建园区。充分用好虹桥枢纽"聚"创新之势的功能，积极参与G60科创走廊建设，协同共建长三角科技创新共同体，高水平建设合肥综合性国家科学中心。

三、全力推进升级版政策措施在商务区落地实施

商务区积极沟通对接市级相关部门，结合落实市委市政府领导重要工作指示，以及本市重点任务分工方案，全面梳理涉及商务区的16项工作任务（其中2项牵头、14项配合），深入挖掘应用场景和企业案例，先后赴新虹桥国际医学中心、中国上海人力资源服务产业园区虹桥园、上海虹桥临空经济园区等开展政策摸排，并就落实社会办医疗机构配置大型医用设备和临床进口医疗器械等政策，征集百汇医院、泰和诚肿瘤医院、美中嘉和影像中心等企业相关政策具体诉求，排定应用场景建设方案和详细节点计划，研究制定挂图作战分工表和行动方案。同时主动对接市级责任部门和闵行、长宁、青浦、嘉定四区政府，配合联动市区有关部门进一步推动深化政策内涵研究、

加强宣传解读、挖掘应用场景、明确落实路径、细化操作流程等工作，全力做好《若干政策措施》在商务区的落地工作，确保升级版政策红利转化为商务区提升能级的动力和活力。

专栏2-3 ▶▶▶
本市贯彻升级版政策重点任务分工方案中涉及商务区的16项工作任务

2项牵头工作："支持虹桥商务区引进更多贸易促进机构、商会协会等国际经贸组织功能性机构落地。"商务区加大工作力度，加快政策优化和功能集聚，在已集聚各类国际贸易投资促进机构37家的基础上，将跟进完成新加坡亚洲公益投资网络、澳门中小型企业联合总商会、亚美尼亚中国合作关系发展中心等3家境外机构入驻商务区，初步形成联系全球超过150个国家和地区的全球化贸易及投资服务网络，充分发挥海外贸易中心境内外双向投资贸易的促进服务能力，打造支持国内企业走出去的国际化、专业化通道。

"支持虹桥商务区为长三角地区开展招商引资、国际人才招引，以及设立城市展示中心、研发中心、营销公司、外事联络处等功能性机构预留空间、创造条件。"经过调研摸排，苏州、嘉兴两地国资企业在商务区约有5.15万平方米的商办载体空间，用于城市展示、招商引资、人才招引、营销联络等功能。商务区将继续深入调研摸清底数，结合核心区城市更新等工作，推动部分楼宇改造提升，以搭建平台、制定规则、双向互动等方式，充分发挥商协会作用，有序引导长三角周边区域在商务区范围内设立有关机构，实现区域互动双赢。现阶段浙江商会已入驻海外贸易中心，近期正在积极对接上海市安徽商会，沟通徽商长三角总部基地进驻商务区等相关合作事宜。

14项配合工作：在强化虹桥商务区核心功能方面，配合市商务委制定《上海市关于创新"丝路电商"合作先行区方案》并摸排梳理有关跨境数据流动、国际电子发票等应用场景；与市卫生健康委跟进商务区内企业关于进口核磁弹性成像医疗器械、质子设备、进口PSMA造影剂用药等政策内容申请。在促进"一核两带"融合发展方面，会同市出入境管理局研究推进移民政策实践基地建设，推荐符合要求的外籍高层次人才办理外国人永久居留，会同闵行、长宁进一步提升外国人办事窗口的服务功能，做好外籍人才就业及居留许可单一窗口办理等服务保障工作。在引领长三角高质量一体化发展方面，主动对接市科委，重点围绕吸引一批具有投资功能的科技中介服务机构在商务区集聚，进一步支持强化现有INNOMATCH等平台，加快推进南虹桥生物医药产业园区项目，支持东虹桥创建中德科技交流服务平台，加快建设北虹桥北虹之云科技创新孵化器，完善北斗西虹桥基地综合服务功能。

第三节 构建现代服务业集聚区

商务区着力提升经济密度和产业能级,商务会展等现代高端服务业快速发展,总部经济资源配置能力和国际竞争力进一步增强,临空服务、健康医药、人工智能、北斗导航等特色产业稳步发展,新业态新模式不断涌现,国际化中央商务区的功能框架初步确立。

一、会展品牌效应不断放大

持续做大会展经济。进博会连续六届成功举办,国际化、市场化、品牌化程度进一步提高。在多方资源整合下,上海市国际展览(集团)有限公司成功组建,目前已拥有30多个颇具国际影响力的品牌展览和专业会议,5个UFI认证展会。虹桥国际会展产业园正式投入使用,集聚了上海市会展行业协会等会展促进机构、英富曼会展集团等国际知

图2-2 第四届长三角国际文化产业博览会

名会展公司及各类会展产业链上下游企业，共计250余家。近两年来，中国国际建筑贸易博览会、第二十届上海车展、两届长三角国际应急减灾和救援博览会和首届"碳博会"等一系列品牌展会先后在国家会展中心（上海）举办，虹桥会展品牌持续打响。

全面提升会展产业能级。研究《虹桥国际中央商务区关于促进会展经济发展的扶持意见》，努力形成更加完善的产业发展政策体系，推动会展行业更快更好发展。发挥会展在消费促进中的重要作用，积极承接和放大进博会溢出带动效应，推动进博会"展品变商品"，成功举办国别商品文化缤纷月等进口主题活动，累计拉动进口消费超百亿元。推动会展行业数字化升级，成立国内首家线上展会龙头企业——云上会展有限公司，不断完善"云展示""云对接""云签约"等线上服务功能，打通线上线下会展服务体系。上海车展、长三角应急展、上海国际养老展等重点展会，实现线上线下同步办展。

二、特色产业园区稳步发展

持续做强高端临空服务业集聚区。"十四五"以来，虹桥临空经济示范区围绕"国际航空枢纽、全球航空企业总部基地、高端临空服务业集聚区、全国公务机运营基地和低碳绿色发展区"五大功能定位，推动高端临空服务业快速发展，年均税收增速达20%。东航系、春秋系、机场系等关联企业、新业务板块不断集聚，累计入驻航空企业近150家，包括5家总部型基地航空公司、8家公务航空企业及若干功能机构，产业生态进一步丰富。通过建立与机场东片区五大主体的日常联系沟通机制，加快研究编制专项规划，机场东片区综合改造有序推进。特色产业"园中园"活力迸发，虹桥临空跨国公司（总部）科创园已入驻跨国企业30余家，八成以上为总部企业。

持续做大医疗健康产业园规模。新虹桥国际医学中心加快推进建设，园区一期已形成包括1家医技中心、近10家国际国内高品质医院、10多家医技/门诊机构的多元办医布局；园区二期集聚信达生物、云南白药等10多家生物医药研发总部，累计投资额超过150亿元，初步形成集研发、临床、服务于一体的生物医药产业集群。虹桥国际创新医疗器械产业园建设完成，已经集聚了以康德莱为代表的13家相关企业，建立起医生创新平台和动物实验研究中心，医械产业初具规模。

逐步形成人工智能创新发展集聚。东虹桥片区围绕科大讯飞上海总部功能，持续引进更多优质人工智能企业，推动人工智能研究院、人工智能企业研发中心等创新业务总部和功能落地，临空人工智能产业园（IBP）正在加快建设。西虹桥片区同联创新

图2-3 临空人工智能产业园

产业园立足基础,进一步拓展人工智能产业发展规模。北虹桥片区启动虹桥国际在线新经济生态园,集聚了智臻智能网络、纳瓦电子等重点人工智能企业,时尚创意园构建"社+商+学"三位一体资源优势,形成以文创产业为核心的产业特色,获得首届"时尚100+"大奖。

有序推进北斗导航产业创新。北斗西虹桥基地发挥全产业链布局优势,鼓励优质企业联合产业链上下游共建,形成"一平台多基地"的北斗产业集聚新模式。目前已引入高分遥感、核建科技、新能源汽车、数字经济、人工智能等战略新兴产业,集聚500余家位置服务领域科技企业,已上市和拟上市企业超过10家,相关产品国内市场份额超过25%,服务"一带一路"沿线30多个国家和地区。依托北斗导航研发与转化功能型平台,加强核心能力建设与共性技术攻关,推动北斗卫星导航系统在应急管理、港口码头、智慧园区、北斗工厂等场景的规模化应用,累计孵化培育企业13家。

不断涌现新业态新亮点。投资超50亿元的上海国际新文创电竞中心加快建设,联动皇族电竞等龙头项目,为重大电竞赛事引进与电竞全产业链发展打下坚实基础。"虹桥之源"在线新经济生态园正式揭牌,成为继"张江在线""长阳秀带"后的第三个市级在线新经济生态园,目前已集聚1500余家数字经济领域企业。蟠龙文化休闲与创意产业集聚区在保护、修缮原有历史文物基础上"古为今用",仿照旧时风貌打造文化休闲商业片区。

图2-4 蟠龙文化休闲与创意产业集聚区

三、优质商务活动竞相举办

不断提升虹桥国际经济论坛影响力。作为进博会的重要组成部分，第六届虹桥国际经济论坛成功举办。积极承接虹桥国际经济论坛溢出效应，举办虹桥国际经济论坛专题对话活动。上海国际仲裁中心主办"中国上海'一带一路'知识产权保护论坛"等高规格、国际化的争议解决专业论坛，促进企业和行业协会的交流合作。

打造投资促进工作品牌，深入推进"虹桥财金汇"等活动，吸引和集聚各类高端商贸要素。成功举办2023年两届"潮涌浦江 投资虹桥"活动，发布重大项目，进行集中签约，全面展现商务区发展动能。

持续加强国际商务旅游示范区建设。成功打造虹桥天地世界音乐节、"虹桥之秋"文化旅游购物节、咖啡文化节等品牌活动，助力打造国际文化旅游交流新窗口。国家会展中心（上海）周边集聚会展配套服务资源，酒店业、餐饮业、休闲娱乐等产业快速发展，青浦西虹桥环国家会展中心（上海）都市旅游区成功创建为上海市全域旅游特色示范区域。

四、专业服务配套日趋完善

虹桥国际商务人才港获得国家级产业园授牌批复，中国上海人力资源服务产业园虹桥园开园以来，截至10月31日累计落地165家人力资源服务类企业，形成了集招聘、培训、人才测评、人力资源服务外包、信息软件服务等业态于一体的人力资源服务全产业链。虹桥国际中央法务区正式揭牌，累计引进81家法律服务机构和泛法律服务机构入驻，初步形成规模效应，商务区仲裁及争议解决功能持续完善。

图2-5 虹桥国际中央法务区

第四节　提升总部经济能级

深入实施总部"虹聚"计划，不断完善政策体系，用好商务区贸易型企业总部和民营企业总部政策，支持各类总部企业加快发展，组织开展专场招商抓增量稳存量，加大贸易型企业总部和民营总部、外资研发中心引进力度，推进麦肯食品、邓白氏、汉德克斯、瑞仕格医疗等申报外资总部或研发中心，开展2023年贸易型总部认定，新增跨国公司地区总部2家，外资研发中心和外商投资性公司4家。积极落实"加快打造长三角民营企业总部集聚区"要求，相继出台围绕做强行业引领功能、支持总部企业国际化发展、支持引进国际化人才和开展国际商务合作等方面政策，集聚了一批具有一定引领性的总部企业，新培育商务区民营企业总部17家。

陆续出台支持内资总部企业、贸易型总部企业发展的政策举措，推动优惠政策落实落地。投资性公司便利化政策落地生效，亚投（上海）私募基金管理有限公司成功设立。持续优化跨国公司资金使用、跨境贸易、跨境研发、人员出入境等便利化措施，

图2-6　虹桥临空经济园天会广场

总部企业全球资源配置能力不断提升。同时，推动产业链、供应链、贸易链不断畅通，商务区功能优势不断放大。累计吸引总部类企业500多家，其中经认定的内资总部企业51家，涵盖新能源、新消费、生物医药等重点产业，总部企业综合贡献不断提高。

从企业投资规模来看，51家内资总部企业的年度纳税总额近35亿元，占商务区总税收规模的比重约8.7%，是商务区着力做强区域核心功能、形成经济发展新活力的重要增长点。从产业生态布局来看，七成以上企业与商务区产业导向高度匹配，包括：以天合光能、晶科能源、重塑能源为代表的新能源，以兰卫医学、先声药业、鱼跃医疗、惠泰医疗为代表的生物医药，以安踏、美的、百秋、波司登为代表的时尚消费，以格创东智、广联达、圆擎科技为代表的生产性互联网服务业和数字经济，等等。伴随着特色鲜明的产业生态体系加快形成，商务区新兴产业发展呈现耦合共生、集聚升级态势。

从长三角协同发展来看，产业联动更加紧密。通过总部设在虹桥，分支机构与生产基地布局长三角，实现能级跃升；或是集团授权，管理和研发型总部入驻虹桥，接轨上海优势，"总部+基地"的产业联动发展格局日益清晰，逐步成为总部企业发展的新路径。2023年7月，大虹桥光伏产业联盟成立，东渐数能、协鑫集团等高能级总部加快引进，商务区已成为总部经济成链发展的热点地区。

图2-7　大虹桥光伏产业联盟成立仪式

在全力打造总部经济新高地上，商务区以精准的政策支持和营商服务，不断做大经济规模、做强核心功能、做高经济密度，持续加大企业"走出去"支持力度，赋能总部企业国际化发展，依托"上海市'一带一路'综合服务中心"等功能平台，与虹桥国际商务伙伴加快形成国际化经济组织服务集群，围绕信息资讯、融资平台、专业服务、项目投资、人才服务、风险防范等六大服务功能，着力打造企业"走出去"一站式服务窗口。此外，商务区加快研究出台企业"走出去"政策服务体系，举办系列政策培训宣讲活动，为企业"走出去"国际化发展提供有力支持。

在吸引培育高能级总部机构上，商务区不断创新招商引资模式，提高招商引资效率，通过持续举办"走出去"企业家圆桌会和"引进来"高水平投资促进活动，提升虹桥对企业投资的吸引力和影响力，形成招商引资的品牌效应，凝聚四区合力招大引强，建立各片区专人对接机制，持续做好项目跟踪和对接，近50家企业正在对接商洽或已开工、注册落地。

第五节　赋能数字新经济

商务区从自身禀赋优势出发，发挥商务区特有优势，强化"大科创"功能，推动长三角协同创新。依托优越的经济地理位置和总部类研发中心集聚优势，提升企业总部研发和创新策源功能，形成长三角产业协同创新平台，赋能长三角区域产业链高质量发展。不断汇聚创新主体，推动提高商务区创新浓度。依托进博会大平台，国际企业竞相发布新产品、新技术、新服务，多款全球医疗创新技术成功落地国内。上海国际技术交易市场建设成效显著，通过长三角技术市场协同一体化机制，联动33个国内技术转移分中心、长三角300余家服务机构和海外11个分中心；累计主办、引进国际大型技术转移展会论坛12场，主办、承办科技成果路演对接会51场，上线发布超1万条需求信息；成功撮合实现近135项科技创新合作，协同网络内机构直接促成国际技术转移项目交易金额达到11亿元，引入多家高新技术企业落地商务区。上交会常年服务工作站正式揭牌，上海国际医学技术转化创新中心签约落地，推动国际国内前沿技术成果转化。

以实施《虹桥国际在线新经济生态园规划建设方案》为抓手，聚力培育在线新经济，激发产业新动能，深耕在线新经济领域，产业数字化和数字产业化稳步发展。涌现出以携程、拼多多、联影、华测导航、云上会展、超竞等为代表的一批领军企业和独角兽企业，以仪菲为代表的一批平台型企业，以锅圈、洋妆源、斑马智行、芯易荟、库卡机器人、亭东影业为代表的一批新锐企业，在数字贸易、智能网联汽车、工业互联网、数字内容等领域培育产业发展集群。商务区范围内长宁、闵行、青浦、嘉定四大片区积极引导作为，呈现出各有侧重、优势合作、态势良好的数字经济发展新局面。商务区已集聚科学研究和技术服务业企业超1.4万家，占比17.5%，是全市平均水平的3.4倍，集聚了信达生物、云南白药等为代表的集研发、临床、服务于一体的现代创新药产业集群，数字内容分发、知识产权交易等知识密集型产业初具规模，形成特色。北斗西虹桥基地、苏河汇等现有孵化器能级提升，开展垂直孵化、深度孵化。博世、联合利华等知名跨国公司总部以及携程、爱奇艺等行业龙头企业，围绕自身产业链建设专业孵化器。第七届中国创新挑战赛（上海）长三角区域一体化发展专题赛现场赛暨年度分享会成功举办，推动形成良好的创新创业氛围。

着力打造数字特色产业集群，加快建设全球数字贸易港、国家数字服务出口基地。加强数字基础设施建设。持续推进5G示范区建设，加速推动宏基站加密布局、人工智能等产业平台和应用场景落地，建设服务全球数据流动汇聚的功能性枢纽型高等级设施，积极推进重点园区、特色楼宇室内分布网，打造通达全球、高速泛在、智能融合的数据港。营造数字产业生态。着力引进和培育数字贸易、数字会展、数字内容、数字健康、工业互联网、数字出行、元宇宙、量子信息、大数据、空天信息十大领域在线新经济龙头企业。聚焦集成电路、新型显示、通信设备、智能硬件等重点方向，加快引育一批具有国际竞争力的大企业和具有产业链控制力的生态主导企业。打响数字贸易品牌。加快打造一批具有国际化基因和发展潜力的数字贸易品牌，吸引数字领域跨国公司的地区总部、研发中心、交付中心和重要平台落户。发挥贸促机构的作用，通过展会、峰会、双边合作等方式，加大虹桥数字贸易品牌宣传力度，搭建海外宣传渠道，不断扩大海内外影响力。

图2-8 苏河汇创业孵化基地

案例1

苏河汇全球共享经济数字贸易中心暨苏河汇创业孵化基地位于长宁区金钟路633号A栋、B栋，地处上海虹桥北临空经济园核心地段，面积6 573平方米，孵化企业使用场地面积占基地总面积2/3以上，基地为企业提供创业孵化相关政策、财税、法律、投融资、人力资源、孵化运营、市场推广等专业服务。2021年5月以来孵化企业落地达211家。先后荣获上海众创空间、上海创业学院、上海市科技创业苗圃、上海科技创新创业服务先进集体等。

第二章 国际化中央商务区

第五节 赋能数字新经济

案例2

携程智慧出行产业园是携程集团针对未来出行领域的发展趋势和需求，打造的由智慧出行产业链相关企业聚集的数字科技园区。该园区聚焦智慧交通、智慧旅游、智慧商旅、智慧物流等领域，集聚优质创新产业和创新人才，推动智慧出行行业升级和创新发展。园区主导产业在线旅游，自园区创建起便全力支持企业发展，在多方面为企业提供专业服务及解决方案。截至2023年10月底，携程智慧园区落地率达70%，承租率高达100%。

图2-9 携程智慧出行产业园

未来商务区将持续优化创新创业生态，围绕优势产业和优势产业门类，提升企业和研发机构的核心竞争力和创新能力，增强市场化科技创新力量的策源能力。同时，聚焦政策制度突破，推动打造配置创新要素平台，搭建更多高质量合作平台，推动打造国际人才港、技术交易功能、知识产权保护中心、全球数字贸易港等重要载体平台，持续推动政策创新，提供更为便利的创新要素等配套支撑，更好地把人流、物流、商流的价值转化为经济价值和创新价值，支持企业加快技术创新、加快业务创新，助推商务区高质量发展。

第六节　打造一流城市品质

按照国际化新城区建设目标，商务区全面推进产城融合发展，加快完善生活空间功能布局和基础设施支持，进一步增加优质服务供给，公共服务更有品质、居住空间更加宜人、城区运行更有韧性、城市管理更加精细，国际化新城区舒适度不断增强。

一、完善高品质生活圈

高端国际化社区得到高标准规划建设。虹庐湾、首创禧瑞荟完成建设并入住，碧桂园柏悦前湾、大华紫樾府、南山前湾拾缦等高品质国际社区项目稳步推进，北虹之星国际化社区已完成控规修编草案。

多层次住房供给加快推进。各片区通过非居住存量房屋改建、城中村改造、新建、配建等多途径增加住房供应，动迁房、租赁住宅、人才公寓相结合的多元住房供应体系加快构建。博雅苑、舒雅苑、茗雅苑、润雅苑、泽雅苑等动迁房已完成建设投入使用，虹桥莲花景苑、虹桥玉兰馨苑、虹桥紫荆雅苑等动迁房项目持续推进建设，为本地动迁居民提供优质居住环境。2022年以来，东虹桥已供保障性租赁住房共计9 600多套，南虹桥已供保障性租赁住房867套，西虹桥配建7 426套租赁性住房，北虹桥新增保障性租赁住房1 042套。虹桥乐贤居城家公寓顺利交付并投入运营，为商务区增加1 701套保障性租赁用房。宏伊安泊芮公寓、可遇公寓等租赁住房项目和璟智公寓等保障性租赁住房项目投入运营，虹尚安雅居租赁房即将试运营，为就业人群提供良好安居环境。推动虹桥良华广场改建项目建设，计划可提供583套酒店式公寓。加快商务区内已建低效商办楼宇改造为租赁住房研究。

高端医疗康养机构加快集聚。新虹桥国际医学中心的高能级医疗健康服务供给能力进一步提升。支持外籍医务人员执业，将外籍医生执业审批从20个工作日缩短为6个工作日。新虹桥国际医学中心美中嘉和影像中心的PET-CT取得社会办医乙类大型医用设备配置批复。远大健康城、德达医院、上海冬雷脑科医院、览海康复医院等项目投入运营。上海市疾病预防控制中心新建工程项目加快推进。

高质量教育资源加快布局。扩大公办教育资源，新增徐和路幼儿园、尚鸿幼儿园、尚泰幼儿园、徐泾第三幼儿园和尚鸿小学。加快豪葳国际双语幼儿园建设。引进世界外国语学校青浦校区。积极引进全市优质基础教育，推进华东师大新虹桥基础教育实验园落地，其中：10-07幼儿园加快建设，07-04小学、06-02幼儿园和华东师大初中项目方案研究加快推进。商务区内一批外籍学校自主面向全国招收外籍人员子女。

优质文体资源加强供给。虹桥国际文化艺术中心、虹桥国际城市文化展示中心等项目前期工作加快推进。上海国际新文创电竞中心项目加快建设。虹桥体育公园完成建设。国家会展中心（上海）虹馆举办麦浪魔都演唱会、Boystory演唱会等活动。举办虹桥天地音乐美食节、淀山湖文化旅游节等文旅节庆活动。"乐游长三角"旅游专列在虹桥火车站首发。2023上海女子半程马拉松赛、2023环意RIDE LIKE A PRO长三角公开赛等国际赛事成功举办。

二、健全区域交通联系网络体系

公共交通体系建设加快推进。加快推进市域铁路嘉闵线、上海示范区线，机场联络线以及轨道交通2号线、13号线等线路西延伸工程建设。轨交14号线嘉定段已完成地下通道的全线贯通。轨交25号线正在开展前期方案研究，原17号线通道利用形成规

图2-10　立体慢行系统

划方案。枢纽西交通广场综合改造提升工程加快建设，开通并优化了虹桥商务区2路，71路中运量公交西延伸工程专用道正式启用，推进中运量通道的规划和预控，规划构筑"核心放射+切向加密"的中运量网。推进临空区域"七下八上"立体慢行系统建设（包括4座景观步行桥、4座人行过街天桥、7处地下人行通道），其中协和路地下通道、北翟路地下通道、北翟路天桥等设施已建成开放。建成国家会展中心（上海）配套停车场约6 000个停车位，含内部配套4 000个和5号停车场2 000个。

路网体系进一步完善。S20外环西段功能提升工程加快推进。临洮路跨吴淞江大桥（临洮路—绥宁路）建成通车，为商务区增加了一条重要的南北向干道。申长北路—金园一路、申昆路—金运路、龙联路、兴虹西路、天山西路、临虹路、朱建路、闵北路、徐德路等区区对接道路加快建设。开展联友路、纪宏路、翔江路、迎宾三路西延伸、纪秀路—纪梅路等5条区区对接道路规划研究。G15公路嘉金段改造已开工，迎宾三路东延伸工程前期工作加快推进。推进会展匝道建设，增强对会展抵、离场交通的快速直接服务。

三、推进重大工程项目建设

推进完成商务区2022年度总控计划评估和考核评价工作、2023年度总控计划编制工作。2023年前二季度，先后组织召开了2023年度总控计划一季度、二季度和三季度全体会议，部署落实相关工作，重点狠抓三个关键，即土地收储、土地出让和项目连续施工、项目新开工，强化投资强度，营造投资热土氛围，尽早尽快释放建设载体。6月中旬，商务区开展了中期调整、中期评估等工作，在四区两企业报送的2023年度总控计划中期调整计划的基础上，经多次会商研判，调入项目29个，调出项目16个。中期调整后，2023年度总控计划共列入202个项目。截至2023年9月底，总控计划累计完成固定资产投资209.55亿元，同比2022年增长50.6%，同比2021年增长31.5%。通过现场调研信达生物、新文创电竞中心、恒力项目、天合光能项目、申昆路地下停车场、西交广场综合提升、虹桥人才公寓、申昆路—金运路等重大项目，商务区督促总控计划项目有序实施。

商务区以总控计划为重要工作抓手，加快城市配套项目建设，持续推动城市基础设施完善、基础服务供给，增强城市能级品质。基础配套设施方面，精准施策推动西交广场综合提升及机场联络线申昆路停车场、国家会展中心（上海）配套停车场、丰虹路地下连通道建设，保障交通安全畅通；实施机场东片区综合改造市政配套二期工程，优化道路、河道、绿化等基础配套设施；推进绥德公园改建工程、长宁环城公园带驿站等项目，提升公共空间品质。新型基础设施建设方面，加快建设长三角数字干线"首发站"，依托北斗西虹桥基地，拓展北斗产业链和应用场景，开展智慧园区管理系统建设。2023年商务区四个片区及两家企业基础设施建设项目情况见表2-4。

表2-4 虹桥国际中央商务区2023年基础设施建设项目情况统计表

所属片区	基础设施建设项目数量（个）	总投资额（亿元）	区级投资额（亿元）
闵行片区	14	21.89	13.43
长宁片区	2	2.55	2.55
青浦片区	10	11.56	11.56
嘉定片区	11	10.99	6.77
地产集团	1	2.10	0
机场集团	1	10.23	0
总　计	39	59.32	34.31

注：表中投资额为年度计划目标。

四、深入推进绿色低碳发展

供能系统加快建设。3号能源中心项目已投运，将与1号、2号能源中心形成良好的能源供应互补效应，基本满足商务区核心区内260万平方米公共建筑用能需求。国家会展中心能源站、国际医学园区能源中心、西虹桥能源中心等已建成投运。

绿色生态城区建设加紧推进。虹桥商务区机场片区、嘉定封浜新镇获得三星级上海市绿色生态城区（试点）称号。南虹桥片区绿色生态城区专项规划获批复。截至2023年9月底，虹桥商务区核心区共有14个项目已获得绿色建筑运行评价标识认证，推进1个项目按照新绿标提升并开展运行标识申报工作。绿色运行面积达到298.76万平方米，其中三星级面积占比达到82.5%。

高品质生态空间加快构建。苏州河生态廊道绿化项目（一期）已完成实施建设。吴淞江生态间隔带加快启动国际方案征集。前湾公园一期已正式开工。临空音乐公园、中新泾公园、临空滑板公园、泗沙林地公园等公园建成开放。新建天山西路北、国家会展中心（上海）绿地公园等城市公园绿地。苏州河绿化景观带、外环景观带等滨水绿道加快品质提升，水系网络得到优化，完成华东政法大学段全部"一带十点"提升。推进实施景观灯光打造工程提升项目，全面提升区域形象。启动绿植铺装与工程建设，积极推进建筑与小区、道路与广场、河道与水系、公园与绿地等进行源头绿色基础设施改造提升。

五、城市精细化管理水平不断提高

虹桥标准管理体系进一步建立健全。推动编制《上海虹桥国际中央商务区景观照明设置导则》《上海虹桥国际中央商务区河道分类治理导引》《上海虹桥国际中央商务区城市家具设置导则》《上海虹桥国际中央商务区街道景观提升导引》《上海虹桥国际中央商务区精细化示范区建设导引》等文件，并推进落地实施。以新虹街道为试点，推进户外广告招牌设置导则编制，创新户外广告招牌管理办法，设立江桥镇户外招牌行政许可受理窗口。

城市管理智能化水平加快提升。搭建服务保障进博会"一网统管"指挥平台，强化进博会城市生命体征实时数据监测，"进博体征"已拓展至9大类近百项指标。接入"西虹桥一体化智慧管养平台""餐饮卫生明厨亮灶"等智能应用场景，整合视频共享平台、5G车载、17号轨交诸光路站等近4 000路视频资源至移动端进博保障APP，实现对进博会城市运行"人、物、动、态"的全维度"智"理。

第三章　国际贸易中心新平台

第一节　"丝路电商"合作先行区

创建"丝路电商"合作先行区是以习近平同志为核心的党中央作出的重大决策部署，是深入贯彻落实党的二十大精神、在新时代新征程深化改革开放的重要任务，是推进高质量共建"一带一路"、积极推动电子商务国际合作的重大举措。习近平主席在第五届进博会开幕式致辞中提出"创建'丝路电商'合作先行区"；在2023年第三届"一带一路"国际合作高峰论坛上，又将先行区创建列为支持高质量共建"一带一路"八项行动举措之一。李强总理在第六届进博会开幕式主旨演讲中，强调支持上海建设"丝路电商"合作先行区。10月17日，国务院发布《关于在上海市创建"丝路电商"合作先行区的批复》。根据《关于在上海市创建"丝路电商"合作先行区的方案》（简称《方案》)，明确在虹桥国际中央商务区打造"丝路电商"辐射引领区。

一、《方案》主要内容

《方案》聚焦制度开放先行、主体培育先行和机制合作先行，加快对接国际高标准经贸规则，探索体制机制创新，扩大电子商务领域对外开放。总体目标可以概括为"四个一批"，即到2025年，形成一批具有示范引领作用的制度型开放成果；集聚一批具有国际竞争力的电子商务经营主体；打造一批各具特色的区域载体；建成一批促进"丝路电商"伙伴国共同发展的公共服务平台，电子商务交易和国际合作交流更加活跃，综合服务功能显著增强，为发展"丝路电商"提供成果支撑和实践经验。聚焦扩大电子商务领域开放、营造先行先试环境、大力推进国际和区域交流合作等3个方面共19项具体任务。

一是扩大电子商务领域开放。共7项任务，包括拓展国际数据服务、实施高标准贸易便利化措施、推动电子单证国际标准应用、探索数字身份和电子认证跨境互操作、扩大跨境电商进口、促进跨境电商出口创新发展、推动"丝路电商"跨境人民币结算。提出建设数据交易登记服务体系和数据交易国际板，参与数据流通国际标准合作；推进国际贸易"单一窗口"国际合作，通过通关数据共享互通，支持"一单两报"等贸易便利化措施；建设跨境电子发票互操作平台，支持银行将电子发票作为进口付汇凭证并推广使用；推动提单、仓单等电子可转让记录境内和跨境使用；支持建立数字身份跨境互操作平台，探索跨境服务规则衔接；支持建立电子认证服务互通平台，满足电子合同、电子化原产地证书等数字化单证业务在线交换及验证需求；结合伙伴国商品出口需求，引入培育更多优质商品；支持跨境电商企业、传统外贸企业和物流企业等各类主体以多种形式建设海外仓，搭建海外仓综合服务平台等先行先试举措。

二是营造先行先试环境。共6项任务，包括在自贸试验区及临港新片区的海关特殊监管区域打造中心功能区、在虹桥国际中央商务区打造辐射引领区、建立跨境电商全球集散分拨中心、培育壮大"丝路电商"企业、完善"丝路电商"基础设施、打造国际人才集聚地。提出推动海关特殊监管区域开展保税展示，拓展跨境电商模式，为伙伴国企业提供一站式进口服务；在虹桥国际中央商务区集聚伙伴国贸易投资促进机构，组织开展"丝路电商"国别文化交流、商贸对接、商品展销等活动；在海关特殊监管区域搭建兼具多种海关监管功能的全球分拨中心，研究探索货物进出仓海关监管新模式；推进电子商务平台和专业服务机构集聚发展，建设跨境电子商务独立站；完善仓储、物流、支付等电子商务基础设施建设，健全跨境电商结算体系；优化完善电子商务领域人才引进重点机构范围，对优秀外籍电子商务人才，给予申请办理多年期工作许可和工作类居留证件便利等先行先试举措。

三是大力推进国际和区域交流合作。共6项任务，包括开展"丝路电商"智库交流、开展"丝路电商"数字技术应用推广、促进"丝路电商"研修交流、畅通伙伴国电子商务交流合作、推动"丝路电商"区域合作、构建"丝路电商"国际服务体系。提出发起成立"丝路电商"国际智库联盟，开展跨境电商规则、产业对接和知识产权保护等研究；打造"丝路电商"数字技术应用中心，推进云计算、区块链、大数据、物联网、数字孪生等技术应用，开展进口宝玉石商品溯源试点工作；设立"丝路电商"合作研修中心，构建政府、高校、社会、企业多方联动的电子商务人才培养体系；设立集商品、旅游、文化展示等功能于一体的国家馆，举办"丝路云品"主题促消费活动；推动长三角地区跨境电商公共服务平台在货物通关、物流跟踪、企业咨询等方面加强合作,鼓励长三角地区跨境电商行业商协会合作;建设"丝路电商"跨境服务平台和境外投资服务平台,实现全周期、全链条服务等先行先试举措。

二、商务区打造"丝路电商"辐射引领区的优势和特色

依托长三角一体化发展、进博会和虹桥国际开放枢纽等国家战略,商务区推动虹桥进口贸易促进创新示范区纵深发展,一半以上企业与"丝路电商"国家开展贸易往来,已经形成了以"丝路电商"助推新发展格局、助力高质量发展的良好基础。

内联外通,进博会溢出带动效应明显。依托"6天+365天"常年展销平台,虹桥品汇、绿地全球商品贸易港在全国特别是长三角设了分中心36个;国家馆63个,其中"丝路电商"伙伴国国家馆19个;虹桥国际咖啡港、国际酒窖运营有序;依托虹桥保税物流中心(B型),成功助力"丝路电商"伙伴国特色展品以"展后转跨境电商"方式进入中国市场,在"丝路电商"分销渠道、国家馆建设、品类集聚上有较好基础。

服务为先,中国品牌和企业出海优势突出。商务区集聚数字贸易企业超7 000多家,总部类企业超500家,特别是安踏、美的、报喜鸟、雅戈尔等民营总部将国际业务

图3-1 进博好物畅购集

板块落地商务区，对外开展投资贸易需求大。同时，依托上海市"一带一路"综合服务中心、虹桥国际商务人才港、虹桥国际中央法务区、知识产权保护中心、RCEP企业服务咨询站、企业国际化服务工作站等平台，形成企业"走出去"服务矩阵，特别是虹桥海外贸易中心已集聚丝绸之路国际总商会上海代表处、中国瑞士中心、新加坡企业中心、法中经贸企业等海外投资贸易促进机构37家，连接国际国内市场。

优化配套，贸易流通综合大节点功能显现。商务区物流体系完善，集聚三通一达、德邦、顺丰等快递企业174家，全国12.7%、全市80.3%的货物通过虹桥这个国内大循环的枢纽节点集散各地，为"丝路电商"国家贸易投资往来提供专业服务。

三、商务区参与创建"丝路电商"合作先行区工作举措

为深入推进《关于推动虹桥国际开放枢纽进一步提升能级的若干政策措施》《关于在上海市创建"丝路电商"合作先行区的方案》，推动商务区打造联动长三角、服务全国、联通国际的"丝路电商"合作先行区的辐射引领区，建成上海"丝路电商"合作先行区的重要载体，商务区制定《虹桥国际中央商务区关于全力推进"丝路电商"合作先行区的三年行动方案》。到2025年，商务区"丝路电商"伙伴国进出贸易同比增长显著高于全市平均水平；探索"丝路电商"伙伴国优质特色产品和服务对接中国市场的一站式服务模式，形成"丝路电商"专业展销、"丝路电商"国家馆、"丝路电商"直播经济样板间；引进和培育一批引领"丝路电商"发展、具备产业链整合能力的龙头企业和平台；全力构建以消费为牵引的电子商务生态圈，打造有利于"丝路电商"发展的国际贸易特色营商环境，成为连接长三角城市群和"一带一路"国家的节点门户和上海国际贸易中心新高地。重点做好以下三方面工作：

一是持续放大进博会综合效应。依托虹桥品汇等常年展销平台，推动"丝路电商"国家馆和专业展销平台升级，并增设更多分中心，引领更多的区域参与到"丝路电商"合作中。大力发展"丝路电商"直播经济，比如，支持俄罗斯酒、新西兰蜂蜜、柬埔寨腰果等通过虹桥品汇直播基地进入国内市场。依托上海国际友城港等平台定期组织国别文化交流、商贸对接、商品展销。举办"丝路云品"主题促消费活动，构建以消费需求为牵引的电子商务生态圈。

二是加强聚焦专业服务能力打造。切实发挥虹桥海外贸易中心优势，在已集聚37个国际贸易机构和组织的基础上，再引进一批"丝路电商"伙伴国贸易机构和组织。加快推动RCEP等新一轮国际经贸协定在商务区实质性落地，建设RCEP企业服务咨询

图 3-2 "丝路电商 云品海购"启动仪式

站,围绕进口市场准入、通关便利、人员流动等方面在商务区先行先试。鼓励政策性和市场化金融机构为"丝路电商"贸易往来、海外仓建设、跨境贸易、仓储物流等提供金融服务。比如,通过跨境电商保单和海外投资保险保单减少企业风险。大力发展生产性服务业,实施跨境电商国际人才培养计划;完善法律、人才、知识产权、咨询等专业服务支撑,全方位助推内资企业国际化转型以及跨国公司深耕国内市场,促进信息流、资金流、贸易流、国际化人才等高端商贸要素高效便捷流动,成为本市和长三角企业拓展"丝路电商"海外市场的重要通道。

三是高质量推动数字化转型重点平台建设。重点打造"丝路电商"数字技术应用中心,通过区块链、大模型、大数据、物联网等技术在"丝路电商"业务中的应用,探索实现"丝路电商"重点商品全程溯源,做好交易真实性审核等,在跨境贸易通关、电子发票、风险监测等技术方面形成示范。支持虹桥贸易数字化赋能中心推动研发制造、跨境通关、物流仓储等贸易全环节数字化改造,赋能"丝路电商"企业中小品牌在中国市场发展。

第二节　内外贸一体化

围绕"强化国际定位、彰显开放优势、提升枢纽功能"发展主线，努力将商务区打造成为国内国际双循环战略链接的新支点、长三角一体化高质量发展的驱动轮，加快推进内外贸一体化工作。

一、在服务新发展格局中体现新成效

《总体方案》发布以来，商务区以国家进口贸易促进创新示范区建设为契机，持续承接和放大进博会溢出效应，深化推进一批交易类、服务贸易类、贸易支撑类国际贸易中心功能平台，虹桥进口商品展示交易中心、新虹桥国际医学中心、虹桥海外贸易中心、虹桥国际会展产业园等能级持续提升。围绕会展经济、总部经济、服务经济等打造特色产业园区，高端医疗服务贸易、离岸贸易、数字贸易、跨境电商等新型贸易形态创新发展。强化新赛道布局和终端带动，新兴产业和行业龙头加快集聚，引进跨国公司地区总部、民营经济总部、研发中心、贸易型总部、上市公司、央企二总部等总部类企业超500家，形成以泰森、米其林、博世等为代表的外资总部生态圈；以波司登、报喜鸟、恒力等为代表的长三角总部生态圈；以美的、安踏、锅圈等为代表的民企总部生态圈；以统一、太太乐、携程等为代表的贸易总部生态圈；以中核建、中电投为代表的央企二总部生态圈，区域开放度、功能引领性、产业显示度不断加强。

二、推进内外贸一体化发展

以海外仓国内保税仓联动为重点，推进内外贸一体化各项试点工作。组织召开试点开题会议。4月份，来自包括广东、浙江、上海等19家细分领域的头部企业代表，在虹桥召开基于实物互联网的内外贸一体化重点试点课题启动座谈会，一起探讨实物互联网在中国落地的施工图，探讨推进传递标准化、数字化的实物包的试点目标任务的落地路径。探索构建内外贸一体化天网。5月份，组织了国内近50位各省市的批发商，与部分海外华商会代表，在虹桥这个联通国际国内的关键节点，以内外贸一体

图3-3　实物互联网PI全景图

化重点试点课题为牵引，在全球产业链供应链争夺激烈、重塑加剧，加快构建区域统一大市场、国内大循环的大背景下，探讨在畅通国内国际双循环中，打造内外贸一体化的网络，助力经销商向供应链服务商的转型发展。

三、促进国际贸易模式创新

商务区围绕承接进博溢出、贸易促进创新和对接国际规则三大重点领域聚力突破，在高水平对外开放中形成市场相通、产业相融、创新相促、规则相联的良性循环，服务国家经济高质量发展。

畅联国内国际市场，全力打造进博会成果集中展示地。搭建一批面向"一带一路"国家和地区的商品直销平台、国别商品交易中心和专业贸易平台，吸引了来自150余个国家和地区近400家客商、2.6万个品牌、15万种商品入驻、销售，开设国家馆63个，累计开设虹桥品汇、绿地全球商品贸易港分中心36个，打造进博直播经济生态，深化咖啡、酒类等专业平台，加速打造联动长三角、服务全国、辐射亚太的进口商品集散地。探索形成进口商品保税展示交易常态化机制，开出保税展示交易面积1.2万平方米，47个国家和地区1 000多个品牌通过保税展示交易试水中国市场。

图3-4 虹桥品汇

强化产业发展核心功能。抢抓数字新经济、时尚新消费、生命新科技、低碳新能源、汽车新势力、贸易新平台等新赛道,集聚行业龙头和独角兽企业。推进全球数字贸易港率先成势。成功推动中国北斗产业技术创新西虹桥基地获评国家级地理信息服务领域特色服务出口基地,积极支持临空经济园区创建国家数字服务出口基地,推动国际互联网数据通道落地,探索高水平的跨境数据流动开放体系。加强贸易创新政策研究,积极推动飞机保税维修等政策落地,争取飞机融资租赁政策,促进航空要素集聚和发展。深化发展离岸贸易、转口贸易等新型贸易业态。依托新虹桥国际医学中心,研究大型甲类医疗设备、进口药品和器械等方面创新政策。

第三节　助力企业"走出去"

为落实《总体方案》要求，建设高标准的国际化中央商务区，加快提升商务区服务企业"走出去"能级，市商务委、商务区管委会联合制定了《加快提升虹桥国际中央商务区服务企业"走出去"能级的若干措施》。以长三角企业借力商务区更高质量"走出去"的服务需求为导向，充分发挥商务区的区位、商务、政策、服务优势，整合长三角一体化发展、进博会及虹桥国际开放枢纽"三大"国家级战略发展平台功能，为长三角企业"走出去"提供更高质量的服务支撑。力争到2025年底，进一步提升商务区服务企业"走出去"的总部机构集聚发展能力、专业服务国际竞争能力、要素资源统筹配置能力、公共服务支撑保障能力，打造商务区助力企业"走出去"的高能级服务高地，并提出6个方面15项主要任务。

一、支持"走出去"总部集聚发展

支持各类总部企业提质升级。建立完善支持总部企业"走出去"的政策服务体系，发挥虹桥贸易总部园区等总部经济培育和孵化功能，鼓励已落户商务区的各类总部提升能级，发展成为"走出去"的亚太总部或全球总部。对总部企业新增海外营业收入给予奖励。对经认定的各类总部给予包括营运专项补贴、人才专项补贴等资金支持。对企业开展境外投资合作业务所得，按规定适用盈亏弥补及税收饶让抵免等政策。

打造长三角企业海外投资总部基地。发挥长三角企业国际市场竞争优势，鼓励长三角企业在商务区设立海外投资业务板块，支持建立以长三角区域为重点，总部在商务区、基地在长三角、业务在全球的企业国际化经营模式，重点推动生物医药、医疗健康、软件信息、数字文创与数字融合、智能制造装备等"链主"企业、数字经济和高端项目总部落户商务区，打造与一体化高质量发展要求相匹配的长三角企业海外投资总部基地。

订制"走出去"企业总部服务包。统筹政府公共服务与市场专业服务资源，加强对企业"走出去"总部提供相关政策匹配、诉求响应、供需对接等精准服务。发挥商务区政企沟通对话会作用，进一步畅通政企沟通机制，开辟问题协调"绿色通道"。

二、强化专业服务配套支撑

打造虹桥专业服务机构集聚区。鼓励具有国际化服务能力的专业服务机构在商务区集聚，制订商务区专业服务机构名单，引导其为商务区企业提供就近高质量服务。支持中国上海人力资源服务产业园区虹桥园、虹桥国际中央法务区等园区建设，探索打造虹桥国际会计事务中心、虹桥国际金融税务中心等专业服务业新载体。积极争取复制推广中国（上海）自由贸易试验区关于律师行业扩大开放的相关举措。支持在商务区试点建立调解、仲裁、诉讼相衔接的涉外商事纠纷一站式解决机制。

提升专业服务机构国际化能力。支持商务区的专业服务机构通过兼并收购、联营合作、自建等方式，加快构建国际服务市场网络，提升跨境服务能力，对在境外设立分支机构或服务网点，符合一定要求的机构给予支持。举办"一带一路"知识产权保护论坛，提升上海市知识产权保护中心维权援助工作站能级，推进海外知识产权服务工作站建设，拓展海外纠纷应对服务网络。支持商务区专业服务机构与"走出去"企业开展业务对接合作，以跟随出海的方式提供高质量服务，拓展国际业务。发挥好RCEP、CEPA作用，支持商务区探索推进职业资格、服务标准、认证认可等领域国际规则对接。

三、打造国际经济组织集聚区

支持国际经济组织集聚发展。大力引进国际影响力大、国际知名度高、资源配置能力强的经贸类国际组织落户虹桥海外贸易中心，对新落户且符合一定条件的国际经济组织，给予租金、开办费、营运及人才专项补贴等支持。对符合一定条件的境外贸易投资促进机构、国际知名商协会等落户商务区给予落地服务、人员出入境便利等支持。鼓励国际经济组织及境外贸易投资促进机构在虹桥国际中央商务区举办各类投资促进、国际性论坛等活动，为商务区企业提供"引进来"与"走出去"双向信息服务。对在商务区举办高水平国际交流活动给予支持。

支持行业协会提升国际影响力。支持商务区的专业行业协会进一步加强与境外行业协会、国际组织开展交流与合作，为"走出去"企业开展业务提供境外事务协调与市场拓展信息支持。支持行业协会负责人在国际组织或国际行业协会中任职。

四、增强跨境业务要素支撑

吸引高端人才集聚。以虹桥国际商务人才港和中国上海人力资源服务产业园区虹桥园为载体，加快启动实施人才吸引专项计划，为各类人才提供包括人才公寓、公租房、子女教育、医疗等服务，加快完善相关配套服务设施。加大对外籍人才吸引力度，提供长期工作居留、永久居留等便利措施。为需紧急入境开展商务活动的外籍人才，提供口岸签证便利。支持需多次临时入境的外籍人才申请办理多次签证。

创新金融服务和产品。探索各类金融机构为商务区内企业提供专项信贷额度等支持。鼓励各类股权投资机构加速集聚商务区，支持合格境内有限合伙人（QDLP）试点在区内落地。鼓励金融机构依托自由贸易账户等为区内企业深化跨境金融服务，加大本外币一体化资金池等产品推广力度。支持商务区管委会与中国出口信用保险公司合作研发针对区内企业"走出去"国际化发展的以人民币计价的跨境保险产品。支持区内金融机构助力商务区企业赴境外上市、发行债券，不断拓宽融资渠道。支持商业银行为符合条件的商务区内企业及专业服务机构提供贸易外汇收支便利化、资本项目外汇收入支付便利化等服务。

五、加强公共服务保障能力

优化"走出去"综合服务。整合市企业"走出去"综合服务中心、市"一带一路"综合服务中心等平台功能，集聚"走出去"相关的金融、法律、会计、广告等专业服务机构，优化商务区内"走出去"企业项目申报、政策咨询、人才发展等"一站式"综合服务。在商务区内建立"一站式"办事大厅，设立"走出去"服务专窗。

探索设立虹桥海外发展中心。借鉴国际成功做法和经验，探索设立由商务区管委会主导、企业化运营的"虹桥海外发展中心"，全方位支持企业开拓海外市场，助力企业"走出去"行稳致远。

发挥专项资金的引导作用。用足用好商务区专项资金政策，统筹用好国家外经贸发展专项资金、市商务高质量发展专项资金、市服务业发展引导资金等专项资金，支持各类企业、专业服务机构、国际经济组织落户商务区，进一步提高资金使用效益。

加强风险防控与海外维权。加强对境外国家地区经济形势、投资环境、行业趋势、文化习俗等分析，发布国别投资指南、政策法规汇编和市场分析报告等。组织开展"走出去"专项培训，帮助企业解读国际市场规则、经贸投资政策、法律环境，引导企业遵守东道国相关法律法规和投资规范，增强社会责任意识。发挥本市海外安全工作机制及市海外救援服务中心作用，指导企业健全海外安全风险防范和处置机制，助力维护企业海外合法权益。探索建立企业海外风险应对能力评估体系，为企业"走出去"

提供事前能力评价报告,帮助企业补齐海外风险防范短板。

六、搭建国际合作交流新平台

放大国际会展溢出带动效应。依托国家会展中心的综合展示交易功能,大力吸引国内外知名会展企业及其总部、专业组展机构、品牌展会、论坛会议及配套企业落户商务区。推动各类会展资源要素在商务区交流、交互,汇聚人流、物流、信息流,带动投资贸易发展。积极推动创建"丝路电商"合作先行区,发挥商务区在"一带一路"跨境电商产品集散地的功能优势和辐射带动作用,用好虹桥进口商品展示交易中心、绿地全球商品贸易港等"6+365"平台资源,为境外企业打通展品变商品的链接。高质量举办各类对接配套活动和投资贸易促进活动,开展"品牌展会走进长三角"系列活动,为长三角企业了解虹桥搭建沟通交流、信息共享、国际合作新平台。

发挥生产性互联网服务平台的资源整合功能。依托"走出去"企业资源网络,完善大宗商品价格发现功能,提升商务区重要大宗商品交易服务平台的国际市场影响力。支持区内工业品电商服务平台与长三角制造企业开展合作,形成"平台+园区"融合发展优势,提升供应链效率。支持数字化转型服务平台为"走出去"企业提供研发、生产、管理、贸易等全过程对接服务。加快打造与生命健康、先进材料、时尚消费等重点产业紧密相关的专业服务平台,为"走出去"企业提供"技术+市场"的增值服务。

第四节　生产性互联网服务平台

2023年7月，上海市人民政府办公厅印发《关于促进本市生产性互联网服务平台高质量发展的若干意见》，明确推进浦东新区、宝山区、普陀区、临港新片区、商务区等区域打造生产性互联网服务平台集聚发展新高地，促进"平台+园区"融合发展，加快生产性互联网服务平台集聚。在市商务委指导下，商务区会同四区相关单位挂图作战，统筹协调推进各项工作。

一、发展目标和重点

到2025年，培育3家以上具有全球影响力、资源配置力和创新驱动力的龙头型平台企业；集聚10家以上具备产业链、供应链、价值链整合能力的高成长性企业；培育若干"小型化、快速化、轻量化、精准化"的数字化系统解决方案和产品；争取数个国家级和市级平台落地，建成以数字化转型示范和专业服务为特色的生产性互联网服务平台集聚区，成为链接长三角城市群、"一带一路"沿线重要城市的上海国际贸易中心建设新高地。

重点培育一批标杆数字化转型和专业服务平台，以服务实体经济为核心，以完善产业生态为重点，以优化发展环境为关键，建设联通全球的生产性互联网服务平台示范枢纽、进博会溢出效应转化中心与长三角生产性互联网服务平台"走出去"促进中心。辐射带动"四区"，即闵行片区聚焦法律服务、人才服务、数字健康等领域，重点做强专业化数字服务平台集聚；长宁片区重点布局数字消费、数字出行、大数据等新赛道，做大数字商贸服务平台品牌；青浦片区聚焦会展贸易、工业互联网、空天信息、数字物流仓储等领域，做优物流仓储服务平台功能；嘉定片区围绕人工智能技术创新，做实技术创新服务平台特色。

二、重点举措

制定实施方案，加快培育应用场景。制定《虹桥国际中央商务区全力创建生产性互联网服务平台示范枢纽的实施方案》，明确了三年发展目标，以及"补要素强生态、做优会展产业整合平台、推动平台要素交互对接、促进平台+园区融合发展"等四方面16项重点工作。聚焦数字化转型和专业服务，结合商务区"大交通、大商务、大会展、大科创"核心功能，培育应用场景，如引导虹桥国际咖啡港与亿通合作打造线上贸易平台，支持云上会展利用阿里云计算、大数据、人工智能技术推动会展产业链数字化转型，支持打造以物流仓储为特色的上海虹桥数字供应链集聚区集采平台等。

梳理首批22家培育清单和若干家招商引资清单，形成梯度发展体系。首批重点培育企业22家，其中列入市级重点培育清单3家。从行业类别看，大宗商品交易服务平台企业1家；工业品电商服务平台企业1家；数字化转型服务平台11家，涵盖数字建筑、泛半导体、智慧物流、时尚消费、会展数字化等领域；专业服务平台企业9家，包括法律、外贸服务、人力资源、技术交易等领域的服务平台。从发展阶段来看，龙头型企业7家、高成长型企业4家、潜力型企业8家、储备型企业3家。例如，广联达为国内数字建筑领域第一，锅圈为预制菜头部品牌。从平台影响力来看，重点培育有国际资源配置能力的平台，如：携程eBooking服务了全球范围内120万家酒店合作伙伴，震坤行聚焦北美、欧盟和东南亚市场自建平台，InnoMatch在多个国家设立海外分中心。同时，商务区结合"企业家圆桌会"走出去活动，形成首批招商引资清单7家，其中诺力上海国际总部项目进入拿地流程。

重点围绕"一批园区平台、一批应用场景、一批制度政策"推进工作。一是开展"一区一特"专项行动。引导四片区结合自身功能定位和产业基础，打造有区域鲜明特色的数字化服务高地。其中，闵行片区做强专业化数字服务生产性互联网服务平台集聚，长宁片区做大数字商贸生产性互联网服务平台品牌，青浦片区做优物流仓储生产性互联网服务平台功能，嘉定片区做实技术创新生产性互联网服务平台特色，加速高能级主体引进和产业集聚。二是实施"园区+平台"赋能计划。培育一批以龙头企业为核心集聚上下游产业链的特色楼宇和园区，重点引导园区运营方和龙头企业搭建数字化服务平台，通过数字化赋能加快形成产业生态，打造3—4个有显示度和集中度的"园区+平台"。如中国北斗产业技术创新产业园区、康德莱虹桥国际创新医疗器械产业园、虹桥国际咖啡港、虹桥国际会展产业园等。同时，积极参加市级生产性互联网服务平台产业地图的制定。三是持续完善政策制度创新体系。在已有关于功能性平台、大宗商品、互联网+生产性服务业等市区两级支持政策的基础上，用好市级"1+X"支持政策，结合虹桥新一轮专项资金的调整优化加大对平台的支持力度，并引导四个区出台针对性产业政策。四是加大宣传强化招引能力。在"潮涌浦江 投资虹桥"投资促进大会上推出一批重点平台，做好典型案例等系列专题宣传报道。会同四个区开展"企业家圆桌会"走出去活动，动态更新招引清单，实施"一企一策"，加大重点平台引进力度。

三、典型案例

InnoMatch全球技术供需对接平台创立于2022年8月，由科寻科汇（上海）科技服务有限公司提供平台建设及运营，由国家技术转移东部中心技术转移生态支持。平台以产业端技术需求和科技成果对接为基本模式，融合全球技术、人才、服务、资本等创新要素，丰富多种业务场景，提升技术供需对接效率，以科创资源数字化赋能线下科技成果转化业务，旨在建成具有全球影响力的技术交易枢纽性平台，形成科技领域数字经济的新增长极。

图3-5　InnoMatch全球技术供需对接平台

广联达科技股份有限公司作为数字建筑平台服务商，专注于建筑信息化行业20余年，围绕工程项目全生命周期的业务领域，面向建筑产业链各参与方，以及城市运营、金融、教育等领域，提供以建设工程领域专业化应用为核心基础支撑，以产业大数据、产业链金融等为增值服务的数字建筑全生命周期解决方案。

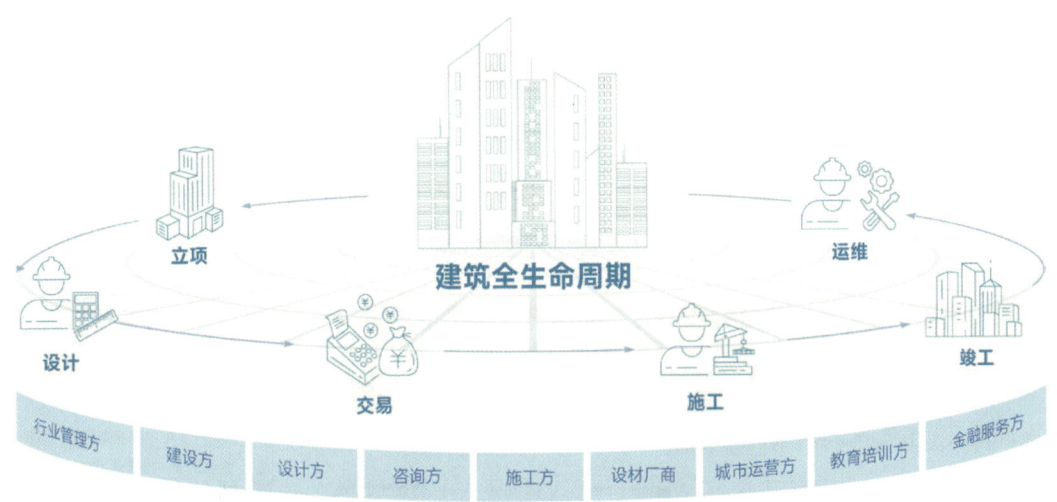

图3-6 数字建筑全生命周期解决方案

震坤行工业超市是国内领先的基于数字化的一站式工业用品采购与管理服务平台。通过"数字化的采销协同网络"实现工业用品供应链的透明、高效、降成本。从管理工具到商业智能,提供标准化软件运营服务(SaaS),帮助中小企业快速完成数字化转型。利用物联网技术与数据智能,提供通用设备的在线监控、租赁及维修保养等服务,实现工厂物料的智能化管理。

图3-7 数字化一站式工业用品采购与管理服务平台

上海黑湖科技有限公司是一家专注于工业互联网软件领域的科技公司，为制造企业提供基于算法驱动、灵活可配置的云端制造协同平台，让生产、质量、物料、设备等关键生产要素实时聚合、协作，让制造云端在线，产业链上下游互联互通、高效协作，帮助制造企业提升运转效率、质量及柔性制造能力，灵活快速响应多变的市场需求。

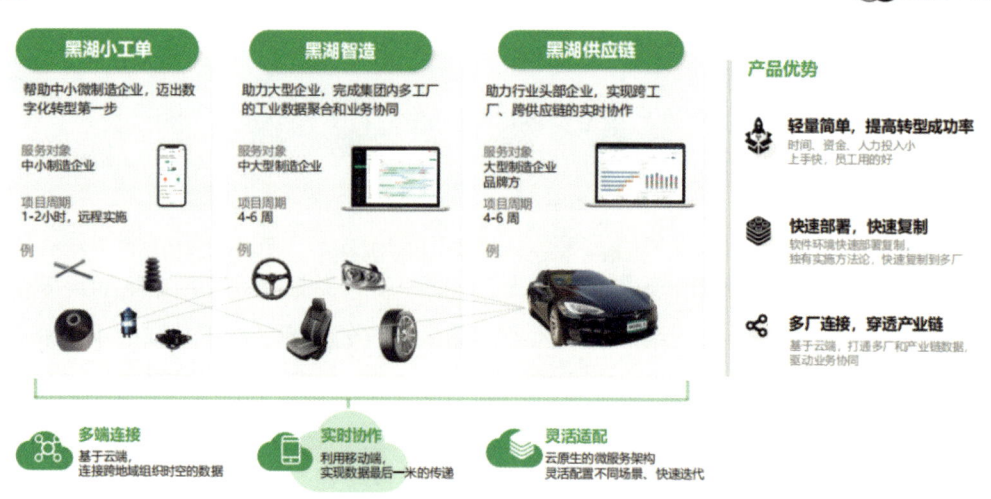

图3-8 云端制造协同平台

第五节　上海西片国际级消费集聚区

商务区加快推进《上海市商业空间布局专项规划（2021—2035）》在虹桥落地，进一步集聚高端消费资源，不断强化集聚区对全球消费资源的配置能力，努力打造成为国际品牌进入中国的加速器、国内品牌出海的桥头堡、新国货潮流品牌的孵化器和进口商品汇聚的集散地。

一、提升商业能级，进一步完善消费布局

商务区围绕商业重点项目建设、数字商圈、夜间活动开展等加强指导。推动虹桥天地、虹桥天街、长宁ARTPARK大融城、青浦万科天空之城等重点商圈消费载体微更新和青浦上海蟠龙天地项目建成开业。探索国家会展中心特色消费地标建设新模式，集结各大知名品牌，形成品牌聚集效应，优化消费空间。依托商务区在电竞、文化、数字方面的集成优势，打造特色生态产业园，不断拓宽EDG等超级IP与消费的融合边界，加强文旅赋能商业，培育年轻一代的消费潜力。

虹桥天地作为商务区直连虹桥交通枢纽的项目，用商业激活地下公共空间，打造为多元文化体验"第一站"——hubo项目，除了装修风格更加新潮，还引进了"只二透明仓"（近万平方米的奢侈品寄卖及零售空间）、"左右艺术超市"（艺术展览陈列式的潮流文化超市）等特色品牌，通过全新概念店、限时快闪店、策展与体验空间以及多功能活动区，打造上海潮流站点，营造国际消费创新体验。

龙湖虹桥天街围绕"城市灵感策源地"进行新一轮升级，通过场内项目调整和"一里九巷""一里绿洲"的改造，全新搭配购物、餐饮、休闲娱乐等业态，以更创新的商业空间、更差异化的品牌组合、更丰富多元的新场景，满足当下Citywalk沉浸式体验等消费新需求。

上海蟠龙天地于2023年4月29日正式开业，作为瑞安集团打造的UrbanRetreat城市微度假目的地，蟠龙天地集商业、住宅、酒店、绿地于一体。延续新天地开放式街区的商业形态，整体规划超50万平方米，商业体量5.3万平方米，公共绿地23万平方米，并规划3千米环形步道和近万平方米户外运动空间，共同打造"公园里的新天地"，探索"生活的另一种写法"。

图3-9 多样化的消费体验

虹桥天地演艺中心是上海首个设在商业综合体内的独立演艺建筑，集演出、会议、活动于一体的多功能平台，目前已经成为"英雄联盟"电竞职业赛事的官方举办地。此外，商务区在建和待建文娱项目包括百老汇综合演艺中心、虹桥国际文化艺术中心、国际新文创电竞中心等，这些重点项目将助力商务区商旅文体展一体联动，加快推进西片国际级消费集聚区建设。

表3-1 虹桥国际中央商务区重大文娱项目

序号	项目名称	板块	现状
1	虹桥天地演艺中心	集聚区	已建
2	国家会展中心演艺馆虹馆	集聚区	已建
3	百老汇综合演艺中心	西虹桥	在建
4	虹桥国际文化艺术中心	南虹桥	待建
5	国际新文创电竞中心	南虹桥	在建

二、打响"虹桥购物"品牌，进一步优化消费环境

商务区不断发挥作为上海面向长三角门户的优越地理位置优势，联动市级"五五购物节"，展示推广全球消费新理念、新模式、新业态、新品牌。不断提升国际影响力。充分利用虹桥特色消费资源，加强集聚区自有品牌宣传推广力度，培育自有品牌消费环境，提升自有品牌形象。聚焦进口消费、餐饮消费、汽车消费、数字消费等重点领域，强化与市级主管部门信息联动互通机制，积极承接上海咖啡文化周、上海数字生活节、上海进口嗨购节、上海信息消费节等市级标杆活动IP。着力增强消费供给的品质化、多元化、高端化，积极推动商家与银行、电商平台的合作，全力动员各类市场主体开展促进消费回补和潜力释放的各种活动，进一步集聚商贸企业和消费者目光，扩大虹桥消费品牌整体影响力。

虹桥天地举办首届虹桥数字黑科技嘉年华，该活动作为2023年闵行"五五购物节"亮点活动之一，通过数字游乐园、电竞游戏、数字消费等六大板块，汇聚AI人工智能、区块链、云计算、5G等数字科技，融入文旅、娱乐、教育和生活等应用场景，创新探索信息消费数字生活，为消费者带来"数字技术"的新体验。据统计，活动期间共吸引了超过57万名参观者前来参观，日均参观人数约为11.4万人次。此外，还举办了"膨胀面包节""泡泡萌粒星愿嘉年华""我i吃冰节""微醺啤酒节"等活动，提供更多元的消费社交场景。龙湖虹桥天街举办"新春游园会·非遗市集"，让消费者打卡旧报刊馆、黄包车、珍藏版旗袍等，领略老上海风情；丽宝广场举办"闪光运动会"，为消费者带来室内外潮流运动体验，助力亚运会等。

三、加快进博溢出效应承接，进一步推动消费创新

丰富消费业态，大力发展保税、免税、离境退税、即买即退、跨境电商新模式等，做大做强虹桥品汇、绿地贸易港等"6天+365天"交易服务平台，打造国别（地区）中心及全球消费中心集中展示基地，支持市场主体对接进博会，推动进博会红利惠及广大消费者，让消费者不出国门，在商务区内一站打卡全球文化。今年上半年就引进了"一带一路"国家供应商42家，其中包括俄罗斯酒、韩国洗护品、塞尔维亚果汁、印度尼西亚燕窝等新品。虹桥品汇直播基地发挥载体和运营优势，扩大丝路电商覆盖半径，前三季度，基地共实现直播电商销售交易额约1.1亿元，已入驻开播客户17家，直播间使用率达到85%以上。包括自营的德国WMF官方旗舰店、瑞士MIDO品牌专卖

图3-10 直播经济新高地

店、梅龙镇官方旗舰店、进宝汇买手团等。进宝汇买手团联动虹桥品汇入驻进口品牌形成"买手店",为"丝路电商"伙伴国、"一带一路"沿线国家企业和商品开展带货专场,推介柬埔寨腰果、新西兰蜂蜜、埃塞俄比亚咖啡等近百款商品,形成洋主播带货特色,助力海外企业走通"数字丝路"。

建设直播经济新高地。受移动互联网快速发展和疫情的影响,直播经济已成为上海在线新经济发展的新名片。携程、唯品会、驴妈妈、爱奇艺等商务区数字经济龙头企业纷纷通过自有平台发展直播经济。截至2023年9月底,商务区有5家企业店铺进入"上海TOP100"(在点淘、抖音、快手三大直播平台销售额前100位的店铺),包括华硕官方旗舰店、迪桑特官方旗舰店、欧普照明官方旗舰店、薇诺娜旗舰店、奥伦纳素旗舰店。商务区内直播经济产品涵盖旅游、服装鞋包配饰、化妆品、电子设备、电器设备、家居、食品等品类。进宝汇、我爱我秀、银科创展等项目开始汇聚网红和内容资源,百秋尚美集团旗下容么么直播中心为直播经济提供专业配套服务。

举办虹桥国际咖啡文化节。作为上海咖啡文化周的重要组成部分,上海咖啡产业高峰论坛暨2023虹桥国际咖啡文化节5月26日在商务区闵行片区开幕。开幕式上,

图3-11　虹桥国际咖啡文化节

《2023中国城市咖啡发展报告》《咖啡产业白皮书》发刊，虹桥国际咖啡港的"百商万店"计划发布，上海市咖啡师职业技能等级社会评价机构揭牌，沪滇合作及金融合作签约，虹桥国际咖啡港与云南国际咖啡交易中心达成合作，并与上海中心"牵手豆"采购签约。咖啡周期间，市民也可深度参与各项活动。另外，虹桥国际咖啡港发布了"百商万店"计划，旨在整合优势资源，构建一站式供应链和内容赋能平台，推动行业整体提升。该计划将为独立咖啡馆提供从精品豆子到专业机器，从烘焙技术到人才培训、从资金到政策等全方位的支持和服务，以优化咖啡馆创业环境，促进咖啡馆生态繁荣。

第四章　第六届中国国际进口博览会

第一节　基本概况

第六届进博会按照"越办越好"总要求,延续"新时代,共享未来"的主题,积极发挥国际采购、投资促进、人文交流、开放合作平台功能,取得丰硕成果。虹桥论坛开放主题更加突出,持续为构建开放型世界经济贡献智慧。来自154个国家、地区和国际组织的政商学等各界代表约1 500位来宾出席开幕式,72个国家和国际组织亮相国家展,128个国家和地区的3 486家企业参加企业展,集中展示442项代表性首发新产品、新技术、新服务。

一、锚定越办越好总要求,全方位展示进博风采

开幕式发出以中国新发展为世界提供新机遇的开放强音。11月5日,习近平主席向第六届进博会致信,强调当前世界经济复苏动力不足,需要各国同舟共济、共谋发展。中国将始终是世界发展的重要机遇,将坚定推进高水平开放,持续推动经济全球化朝着更加开放、包容、普惠、平衡、共赢的方向发展;希望进博会加快提升构建新发展格局的窗口功能,以中国新发展为世界提供新机遇;充分发挥推动高水平开放的平台作用,让中国大市场成为世界共享的大市场;更好提供全球共享的国际公共产品服务,助力推动构建开放型世界经济,让合作共赢惠及世界。对进博会"三大定位"提出新要求,为进博会"越办越好"进一步指明方向。习近平主席的致信引发中外嘉宾热烈反响,各方纷纷表示从中感受到中国坚定推进高水平开放、与世界共享发展机遇的信心和决心。

国务院总理李强出席开幕式并发表主旨演讲,与大家分享了几个具体的"进博故事"后指出,经济全球化是历史大势、人心所向,开放合作、互利共赢是最

明智也是最自然的选择。李强总理开幕式前参观了企业展,开幕式后同与会外国领导人共同巡馆。多国领导人和国际组织负责人现场致辞。国务院副总理何立峰主持开幕式。

国家综合展成为综合形象展示重要平台。国家展为不同发展水平的国家增进交流、促进合作、互利共赢提供重要平台,受到参展各国高度赞赏。巴林、中非、多米尼克、冈比亚、几内亚比绍、洪都拉斯、马里、阿曼、塞拉利昂、多哥、津巴布韦等11国首次参展。各参展国积极推介本国投资环境、旅游资源、优势产业和特色产品,举办近200场丰富多彩的展台活动。中国馆以"中国式现代化新成就为世界发展提供新机遇"为主题,聚焦自贸试验区建设十周年成就,重点展示我国推进高水平开放和高质量发展的最新成果,向世界讲述"中国好,世界会更好"的精彩故事。洪都拉斯带来咖啡、可可、水果、海鲜等美味;塞尔维亚运用多媒体方式展现河流、树木等场景,让观众感受当地的美丽风光和特色生活;芬兰以北欧风格"幸福的家"为主题,展现独具芬兰特色的简约设计;斐济展台别出心裁还原沙滩风景,令参观者耳目一新。馆内各类展品和互动展项受到观众广泛欢迎,成为观展热门打卡地。

企业商业展众商云集、新品众多、成效显著。128个国家和地区的3 486家企业参展,其中,世界500强和行业龙头企业达289家,数量为历届之最。六大展区设置聚焦高质量发展和高品质生活,创新引领成为共同主题,科技赋能成为主流趋势,展台展品科技感强、题材新颖、亮点纷呈。442项代表性首发新产品、新技术、新服务集中展示。创新孵化专区吸引来自39个国家和地区的超过300个创新项目参展,超过前两届的总和。专区内小微企业积极参与评选活动,在绿色低碳、医疗健康、数字经济、创新科技等4个赛道内角逐出本届"最具市场潜力奖"。首次举办跨国企业家巡馆、中小企业专场对接会和汽车展区现场成交活动。积极强化对接撮合,通过组织近百场专场对接活动等方式,多措并举促进成交,采购商的"购物车"兼具烟火气和科技感。非洲"甜面包"贝宁菠萝开启中国首秀,成功签下大额订单,大量高科技产品也获专业观众青睐,有望加快进入中国市场,助力产业升级。据统计,本届进博会按一年计意向成交金额784.1亿美元,比上届增长6.7%。

虹桥论坛持续为构建开放型世界经济贡献智慧。开放主题更加突出。聚焦"携手促发展 开放赢未来"这一主题,22场分论坛围绕"开放发展""开放合作""开放创新""开放共享"等4个板块开展深入研讨;重磅发布旗舰报告《世界开放报告2023》,

图 4-1　第六届进博会掠影

第四章　第六届中国国际进口博览会

第一节　基本概况

图4-2 国家综合展

图4-3 企业商业展

公布最新世界开放指数并举办专题研讨会。发言嘉宾阵容强大。副国级以上嘉宾8人，省部级68人，诺贝尔奖和图灵奖得主6人，境内外院士（学部委员）8人，知名专家学者22人，世界500强和行业龙头企业高管118人。政商学等各界发言嘉宾共计345位。创新功能促进"投资中国"。举办"投资中国年"系列活动，包括高峰会议暨上海城市推介大会、自贸试验区专场投资促进活动、外资企业圆桌会议。多场分论坛围绕推介营商环境、促进贸易投资对接等开展深入研讨，放大论坛综合效应。各方参与度大幅提升，虹桥论坛参会人数超过8 000人，为历届之最。联合国开发计划署等国际组织合作主办分论坛，数量创新高。

专业配套和人文交流活动放大展会综合效应。集中举办政策解读、对接签约、投资促进、研究发布、产品展示等各类配套活动122场。其中，由国际组织、有关部门、地方政府（交易团）及中央企业主办的活动占比40%以上。增设配套活动组团观展服务，吸引更多活动嘉宾到展台参观洽谈，进一步强化"以会促展"功能。中华老字号创新发展大会、中国国际石油贸易大会、长三角G60科创走廊高质量发展大会等高层级活动已连续多届举办，形成强大品牌效应。贸易投资对接会邀请近4 000家

图4-4　虹桥国际经济论坛

图 4-5　人文交流活动

展客商参加洽谈对接,达成合作意向416项。组织96场集中签约活动,达成合作意向超过600项。开展71场新品发布活动,展示142项前沿科技产品。738家机构参与人文交流展示,中外演出团体带来展台活动和公益演出超过200场,相关数量均超历届水平。

现场服务凸显科技元素和绿色理念。人员进馆和就餐便利性大幅提升。增设4处直通馆内的安检验证点,电子证件验证通道数量增加45%。在原有商业广场就餐区域外,新增多个临时就餐区,供参展参会人员就近选择,缓解大客流瞬时用餐压力,提升用餐满意度。强化人工智能技术应用,新增机器人问询导览服务,融合线上问询与线下导览,新颖有趣的"数字进宝"机器人成为观展嘉宾的"随身助手",实现更佳导览体验。网上供采大厅发挥重要功能,提供信息发布、贸易配对、行程安排等全流程服务,专业观众发布采购需求逾万次,智能匹配展商22万余家次、展品137万余件次。开展"零碳进博　零塑办博2.0"行动,通过省间绿电交易方式采购绿电800万千瓦时,首次实现100%绿电办展。鼓励各方记录碳足迹,引领"碳中和"时代风尚。结合低碳环保等热点主题,开发相关文创产品,打造绿色办展理念传播新载体。

图4-6 现代科技元素

二、以进博会为契机,再奏开放最强音

始终坚持习近平总书记赋予进博会"构建新发展格局的窗口、推动高水平开放的平台、全球共享的国际公共产品"的三大定位,充分发挥进博会"国际采购、投资促进、人文交流、开放合作"四大平台作用,推进展品变商品、展商变投资商,持续放大进博会溢出带动效应,不断提高开放水平。

一是推进展品签约落地,创造更大的市场机遇。本届进博会,上海交易团加强精准对接与洽谈,举办了集中签约、政策解读、新品首发等25场配套活动。上海交易团达成意向采购订单95亿美元,同比增长5.3%,连续6年居全国各地方交易团首位。意向订单来自35个国别和地区的商品,采购范围进一步扩大。上海不断强化"6天+365天"交易服务平台功能,推进更多进博会展品进入中国市场。比如,发挥全球商品贸易港平台作用,累计促成6 000余款进博会同款商品进入国内25个省市流通市场。再比如,商务区保税物流中心(b型)推进"展转保、展转跨"业务模式,支持参展企业通过保税展示展销模式参加进博会。

二是贡献虹桥智慧，更好对接国际高标准经贸规则。李强总理在主旨演讲中强调要"推进上海自由贸易试验区高水平制度型开放"。商务部、上海市政府共同举办了"投资中国年"高峰会议暨上海城市推介活动，联合国贸发会议秘书长格林斯潘、联合国国际贸易中心执行主任汉密尔顿等嘉宾发表演讲，为上海高水平开放提供真知灼见。上海举办了浦东、虹桥两场分论坛，诺贝尔经济学奖得主让·梯若尔、亚洲基础设施投资银行行长兼董事会主席金立群等学界专家、企业家齐聚一堂，为浦东、虹桥的未来发展把脉献策。浦东将率先构建与国际经贸规则相衔接的制度体系和监管模式，虹桥将持续增强制度创新的辐射力、科技集群的吸引力、产业升级的引领力。

三是加强技术对接，着力集聚创新动能。本届进博会有442项新产品、新技术、新服务集中亮相，创新特征格外突出。创新孵化专区有来自39个国家和地区的300余个项目参展。其中，上海积极支持北欧创新中心、国家技术转移东部中心、启迪之星等3家平台企业，携来自北欧、巴西、澳大利亚等国家和地区的80余个优质项目亮相。"聚前沿　创未来"创新孵化专场活动上，发布了《上海科技创新政策服务指南》，助力创新企业孵化发展。国家会展中心云集全球产品、技术的同时，上海临港则集聚了全球"最强大脑"，在第六届世界顶尖科学家论坛上进行了一场"头脑风暴"。同样是第六届，两者相通的是开放合作与协同创新。

四是拓展务实合作，助力更加包容共享的开放型世界经济。李强总理在主旨演讲中提出"在上海建设'丝路电商'合作先行区"。上海正在加快对接国际高标准经贸规则，探索体制机制创新，扩大电子商务领域对外开放，全力打造数字经济国际合作新高地，服务共建"一带一路"高质量发展。本届进博会，有120个外宾团组和百余名世界500强和行业龙头企业高管，感受了进博热度和上海温度。上海市领导会见了来沪参加进博会的外国政要和企业高管，积极推进企业用好进博会这一国际公共产品，进一步促进经贸、科创、教育等领域的交流合作。此外，上海人文交流馆亮相进博会，以"进博首发彰显溢出效应"为主题，分7个展区展示了90个本土精品和海外优品的进博故事。

三、以精益求精为目标，服务保障再上新台阶

从展客商的视角出发，聚焦智慧、绿色和便利，以高品质服务保障，实现了展会安全有序和观展便捷舒适。可以归纳为"六个首次"和"六个优化"。

第四章 第六届中国国际进口博览会

第一节 基本概况

"六个首次"主要包括：一是首次搭建进博会空间计算平台，精准计算、回溯展馆的实时数字动态，已应用于人流态势实时感知和人群异常聚集告警，应急响应有了新思路和新方法。二是首次推出参展动植物产品、食品特许审批便利举措。第六届进博会共办理特许审批43份，有来自基里巴斯、马耳他等8个国家的展品，涉及水产品、菠萝等多种食品农产品。三是首次实现全绿电办展，通过省份间绿电交易的方式，采购了绿电800万千瓦时。除了实现全绿电办展外，第六届进博会期间还将对建筑运行、餐饮供应等碳排放数据进行核算，采用购买碳配额方式，中和展会温室气体排放，实现零碳办展目标。四是首次设立法律服务保障组。设置涉外法律服务中心、调解中心、知识产权综合服务中心和西虹桥人民法庭一站式服务窗口等4个驻场服务点位，组建法律服务志愿团，提供法律咨询等服务500余次。五是首次在展馆内举办了"进博首发之夜"主题活动，丰富了进博会消费场景，使展客商能够尽享进博精品。线上同步开展"丝路云品"电商节活动，开启"丝路云品"专属直播间，推出了进博会打卡、云逛展等活动。六是首次在国家会展中心周边停车场设置了非预约社会车辆定点下客点，进一步挖潜停车资源、优化停车场功能。搭乘未预约车辆的展客商在此下车后步行10分钟即可到达展馆。

"六个优化"主要包括：一是优化了证件办理程序。2023年，办证流程由串联改为并联，办理时间进一步压缩，应急办证最快24小时内完成。同时，扩大了电子证件的使用范围和时间，遗失、遗忘证件的展客商可以非常便捷地线上申请、快速入馆。二是优化了交通出行举措。轨道交通、包车客运、地面公交、出租汽车全方位保障了展客商的出行需求，集约化出行方式超七成，其中轨道交通占比约45%、包车客运占比约30%。此外，近3 000个停车泊位实行灵活预约，大车泊位剩余时及时调整向小车开放。三是优化了食品供应保障。53个固定餐饮、7个临时餐饮和12辆流动餐车，为展客商提供了丰富的用餐选择。推行适度点餐和"小份菜"，开展自律承诺等光盘行动，餐余垃圾分类实现100%。同时，供博食品安全保障标准全面实施，确保展客商吃得安心。四是优化了接待服务举措。300余名联络官、750辆上汽接待用车等资源，保障了嘉宾接待任务的顺利完成。在进博会官网以及相关旅游平台发布了871家接待宾馆酒店名单，实行价格临时干预措施，确保房源充足、价格稳定。展馆内设置"党群服务站"和"职工驿站"，为展客商以及一线工作者提供服务。五是优化了志愿者服务。近6 000名"小叶子"志愿者分批参加了"啄木鸟"行动等岗位实训，既了解场馆、熟悉场地，又辅助检查场馆设施和标识，为展客商提供了更加准确、细致的服务。六是优化了消费支付方式。上海在包括商业、文旅、机场车站等重点场景已开通外卡POS机超3万台,实现三大场景重点商户全覆盖,以满足来沪境外人员的刷卡支付习惯。同时,国家会展中心和"吃、住、行、游、购、医"等各大场景的商户均支持受理多种支付方式,可满足来沪境外人员在沪日常消费支付便利。

第二节 配套保障

根据《第六届中国国际进口博览会城市服务保障总体方案》相关要求，按照进博会城市服务保障领导小组统一部署，成立虹桥国际中央商务区综合服务保障组。综合服务保障组提高站位，精心筹备，聚焦重点项目，加强区域综合服务保障，加强统筹协调和组织推进，抓紧抓实抓细各项工作任务，以一流城市环境、一流服务保障确保第六届进博会圆满成功。

精心拟定方案，全面督促落实。综合服务保障组编制下发了《第六届进博会虹桥国际中央商务区综合服务保障组工作方案》和《任务清单》。定期向各成员单位下发"工作提示"，督促指导各成员单位提高站位、强化担当，全力以赴、全情投入，提高标准、固化机制，对照任务清单和巡查问题清单，自查自纠、逐条销项。各成员单位密切协同，形成工作合力，把城市管理精细化工作对接机制、虹桥区域城管执法联勤联动等平台作为进博保障工作的重要抓手，深入推进各项任务落到实处。针对《任务清单》中所涵盖的5个大类、20个具体项目，综合服务保障组办公室每周汇总任务进度，每两周召开联络员会议协调进展情况，不定期会同相关责任单位开展现场督导检查。相关单位联合开展进博会前期和其间的检查巡查工作，并做好进博会期间的值守保障工作。

图4-7 进博会志愿者誓师大会

做好承上启下，建立沟通联系。综合服务保障组办公室与市进博城保办保持密切沟通，定期上报工作进展、提供宣传素材，并与长宁、闵行、青浦、嘉定四片区进博城保办，以及闵行绿容局、建管委，青浦区精细办，长宁区建委等行业主管部门建立工作渠道，详细了解各区工作开展情况。同时，与市水务局、市绿容局、市城管执法局等部门，就具体问题进行深入沟通对接，充分利用工作组统筹协调平台的功能机制，确保信息畅通、责任明确、协作高效。

推进配套建设，放大进博效应。综合服务保障组紧紧围绕"配套设施建设、综合交通组织、城市管理精细化、筹办虹桥分论坛、进博会综合效应"等工作，有力在序推进各项配套项目建设，合力放大进博综合效应。统筹协调虹桥综合交通枢纽西交通中心平台改建和虹桥品汇B栋机电设施安装等项目工程，进一步优化"国家会展中心—虹桥枢纽"区域步行交通标识，积极协调推进国家会展中心周边P20停车场更新和P7停车场跨小涞港钢便桥建设。着眼"6+365"进博商品常年展示功能平台优化完善，推进虹桥品汇等的进博商品常年展功能优化和室外空间景观提升方案落地，进一步汇聚进博商务商品流。规划制定虹桥枢纽、商务区楼宇等进博公益宣传方案，形成良好

图 4-8　进博会综合应急演练

图4-9　进博场馆周边城市空间治理

迎博办博氛围。组织开展了"迎进博虹桥西交项目综合应急演练"等科目演练，增强商务区服务保障进博的责任意识和应急处突能力。

提升市容环境，加强巡查力度。综合服务保障组办公室会同四区六街镇聚焦"彩化""靓化""净化""序化""优化"等方面，着重抓好商务区的清洁道路、水系、城市家具，户外广告和招牌整治、景观照明灯光效果提升等10项具体工作。组织开展商务区市容环境专项巡查，共检出涉及道路、水系、绿化等方面的市容环境问题共计1 721处，并以此进行分区、分类形成清单分发各区，要求有关部门对照清单、挂图作战、逐条销项，及时发现和反馈检查中发现的问题，推进问题的整改。对于进博场馆核心区域、重点接待宾馆、重要迎宾通道等市容环境保障节点，分类制定方案落实"检查""巡查""督查""自查"，做到"每周必检、每点必到、每次必评"，推动各片区及虹桥机场、地产虹桥等单位的进博市容环境保障工作。

全面深化城管执法"4+2"联动工作机制。商务区管委会会同市城管执法局，多

图 4-10　道路环境综合整治

次走访各区城管执法部门并召开联勤联动工作会议,加强对区区交界、市区交界、城乡交界等薄弱区域市容环境的联合整治,强化地铁出入口内外和周边的环境综合治理,规范非机动车管理,消除环境短板。

第三节　进博会溢出效应

作为进博会永久举办地，商务区在服务保障好进博会的同时，着力发挥世界级的流量入口优势，用好进博会商品服务展示交易、消费场景体验、投资贸易洽谈、技术解决方案推广等综合功能，建设高能级贸易主体首选地，打造进出口商品集散地和进口贸易促进创新示范区，更好联动"两带"产业升级和消费升级，延伸产业链条，拓展产业深度，不断放大进博会溢出带动效应。

一、以功能平台为支撑，做强亚太进口商品集散地主功能

一是加快"6+365天"常年展示交易服务平台建设。完善虹桥进口商品展示交易中心保税货物展示、价格形成、信息发布等功能。虹桥进口商品展示交易中心（虹桥品汇A栋）作为上海市"6+365天"常年展示交易主平台，累计已集聚全球108个国家和地区的6 000多个品牌8万多种商品，其中包括58个"一带一路"国家的3万多种商品。同时，加速打造联动长三角、服务全国、辐射亚太的进口商品集散地。平台累计在全国开设23家虹桥品汇分中心，实现采购变贸易，发挥了国际国内双循环的战略链接作用。2023年前三季度，平台贸易额超100亿元，同比增长超过20%。虹桥品汇B栋于本届进博会前建成，成为进口工业品首发平台，首期推出"虹桥品汇机车世界"，引入10多个世界主流一线品牌，成为进口高端摩托车的首发平台。

设立于虹桥品汇的"上海国际友城港"，常态化组织国别文化交流、商贸对接、商品展销等活动，打造"国际会客厅"。今年前三季度，累计接待28个国家（地区）55个团组，其中包括古巴、越南、乌兹别克斯坦等13国总领事、斯洛伐克布拉迪斯拉发州州长、南非莎拉巴特曼市市长、洪都拉斯总统访华随行媒体团等高层团组，先后举办韩国全罗南道线上经贸洽谈会、"魅力古巴"推介周、"中俄青年同走友谊路"上海站欢迎会等10场友城活动，承办拉美地区、欧非地区公务人员研修班等28场商贸交流活动，向境内外贸企业引荐了巴西、斯里兰卡、新西兰等国贸易商。

绿地全球商品贸易港为包括"一带一路"沿线国家在内的全球商品搭建"6+365天"常年展示交易平台，已吸引来自76个国家和地区的180家企业和组织入驻，设立

国家馆63个，引进进口商品9万余件，涵盖食品酒饮、数码家电、美妆护理、服饰箱包、家具家居等20余个大类，其中进博会同款商品超过2万款。

二是培育一批进口专业贸易平台。打造珠宝玉石、化妆品、康养医美、服装纺织、食品酒类、咖啡等专业贸易平台，集散全球优质日用消费品，满足消费升级和供给提质。鼓励采购商联盟加大对各国特色化、差异化优质商品的引进力度，扩大进口商品贸易规模。其中，虹桥品汇国际咖啡港已集聚58个国家的咖啡产品，设立了包括古巴国家馆在内的28国咖啡品类的常年展，50家咖啡企业商品销售及活动联动，带动销售30亿元。虹桥国际酒窖引进罗斯柴尔德等精品酒庄、人头马、奔富等知名品牌，引入专业进口商和渠道运营商进驻。

三是进一步提升虹桥保税物流中心（B型）功能。2023年前三季度，一线进出口额为9.34亿元，同比增长16.31%。区内跨境电商网购保税进口业务实现销售订单646万单（占全市43.48%），交易总额达12.3亿元（占全市28.45%），均排名全市第一。为丝路电商国家货物提供保税服务，总货值达2 171万美元，涉及国别有澳大利亚（近960万美元）、越南、泰国、新加坡、意大利等20多个国家。同时，虹桥保税物流中心连续第五年为宝玉石参展和留购提供便利化措施支持，占比金额较高的国家有泰国、

图4-11　虹桥保税物流中心

意大利、巴西和哥伦比亚等国。

二、以数字贸易做赋能，形成进博会溢出效应转化新模式

做强在线新经济服务进博会的功能。鼓励新零售、网红直播带货、社交电商、社群电商等新型智慧营销与跨境电商融合发展，建设直播基地集群和产业平台。虹桥品汇引进进宝汇直播跨境电商基地，聚焦"直播+进博""直播+保税""直播+产业"，提供 KOL 和 KCL 主播、视频制作、内容创作、平台分发、直播培训等服务，打造以进口为主题的在线新经济平台，常态化为"丝路电商"伙伴国、"一带一路"沿线国家企业和商品开展带货专场，获评上海市首批直播电商基地，持续拓宽进博商品国内线上销售渠道。

做强跨境电商业态服务进博会的能级。打造集品牌展示、产品交易、国际营销、配套服务等多功能为一体的全球数字贸易服务平台。集聚一批跨境电商平台、跨境金融、国际物流、综合配套龙头企业，培育一批中小型跨境电商企业。

充分发挥进博会促消费稳增长作用，引导进博会溢出效应重点承接平台企业积极开展进博主题促销活动。如虹桥品汇推出咖啡文化周、国别缤纷月、清酒文化节等系列活动，打响"进口采购到虹桥、消费体验来品汇"品牌；绿地全球商品贸易港结合各国风土人情、艺术人文、美食佳酿等开展"G-Hub全球国别缤纷购"，全渠道推出万国啤酒节、中东异域商品展、土耳其当代摄影艺术展、卡洛芙珠宝节等线上线下互动体验活动；进宝汇通过"直播 High 购季"向全国消费者展示虹桥优质进口商品，增加线上目标消费群体对进博会和虹桥跨境商品资源的认知。

三、以贸易总部促整合，营造国际贸易创新发展的新生态

聚焦进博会参展主体，加快吸引培育高能级贸易主体。支持引进进博展商或其代理商投资设立贸易总部。充分发挥《关于支持虹桥国际中央商务区贸易型总部发展的若干措施》《虹桥国际中央商务区关于支持内资总部企业发展的政策意见》等总部政策效应，吸引跨国公司地区总部、民营企业总部、央企第二总部、产业贸易总部、本土跨国公司总部等各类进口贸易头部企业机构，打造高能级贸易主体首选地。

搭建服务总部经济发展的专业化支撑体系。引导鼓励贸易型总部发展，提升进口贸易与总部经济能级，围绕进博会以及国际贸易链，建设"上控资源、下控渠道"的贸易型总部集群。

集聚国际贸易促进功能机构。支持虹桥海外贸易中心提升能级，进一步加大具有国际影响力的国际经贸组织、境外贸易促进机构、国际贸易商协会等组织的集聚力度。

四、以制度创新为亮点，形成国际化营商环境的新举措

全面提升进口贸易开放水平。主动对接 RCEP 等国际自贸协定，设立 RCEP 企业服务咨询站，落实上海市服务业扩大开放综合试点总体方案，加大数字贸易、金融服务、商品会展等领域开放试点。进口博览会期间的展品税收支持、通关监管、资金结算、投资便利、人员出入境等创新政策依法上升为常态化制度安排，打造进口领域全方位开放的前沿窗口。

提高监管便利化水平。探索开展海关特殊监管区域外重点企业特殊监管创新试点。在一定范围内放宽进口商品准入门槛，为快运货物、易腐货物提供 6 小时通关便利。在保税展示交易中开展多元化保证金、银行保函、企业保函及企业资信担保等担保机制。探索货物的临时准入及无商业价值样品的免税入境政策。

强化金融服务保障。探索推动区域认证企业开立 FT 账户，鼓励商务区符合条件的企业开展资本项目收入支付便利化试点，创新外汇结算，推动符合条件的进口贸易企业搭建本外币一体化资金池，探索建立"政银保"三方合作机制支持企业发展，加强融资和信贷支持。

第四节　2023虹桥HUB大会

11月6日上午，第六届虹桥国际经济论坛虹桥国际开放枢纽建设分论坛暨2023虹桥HUB大会在国家会展中心（上海）举办。本次分论坛由上海市人民政府、商务部共同主办，商务区管理委员会承办，以"深化区域协同创新，赋能虹桥国际开放枢纽高质量发展"为主题，紧扣一体化、高质量、国际化和开放创新，分四方面内容展开：一是区域协同与创新发展，紧紧围绕长三角一体化发展和科技创新国家战略的深度融合；二是区域协同与产业升级，着眼在长三角一体化背景下现代化产业体系升级；三是区域协同与深化开放，着力呈现虹桥作为长三角一体化深化开放门户，主动服务构建新发展格局，诠释高水平开放与深化区域协同的双向成就；四是区域协同与核心打造，讨论作为虹桥国际开放枢纽"一核"的商务区"大交通、大会展、大商务、大科创"高质量开发新路径、新实践等。

图4-12　2023虹桥HUB大会现场

虹桥HUB大会作为进博时刻虹桥的"主场亮相"，上海市委副书记、市长龚正出席大会并致辞。商务部副部长盛秋平、国家发展改革委党组成员郭兰峰、中国银行行长刘金致辞。龚正市长在致辞中说，建设虹桥国际开放枢纽，是我国扩大高水平对外开放、推动长三角一体化发展的重大战略部署。当前，上海正加快建设具有世界影响力的社会主义现代化国际大都市，虹桥国际开放枢纽作为重要的开放平台，要聚焦做强虹桥国际中央商务区、做优南向北向拓展带，持续推动"大科创"赋能"大交通""大会展""大商务"。要持续增强制度创新的辐射力、科技集群的吸引力、产业升级的引领力，加快打造成为提升区域核心竞争力的增长新引擎、具有全球影响力的开放新门户、引领长三角一体化发展的重要动力源。期待海内外专家学者、产业翘楚深入交流，贡献真知灼见，热忱欢迎海内外企业投资虹桥、扎根中国、服务全球，共享发展机遇，共创美好未来。

大会由副市长、商务区管委会主任华源主持。2014年诺贝尔经济学奖得主、图卢兹经济学院经济学教授兼名誉院长让·梯若尔，亚洲基础设施投资银行行长兼董事会主席金立群，国务院发展研究中心副主任隆国强、香港中文大学（深圳）前海国际事务研究院院长郑永年等作主旨演讲。

一、大有可期，开拓创新驱动新局面

新一轮科技革命和产业变革方兴未艾，向科技创新要"新质生产力"已成为全球应对风险挑战和收获高速增长的重要手段。在大会开场演讲中，2014年诺贝尔经济学奖得主、图卢兹经济学院经济学教授兼名誉院长让·梯若尔（Jean Tirole）对于虹桥的科技创新企业如数家珍，他列举了携程、科大讯飞、爱奇艺等一批立足虹桥、具有国际影响力的创新型企业，指出在经济学视角中，创新势在必行，而培育颠覆式创新离不开私人部门和政府的共同助力，也离不开多要素融合的创新生态系统的支撑，以及对互利共赢的国际开放战略的奉行和坚守。

> 虹桥作为国际开放枢纽，公共部门的产业政策已经取得了很大成功。在创建和维护产业集群方面，虹桥已经是打造了一个很成功的产业集群。而且不仅仅做到基础设施的共享，也实现了对信息的非正式的共享。
>
> ——让·梯若尔（Jean Tirole），
> 2014年诺贝尔经济学奖得主、图卢兹经济学院经济学教授兼名誉院长

亚洲基础设施投资银行行长兼董事会主席金立群从亚投行的愿景和"明天的基础设施"角度出发，表示技术和数字基础设施将在未来几十年成为可持续增长的关键驱动力。同时指出，鉴于虹桥正在成为连接长三角与上海，乃至全球市场的重要枢纽，因此虹桥的未来将不仅仅止于商贸和交通的枢纽，还将会成为一个创新和知识的枢纽，推动从经济、贸易，到文化、知识的高质量发展。

旧金山湾区委员会经济研究院院长杰夫·贝利萨里奥（Jeff Bellisario）在演讲中介绍了全球区域协同创新标杆旧金山湾区的创新生态系统，强调了构建开放创新平台、推进全球开放连接的重要性，并且表达了期待未来虹桥和旧金山湾区进一步加强互鉴、深化联动，促进彼此经济高质量发展的愿望。

> 虹桥国际开放枢纽的愿景不仅会成为一个商贸和交通的枢纽，也会成为一个创新和知识的枢纽。
>
> 在今天的知识经济当中，一个城市经济的重要性要大大超过它的基础设施，一个城市的繁荣和竞争力是由它吸引的人才所决定的，没有人才就没有发展。
>
> ——金立群
> 亚洲基础设施投资银行行长兼董事会主席

> 旧金山湾区和大虹桥区域有很多的相似之处。虹桥的制造性企业、高科技企业和创新企业跟湾区也有很多相似之处，在这里能够感觉经济增长创新活力，希望彼此能够深入开展合作。
>
> ——杰夫·贝利萨里奥
> （Jeff Bellisario）旧金山湾区委员会经济研究院院长

此外，在大会开场先导片中，科大讯飞董事长刘庆峰、协鑫集团董事长朱共山、正大天晴药业集团董事长谢承润分别讲述了其基于虹桥的综合生态优势，成为大会议题在虹桥落地践行的生动注脚。

二、大有可观，服务双向开放新格局

虹桥国际开放枢纽叠加承载了一系列国家重大战略部署，深入推动长三角一体化发展，服务构建新发展格局。2023年7月，国家发改委出台关于推动虹桥国际开放枢纽进一步提升能级的24条政策措施，这是继2021年《总体方案》落地之后的一次重大政策升级。对于虹桥在我国双向开放格局中肩负的使命任务，以及所能够做出的更大贡献，与会嘉宾进行了深入的剖析和建言。

国务院发展研究中心副主任隆国强在发言中，以率先推进数字化转型、率先推进绿色转型、率先推进制度型开放、率先打造国际人才高地等"四个率先"归纳了虹桥国际开放枢纽更好承担重大使命、服务国家战略的高质量发展路径，并向虹桥提出了作为国际开放枢纽，要在数字化转型方面走在前面，引领中国在新一轮技术革命和产业变革中抢占制高点的发展期待。

香港中文大学（深圳）前海国际事务研究院院长、广州粤港澳大湾区研究院理事长郑永年在演讲中表示，纵览全球，开放的科教人才系统、开放的企业系统和开放的金融系统推动发达经济体建立了"地域嵌入型"世界级经济平台，他期待虹桥能够立足自身角色，继续加强做好国家现代化建设的重要区域抓手。

正如博世集团董事会主席史蒂凡·哈通（Stefan Hartung）、瑞安集团主席罗康瑞等一众嘉宾在给大会的寄语中不谋而合提到的：虹桥辐射长三角、联通海内外，因此是海外企业设立总部的首选地，也是在上海参与高水平开放合作的重要起点。

> 数字化转型是新一轮技术革命和产业变革的核心。虹桥作为国际开放枢纽，必须在数字化转型方面走在前面，引领中国在新一轮技术革命和产业变革中抢占制高点。
> ——隆国强
> 国务院发展研究中心副主任

> 发达经济体都有三大开放系统：一是开放的科教人才系统，二是开放的企业系统，三是开放的金融系统。这三大开放系统推动了发达经济体建立地域嵌入型世界级经济平台。
>
> 从这个框架来看，上海的角色，虹桥的角色，就非常清楚，是我们国家现代化最重要的区域抓手。
> ——郑永年
> 香港中文大学（深圳）前海国际事务研究院院长
> 广州粤港澳大湾区研究院理事长

三、大有可为，打造产业协同新高地

从全球到中国，协同都是提升区域产业能级的必由之路，数字化、智能化、绿色化也越来越成为新型工业化进程的必然目标。大会演讲环节中，OTIS全球公司董事会主席、首席执行官兼总裁朱蒂（Judy Marks），中国核工业建设股份有限公司党委书记、董事长陈宝智，毕马威亚太区及中国主席陶匡淳等，讲述了世界制造业龙头、骨干型央企、全球现代服务业标杆在虹桥支撑构建现代化产业体系，服务推进新型工业化，推动产业补链延链升链建链协同，促进区域产业能级提升，助力区域产业数字化、智能化和绿色化改造升级等方面的趋势洞察和产业实践。

虹桥国际开放枢纽启动建设两年多来，一批标志性、引领性的龙头企业将总部设在虹桥，促进全球资源汇聚，推进区域产业协同，使中国产品与服务更快走进国际市场，更好参与全球竞争。大会现场，天合光能董事长兼首席执行官高纪凡、上海华测导航技术股份有限公司董事长赵延平、上海神马电力控股有限公司董事长兼首席执行官马斌、CDP董事长兼首席执行官吕威等扎根虹桥的跨领域企业家代表，在德勤中国主席蒋颖的引领下，就"区域协同中的核心竞争力引擎打造"话题，基于高新科技、绿色低碳、总部经济、流量价值等不同视角，从虹桥国际开放枢纽空间侧区位优势、生态侧内生动能等多个层次开展了深入探讨，成为海内外更多企业家、投资人选择虹桥共享发展机遇的决策参考和鲜活案例。

四、大有文章，助推枢纽迈上新台阶

"今天的虹桥不同以往，未来的虹桥不可限量。"2023年，虹桥国际开放枢纽高质量发展成果喜人，两年多来虹桥国际开放枢纽的地区生产总值年均增长超过8%，以不到长三角2%的国土面积，贡献了近10%的经济总量，彰显了长三角强劲、活跃增长极的集中极的作用。而这些成绩也成为所有与会嘉宾有目共睹的共同认知。本次大会凝聚的一系列发展共识，为虹桥国际开放枢纽建设再上新台阶增添了全新动力。与此同时，通过本次大会学术界、产业界的交汇碰撞，合力阐释"创新成于开放，开放赢在创新"的发展精髓，以思想解答时代发展之问，为全球"深化促进区域协同创新"议题，贡献了"虹桥智慧"，沉淀了"虹桥方案"。

本次大会以虹桥为缩影，着力呈现中国式现代化新机遇和新气象，全力彰显高水平开放和高质量发展的光明前景和广阔未来，将进一步提振选择虹桥、投资中国的底气和信心，以更好落实新发展理念，更好推动高质量发展，更好构建新发展格局，使虹桥HUB大会成为商务区面向世界的又一重要门户，为虹桥国际经济论坛增添一抹高规格、高水准的主场亮色。

第五章　四大片区协同发展

第一节　闵行片区

一、总部经济能级不断提升

聚焦总部经济，主动出击、精准招商，进一步放大虹桥国际开放枢纽升级版政策赋能效应，做好补链延链升链建链的大文章。创新成立国际贸易、生物医药、中央法务区、新赛道等4个专业化产业招商事业部，均采取双组长负责制，由南虹桥集团和区相关委办局各委派一名组长，依托专业化精干招商队伍，深入开展精准招商和产业集群研究，完成从全行业招商向产业链招商转变，推动招商效能快速提升。加大"走出去"招商力度，赴北京、广州、深圳、厦门、福州、合肥等重点城市访企业、谋合作、话发展，推动重点企业加快落地。发挥6个楼宇工作站网格化服务优势，建立常态化企业走访机制、诉求解决机制和企业高管及人才关怀机制，积极构建一流营商环境。聚焦招商接待、交易团保障及市容环境保障等方面，梳理保障第六届进博会重点任务12项，对标对表、积极落实，确保第六届进博会顺利举办。成功举办"虹桥之核　未来已来"2023年虹桥国际中央商务区（闵行部分）企业表彰会、"闵行区潮'涌浦江　投资上海'全球分享季——'投资闵行月月签'招商引资项目集中签约仪式"等重大活动，进一步激发区域发展活力。

二、产业集群布局更加优化

发挥产业项目攻坚协调推进机制统筹作用，紧盯项目关键节点，主动对接、跨前服务，推进高能级、引领性总部项目快速布局落地，基本形成重点产业加速集聚、开工建设如火如荼的良好态势。一是生物医药产业集群进一步夯实。威高、云南白药、信达、东软等4个在建项目正抓紧推进建设，其中信达、威高、云南白药完成阶段性

第五章 四大片区协同发展

第一节 闵行片区

图5-1 信达生物全球研发中心项目封顶

工程成果,顺利实现结构封顶,对生物医药产业集群打造具有标志性意义。正大天晴、先声诊断、先声药业等3个项目实现开工。生生物流加快开工前准备工作,美德纳、千麦医疗等重大项目顺利签约落地,启动协鑫集团、石药集团意向用地控规调整,生物医药产业集聚全面进入"加速跑"。二是光伏等绿色低碳新赛道加快布局。天合光能、晶科能源、协鑫集团、阳光电源、润阳新能源等标志性、引领性的龙头企业纷纷奔赴落地,其中天合光能实现开工,着力以总部经济构筑新能源产业新高地。三是其他以数字经济产业为代表的一批重大产业项目抓紧推进。赛意、新易腾加快推进土地出让前期工作,诺力股份完成股权转让。电竞中心商业商办地块、印象城一期顺利实现结构封顶,卓然、印象城二期实现开工。徽商长三角总部中心完成签约,前湾云台项目顺利开工,打造面向长三角地区的研发总部集聚区。

三、贸易功能持续深化拓展

进一步承接放大进博会溢出效应,持续强化虹桥进口商品展示交易中心建设运营,新引进金塑宝、麦肯等贸易型企业近百家,累计达909家。成功举办上海"丝路电商云品海购"、上海咖啡产业高峰论坛、"魅力古巴"推介周、中越企业交流会、日本产酒类B2B商贸洽谈会等活动，搭建展示交流平台，扩大交易中心影响力。依托保税物流中心（B型），做优做强国际贸易产业，积极探索海关便利化措施和创新政策，通过区外保税展示交易业务，扩大服务半径，走通安缦艺术品区外保税展示监管模式。虹桥海外贸易中心持续推动贸促机构建立国际化"朋友圈"，前三季度，已累计引入俄中商务中心、中国瑞士中心、中欧合作促进会、新加坡中心等12家贸易及服务机构入驻。

四、高起点规划打造虹桥前湾片区

前湾片区位于商务区中心位置，面积30平方千米，北青公路以北10平方千米是近期重点建设区域，是商务区中规模最大、最完整的成片可开发区域。规划将前湾片区打造成为虹桥国际开放枢纽核心功能承载区，面向国际国内的世界级"会客厅"，引领高品质生活的人民城市样板区，服务长三角和全国发展的强劲活跃增长极，形成"10+10+10"的区域开发框架，构建"一湾一核、四心四轴"的复合城市结构。"一湾"即"一湾引苏河"形成的C字形前湾公园；围绕前湾公园，打造2平方千米中央活动区（CAZ）活力核；"四心"是围绕4个轨道交通站点形成的TOD开发组团；由中央活动区向外延伸，形成联系周边的4条城市轴线。

图5-2 前湾片区效果图

前湾以"无限城市，未来前湾"为愿景，营造极具魅力的城市形象。前湾将通过"无限渗透的水绿空间、无限魅力的城市形象、无限链接的立体交通网络、无限活力的公共服务设施体系、无限智慧的数字城市系统"5大设计策略，描绘一张"城市友好、高度适宜、路网密集、建筑通透、色彩明朗、线条简洁"的城市蓝图，打造上海西翼具有标识性的区域新地标，统筹商务、产业、生态、公服、居住、交通六大功能，结合城市更新和精细化管理进行区域品质提升，包括产业能级、交通优势以及城市品质等方面。城市空间品质方面，生态和公共配套基础良好，10千米的吴淞江生态廊道已基本建成，多所国际学校凸显国际配套服务优势。依托前湾公园，打造"一湾两湖三区十八景"的景观格局，串联虹桥国际文化艺术中心、虹桥国际会议中心、虹桥国际城市文化展示中心等重大公共文体设施。公园与周边城市功能无界融合，充分构筑前湾片区"五分水绿五分城"的生态格局。

五、专业服务能级加快提升

依托重点功能平台，加快集聚发展与国际化中央商务区相匹配的专业服务业，持续完善全产业链专业服务体系，为各类企业走出去提供专业服务支撑。启用虹桥国际中央法务区法务大厦，出台专项扶持政策，新引进北京炜衡、广信君达、段和段、中夏等龙头法律服务机构，累计达81家。启用综合服务中心，全力提供"一站式"政务服务和"家门口"法律服务平台。成功举办第七届新兴法律服务业高峰论坛等36场活动，吸引超2 000人次集聚法务区，平台吸引力不断提升。制定专项扶持政策，给予开办费、租金补贴、人才保障及开设同城分所等多方面支持。中国上海人力资源服务产业园虹桥园被认定为市服务业创新发展示范区，新引进博尔捷等76家人力资源企业，开园以来，累计实现税收超4亿元。被认定为市服务业创新发展示范区，赋能企业完善人力资源体系。举办虹桥园开园一周年等活动，第六届进博会期间开展"虹桥国际人才会客厅"走进进博会活动，组织8家人力资源龙头企业参展，展现南虹桥国际人才服务优势，在进博会首次提出国际人才服务及国际人才蓄水池理念，促进国际人才交流。

举办虹桥园开园一周年活动，推出六大类56项服务清单和"1+3升级包"服务，形成了集招聘、培训、人才测评、人力资源服务外包等业态于一体的人力资源服务全产业链，服务区域人才能级加快提升。商务区企业服务中心围绕区域定位，拓展出入境受理范围，外籍人员工作签证受理范围由A类拓展至B类，助力引才聚才。积极向重点企业及高端外籍人才推介出入境政策，为专家人才开辟绿色通道，制定一人一方

第五章　四大片区协同发展

第一节　闵行片区

图5-3　中国上海人力资源服务产业园虹桥园

案,成功受理百汇医院、CDP等企业高管永久居留业务。上海国际技术交易市场建设"全球技术供需对接平台"获得市生产性互联网服务平台授牌,形成具有国际引领作用的全球技术展示中心和交易市场,促进高端产业发展技术要素集聚闵行,加快产业孵化。

六、规划优化持续深化

对标国际最高标准、最好水平,持续深入谋划高质量规划方案,形成一批优秀的规划成果。规划实施管控体系基本构建。前湾片区总控实施平台九大专题形成成果,正抓紧推进上报审批及成果发布工作。通过城市风貌、公服设施、地下空间等九大系统,确定建设标准和管控要求,指导前湾片区从开发建设到运营维护等各环节工作,实现"规、建、管、投、运、维"全生命周期统筹管理。一批专项规划形成成果。绿色生态专业规划获区政府批复,为绿色生态城区创建落实规划依据。通信、燃气等专项规划完成专家评审,地下空间、综合交通、供水、水利、污水、雨水等专项规划形成成果,吴淞江两岸生态空间规划国际方案征集有序推进,为区域开发建设提供规划支撑。紧密跟进市轨交线网规划评估及方案优化,推进轨交25号线及25号线支线规划尽快确定。稳步推进城市景观设计和成果展示。优化城市景观方案。前湾公园三期方案基本确定,描绘了公园从古典到未来的时间长卷,奠定前湾片区城水交织的公园城市氛围，打造生态绿色品质标杆；前湾公园桥梁方案完成方案比选，打造系统性、标志性的桥梁景观风貌；前湾生物医药板块绿色空间方案形成阶段性成果，全方位塑造城市表情，营造绿色开发、富有魅力的公共空间。

七、城市品质稳步提升

坚持产城融合发展，发挥虹桥国际开放枢纽专项债赋能作用，推动项目建设提速提质，一批城市配套项目加快布局，构建高品质宜居宜业环境。综合交通项目建设持续推进。13号线西延伸、示范区线等重点轨交加快推进建设。兴虹西路、纪友路等道路实现完工，闵北路等骨干道路顺利开工，持续完善区域周边路网结构，同步促进周边地块开发。绿化水系项目加快推进。按照"一湾、两湖、三区、十八景"景观格局，生态地标前湾公园一二期高标准有序建设，三期方案形成成果。新虹小流域、雄伟河等项目加快推进建设，四大绿地和北横泾环通等重点品质提升项目设计方案深化研究。公服配套设施有序推进。10-07幼儿园、新虹派出所实现开工，07-04小学、06-02幼儿园正加快推进开工前期准备工作，华东师范大学初中项目方案研究加快推进。美丽家园项目抓紧推进。爱博六七村等美丽家园综合修缮项目主体工程年底实现完工。

第二节　长宁片区

长宁作为"大虹桥"上海市域内唯一的中心城区，正举全区之力推进"最虹桥"引领行动，加快落地一批高含金量的政策措施，推动产业发展布局更加优化、枢纽门户功能持续升级。

一、持续做强"最虹桥"品牌，强化国际开放枢纽核心功能

落实"最虹桥"引领行动。2023年2月，长宁召开区推进虹桥国际开放枢纽建设领导小组2023年第一次会议，深入学习陈吉宁书记调研虹桥国际中央商务区重要讲话精神，并提出长宁航空服务、总部企业、数字经济集聚等"十大比较优势"，为"最虹桥"引领行动在东虹片区的深入推进作出战略性部署，持续建设更具竞争力的"最虹桥"品牌。

提升"东虹桥"显示度。5月，商务区"潮涌浦江　投资虹桥"投资促进大会成功举办；7月，"变局　创新"品牌高峰论坛顺利召开；8月，第十届全球投资并购峰会暨第九届金哨奖颁奖典礼隆重举行。"东虹桥"品牌不断擦亮，显示度持续提升。

强化国际定位。一是国际航班回归。2023年3月26日，上海虹桥国际机场暂停三年的国际及港澳台地区进出港航班业务"重启"，夏秋航季计划每周执行国际、港澳台地区航班314架次，相较于2019年同期增加22架次。二是国际航班全面恢复。8月16日，虹桥国际机场涵盖5条国际（地区）航线50架次的计划内航班全面恢复，航班总量和旅客总量已经全面达到了2019年同期水平。高峰小时容量从48架次/小时提高到了50架次/小时，日均出入境人员数量将稳定在9 000人次以上。

彰显开放优势。一是做强"首发、首店"经济。东虹桥中心成为区域内商办综合型首发项目，"盒马跨境GO"新零售模式在此落地。首发经济地标光大安石大融城开业，临空商圈引入首店24个。二是用好对外贸易平台。积极承接进博会溢出效应，推动百秋等"6+365天"交易服务平台将展品变商品，发动携程推出"丝路电商"系

图5-4　东虹桥中心

列直播，带动旅游消费。三是扩大高含金量政策受益面。持续推动虹桥国际开放枢纽高含金量政策在东虹片区落地见效，并涌现多个"首例"。超过25家企业开通了国际互联网数据专用通道，开立自由贸易账户的企业达到77家，汰新生物成为商务区外籍高层次人才持永居身份证创办科技型企业"首例"等。德孚同诚私募基金成为长宁区首例通过虹桥商务区绿色通道完成投资类企业备案项目，营业执照办理时间缩短至24个工作日。

提升枢纽功能。一是总部企业集聚。东虹桥区域目前集聚的经市商务委和商务区认定的各类总部企业达57家，其中跨国公司地区总部26家、外资研发中心3家，合计占各类总部企业一半以上，国际化程度和开放特征愈发鲜明。二是功能性机构集聚。虹桥临空经济示范区集聚了超过60%的落户于上海的基地航空公司。航空案件审判站入驻东虹桥，与航空争议调解中心、航空仲裁院构成国内首个融调解、仲裁、审判于一体的航空争议一站式解决平台。虹桥海外人才一站式服务中心拓展服务功能，成为全国第一家整合人社、公安、科委、侨务、台办、外办等多部门资源的区级人才人事业务综合受理平台，累计服务36万人次。

二、持续铸造"枢纽经济"特色，深耕现代化产业体系试验田

做强重点产业动能。围绕产业链等"四链融合"，聚焦"航空+总部""数字+绿色"两大集群，发挥重点产业链带动作用，支持"链主"企业招引上下游优质项目，推动高水平企业总部、高能级研发中心"两高"项目落地，持续丰富和优化东虹片区产业生态。在航空领域，打造强劲活跃国家级临空经济示范区。强化"国际航空枢纽、全球航空企业总部基地、高端临空服务业集聚区、全国公务机运营基地和低碳绿色发展区"五大功能定位，吸引更多海内外民航总部、通航总部、航空货运总部及关联企业、国产大飞机项目、航空联盟及机构入驻。研究推进开通面向新加坡等全球城市的点对点中远程国际精品航线、加密城际空中快线。在总部领域，打造长三角总部集聚新高地。深入实施"总部增能行动"，持续做好"跨国公司地区总部圆桌会议"品牌活动。加强总部招商力度，吸引跨国公司地区总部、民企类、贸易型等各类总部企业在东虹片区集聚。推动瑞士山特维克矿山公司和丹纳赫集团旗下三家公司迁入，推动浙江天圣上海公司迁入和股权转让。在数字领域，打造上海数字经济转型标杆区。围绕长宁区"3320"战略，聚焦数字消费、人工智能、数字健康、数字出行四大领域，东虹片区已集聚1 500余家数字经济领域企业。依托百秋电商、科大讯飞等龙头企业持续深化"数字长宁"品牌效应，推动天猫生态实验室落地百秋，打造数字创新生态，逐步实现数字经济领域的转型升级。引入随申行智慧交通、萃锦半导体等优质项目，首家数字化全国性保险经纪公司旭升保险已提交进驻计划，京东购物项目新设1家企业。在绿色领域，积极创建上海市低碳发展实践区。大力发展超低能耗建筑，组建双D创新领跑者联盟。完成石领新能源、朗绿科技迁入，朗绿旗下持股平台崇创投资也意向随迁。

完善特色产业园区和功能平台。对标上海市"3+6"新型产业体系，围绕东虹片区"4+6+N"重点产业目录，聚焦临空经济、总部经济、数字经济、开放经济等四大领域，突出航空物流、时尚创意、数字、专业服务、生命健康、金融服务等六大重点产业，培育新能源、智能网联、互联网医疗等若干产业新赛道，深入建设虹桥临空经济示范区、"虹桥之源"在线新经济生态园、虹桥临空跨国公司（总部）科创园等特色产业园区以及大虹桥生命科学创新中心、虹桥财富管理走廊等功能平台。大力推进大虹桥数字中心直播基地（容么么直播中心）、人工智能研究院、智慧医疗产业园、数字出行园等服务平台建设，大力提升苏河汇、东华科技园等现有孵化器能级。加快集聚

培育百秋、东航电商等一批创新主体和百亿乃至千亿级交易平台。截至2023年9月底，东虹片区已建成180余幢商务楼宇，集聚了6 000余家企业。

三、持续优化营商环境水平，砥砺一体化高质量发展磨刀石

完善企业服务。 围绕服务企业发展，全力办好"企业开门七件事"。一是推动政策先行先试。抓牢《总体方案》及市级支持商务区提升能级有关措施赋能的契机，以德孚资本设立为试点，帮助企业在24个工作日内完成从申请到领照，相较常规缩减了两个月的时间。二是提升专业服务功能。设立最虹桥法治研究中心，成立东虹桥检察服务站，挂牌新泾镇营商服务中心，常态化开展知识产权保护行动。开展第三届"科创之星"表彰活动，助力构建动能强劲、要素集聚、活力迸发的大科创生态。三是构建服务企业全方位平台。全力打造东虹桥企业服务会客厅，积极争取商务区更多绿色通道和先行先试项目进驻，不断深化"四心三最"东虹服务品牌建设。初步梳理形成20大类184项服务清单，并启动装修设计，努力打造成综合共享的三级服务体系，提供一站式、一条龙的企业全生命周期服务。

优化人才服务。 围绕服务人才所需，全力办好"白领十大实事"，以打造人才高地支撑东虹桥产业高地建设。一是强化人才服务功能。打造白领服务金牌店小二，建设知识产权保护服务集聚区，促进高端产业、高端人才汇聚。推进出入境便利服务、APEC商旅卡等高端人才绿色通道服务项目，推动落实外国人永居权申报管理便利化。实施留学回国（境）人员租住人才公寓专项政策，前三季度全区已安排的416名入住人中，有120余名海外人才已与拼多多、博世、携程、联合利华等重点企业签约。二是保障人才优质生活配套。推动豪葳国际双语幼儿园开园、虹桥体育公园正式开放、环城公园带驿站投入使用。稳步推进9-1、351街坊等公租房建设，支持招商项目重点产业人才安居保障，开展主播等不同白领人群的运营服务模式研究。会同市、区交警联合开展临空交通调研，着力提升区域对外通达性，为人才出行提供便利交通保障。

抓牢招商引资。 一是坚持寸土必争的招。做到善于争空间，聚焦"新空差变"四个维度（即："新"的空间做好源头招商、"空"的空间实现腾笼换鸟、"差"的空间全力提质增效、"变"的空间乘势二次改造），建立楼宇"三率"中位数偏离分析机制，加强楼宇去化、产出情况的动态跟踪、因情施策。做到主动争企业，用好项目审批绿色通道，持续招大引强。做到持续争活动，加快"走出去"招商步伐，瞄准北京、深

圳等潜在招商目的地和客户群，有的放矢加大宣介，让东虹桥的形象和声音传播得更广更远，争取更多优质企业入驻，并加强"走出去"招商后评估工作。二是坚持滴水不漏的留。在税源方面，加强东虹片区经济数据统计分析研究，争取把经济活动发生地变为纳税地和统计地。在服务方面，服务关心好企业，让企业在每一件小事中感受东虹片区的营商环境。在信息方面，强化协同联动，深入挖掘潜在的招商信息，助推更多项目落地。三是坚持颗粒归仓的增。做好归结工作，精心画好"企业体征图"，梳理企业"家谱"，吸引更多关联企业、上下游企业入驻。与各部门对接联动，争取更多一次性税源落入长宁。做好补缺工作，做好企业涨跌分析研判，开展产业专题研究，细化颗粒度。

强化平台招商。一是依托平台安商稳商。充分发挥长三角企业家圆桌会、虹桥临空企业家联合会、虹桥资产管理论坛等平台作用，组织开展程桥片区早餐会暨女企业家沙龙、"干细胞技术创造健康美好未来"创投沙龙、"工赋meetup"数字化转型企业家沙龙等活动，以平台聚集的高净值群体作为突破口和施力点，助力招商引资工作赋能增效。二是探索平台经济模式。成立临空园区投资家俱乐部，借助资本力量，鼓励金融机构协助开展招商，推动政企间、企业间对接合作。探索发挥区属国企投资平台作用，谋划设立园区产业基金，积极探索"基地+基金"的创新合作模式，推动重大招商项目落地，引领重点产业集群发展。

推进长三角一体化国家战略。一是加强与长三角城市的沟通对接。围绕建设特色园区、培育招引科创企业，东虹办赴合肥高新区、瑶海区、无锡锡东新城商务区等地（园）区学习调研。围绕共享虹桥机遇，参加由商务区主办的宁波企业家圆桌会。二是深化与相关园区的合作交流。推进东虹办与马鞍山、太原、无锡等地相关地（园）区合作协议的落实。坚持共拉长板、互补短板、融合共享，建立长三角产业园区联盟。

四、持续提升城区环境品质，打造宜居宜业产城融合样板间

持续推进重点项目。一是全力打造战略新空间。临空"核心四街坊"建设稳步推进，宜家荟聚购物中心、临空12号地块（虹桥上城）有序建设，中海租赁住宅竣工验收。全力做好光大安石、东虹桥中心、云启中心等新建载体源头招商。二是着力推动存量载体更新。大力推动生命元山（原明基广场）更新提升，打造长三角生命健康产业中心。研究推动工贸小区、置信电气工业厂房等存量空间进行城市提升，加强新老

图5-5　生命元山（原明基广场）

虹桥联动，以城市更新焕活产业生机。

持续改造机场东片区。一是推进规划用地转型。截至2023年9月底，已完成机场集团、东方航空、中航油共计15幅地块的存量用地转型，并签订了土地出让合同。二是加快地块项目建设。机场集团J-01项目和东航K1-01地块年底开工。南北园北块、蓄车厂库改建开展前期准备工作，春秋航空总部办公楼加快建设。

持续改善交通循环。一是规划道路系统。外环西段抬升工程（包括长宁段）年内开工建设。结合外环抬升契机，研究形成东虹片区"四纵十八横"路网建设方案，同步建设配套路网。二是争取轨交设站。积极争取南北向26号线、东西向17号线东延伸在东虹桥区域设站。三是研究优化公交线。建议保留虹桥4线，补足轨交覆盖空白，提升长宁片区南北向骨干公交网络转换能力，与北横西延伸及71路形成网络化运营。四是完善慢行系统。苏州河慢行步道11.2千米全线开放，北翟路地道完成建设，慢行系统建设初具规模。

持续深化绿色低碳。机场东片区新建建筑全面执行绿色建筑二星级以上标准，其中绿色建筑三星级比例达到50%。虹桥体育公园全面投入使用，临空音乐公园正在改造提升并逐步开放。外环林带建成并开放6.25千米生态绿道。

持续提升功能配套。一是居住品质进一步提升。虹桥人才公寓、临空9-1租赁住宅加快建设，区域内精品小区工程和电梯加装工作有效开展，人才住房建设标准及配套设施进一步优化。二是公共服务进一步强化。2023年城市徒步嘉年华、2023年上海女子半程马拉松赛在东虹片区成功举行。新泾镇再次获评2021—2023年度"上海民间文化艺术之乡"。

图5-6　2023上海女子半程马拉松赛

第三节　青浦片区

一、持续强化"大会展"特色功能，打造国际会展之都核心承载区

（一）推动会展产业能级提升

一是会展产业蓬勃发展。持续做好虹桥国际会展产业园建设工作，被评为市级生产性服务业功能区，引进英富曼会展集团、云上会展公司等知名会展企业。支持会展行业加快恢复重振，举行"上海市工商联展览商会成立大会暨首届大会展产业发展论坛"。

二是强化进馆招商。组织企业参加进博会，开展青浦区营商环境考察暨进博会展客商交流座谈会等系列活动。制定全区会展招商方案，指导各经济主体对接并入驻国家会展中心，设立青浦西虹桥商务区"会客厅"及招商办公室，形成长期合作关系，让更多参展企业走进青浦、了解青浦。

三是全力保障第六届进博会。完善第六届进博会服务保障方案和应急预案，增设综合协调"专班"。先后组织3次"走进青浦"系列展前推介活动，通过展前精准对接

图5-7　第六届中国国际进口博览会现场

展商企业，集中展现本区在产业发展、营商环境等方面成果，落实始祖鸟、安踏、万年青等23个品牌参展进博会。

（二）积极承接放大进博效应

一是持续强化"6+365"平台建设。研究制定《青浦区关于承接中国国际进口博览会溢出效应、聚焦上海虹桥国际中央商务区青浦片区促进贸易提升的实施意见（草案）》。

二是持续举办高端国际活动。先后承办联合国采购大会、中国国际公共采购论坛等高端国际性活动，举办青浦区招商推荐会，吸引境外商会、进口国家馆和参展企业落户青浦，有效搭建起国内国际双循环桥梁纽带。

三是持续打响"进博集市"品牌。延伸开设进博集市，提供"永不落幕"的、集聚贸易供需各方的沟通平台，增加开放交往、创新创意、资金技术的商业机遇，为实现"展品变商品""意向变订单""展商变客商"的转化，鼓励有意愿的境外参展商到长三角区域各省市进行展贸活动，把进博会打造成长三角对外开放的重要窗口，完成众采平台"6+365进博集市"在杭州市的首站活动。

（三）加强会展业政策支持力度

落实《青浦区提信心扩需求稳增长促发展行动方案》，紧扣企业需求出台更为精准的支持政策，利用各大展会复展契机，鼓励本区的会展企业"走出去""请进来"，同时大力支持引进优质会展企业，支持开办高水平会展项目等，加速会展业恢复重振。加大会展活动支持，贯彻服务业高质量发展政策，对会展主办方在本区举办的大型展览活动予以扶持，鼓励展会数字化转型，推动会展新基建。加大会展人才支持力度，对会展产业相关人才予以支持，对符合条件的人才在购租房补贴、人才落户、人才公寓等方面均给予大力支持。

二、持续增强"大商务"核心功能，建设功能复合的贸易枢纽

（一）推动总部经济能级提升

一是总部经济引导政策不断完善。完成了青浦片区产业发展规划，明确产业发展目标、发展策略、保障措施及发展行动计划。

二是各类总部集聚日益明显。已形成央企总部、跨国公司总部、民企总部、新兴科技总部汇聚的总部经济集聚升级新高地。立足打造国际贸易中心新平台，跨境电商迅速发展，绿地贸易港创立"进博集市"、在全国开设13家分港。

三是积极布局商贸总部，大力引进金融、法律、会计服务等专业服务功能以及国

家级、市级资源平台，对标一流商务区的要素能级，形成完善的商务生态，打造国际化中央商务区。

（二）推进贸易功能深化拓展

一是积极支持企业"走出去"。制定《青浦区加快发展跨境电子商务实施细则（草案）》，加大对企业"海外仓"和海外营运扶持。

二是大力开展招商引资活动。积极参加广州、深圳、福建企业家圆桌会招商活动专题会，精准对接重点企业，推进在谈项目落地。参加"潮涌浦江　投资虹桥"系列招商活动，新华汇申、中科醒诺2家企业集中签约。

三是积极拓展海外资源。充分发挥虹桥海外贸易中心分平台（西虹桥）以及境外商协会共享办公平台的作用。进一步拓宽海外商品进出口渠道，持续强化跨境电商"1210"出口模式，推动虹桥进口贸易促进创新示范区建设。

（三）聚力打造西片国际级消费集聚区

一是加快引入商业设施配套。结合"一刻钟便民生活圈"示范社区建设，打造智慧早餐、智慧菜市场等商业应用示范场景。

二是积极谋划全年购物活动。通过政府引导、市场主导的方式，依托各大商业、品牌企业，以节日、假日等重要时间点，聚焦首发经济、品牌经济、夜间经济等内容，推出一批线上线下主题活动，精心谋划第四届"五五购物节"青浦区活动。

三是推进重要商业载体建设。持续推进百老汇剧院群、蟠龙天地等大型商业中心、兰韵文化中心项目和沪青平商业带建设。"五一"期间蟠龙天地开业且人流量破110万次、总营业额超2 500万元，"六六夜生活节"期间蟠龙天地、夏都小镇步行街入选"2023上海夜生活好去处"，"十一"国庆期间蟠龙天地共计接待游客超百万人次。

三、持续塑造"大科创"新增功能，提升区域产业协同创新能力

（一）持续完善北斗西虹桥基地综合服务功能

一是有力推进北斗产业平台建设。发挥北斗创新基地全产业链布局优势，鼓励优质企业联合产业链上下游共建，形成"一平台多基地"的北斗产业集聚新模式。拥有北斗企业300多家，包括1家A股上市企业（华测导航）、7家上市培育企业（IPO辅导期）、41家优质企业（年营收1千万—1亿元，年增幅30%以上）。

二是持续提升北斗产业能级。北斗西虹桥基地获批全市唯一的国家专业类特色服务出口基地，为上海首个地理信息类特色出口基地，基地保持年均50%的增长，增速

在国内保持领先，已成为上海北斗产业的集聚中心和全国北斗产业园区的排头兵。持续推进长三角高分遥感数据应用服务中心建设。上海市空间信息产业协会正式落地，承担空间信息领域规划统计、政策建议、标准制定等工作。

三是不断提升专业化服务水平。积极打响科创服务牌、服务北斗生态圈，长三角生态绿色一体化发展示范区知识产权运营大会成功举办，"上海市知识产权运营服务集聚区青浦功能园"、"青浦区专利超市"正式揭牌，成为国内综合竞争力最强、产业链最完整、公共服务平台最完善的"北斗第一园"。

（二）持续推动特色产业与创新深度融合

一是持续推进"上海文化影视科技产业集聚区"建设。已集聚烧糖文化、上象娱乐等一批影视科技龙头企业，加速布局文化影视科技产业发展新赛道，助力上海加快建设全球影视创制中心。

二是加快推动长三角数创先导区（徐泾104区块）建设。实施2.5平方千米园区整体二次开发，全力推进空间腾退和数字产业功能落位，完成长三角数创先导区规划编制。

三是持续打响"虹桥数字物流装备港"品牌。全力支持华新片区建设虹桥数智供应链集聚区，持续推进上海虹桥数字物流装备港（华新片区）改造先行试点项目，打造智能化国家物流枢纽。

图5-8　推进长三角数创先导区建设

四、持续做强"大交通"基础功能，推动城市功能和软实力进一步提升

（一）加快推动交通基础设施提档升级

一是加强规划编制。编制完成《青浦区综合交通"十四五"规划》《青浦区青东片区综合交通规划研究》等，加快推动区域综合交通规划高质量发展，开展《青浦区综合交通规划》编制工作，聚焦优化青浦片区区域路网体系。

二是有序推动轨道交通建设。全力配合推进市域铁路上海示范区线建设，协助推进轨交2号线西延伸、13号线西延伸工程，配合开展25号线延伸至华新镇区的规划方案研究。

三是稳步推进道路交通建设。加快完善高快速路集疏运服务体系，加速推动G15抬升扩容和G50扩容及智慧高速改造，实现"外围环路系统"扩容，启动G318改扩建工程，持续推进区区对接与镇镇对接道路工程。

四是不断完善公共交通网络。结合虹桥单元规划，加快中运量线路方案研究。结合第六届进博会保障，优化进博会停车总体保障方案。

（二）加快推动城市区域品质优化提升

一是有序推进城中村改造项目。实施城中村改造项目控规调整，推进徐泾罗家小区、老集镇、蟠龙等3个城中村改造项目。其中徐泾镇老集镇"城中村"改造项目东至华徐公路、西至明珠路、南至沪青平公路、北至盈港东路，总用地面积35.187万平方米，采用集体经济组织引入合作单位共同改造开发。改造成果包括3个安置房基地、3个商品住宅、4个商办、2个商业及若干基础设施建设项目。改造范围与保留区域犬牙交错、界面复杂。包括在徐泾A2a-04d地块幼儿园新建工程，新建10班规模的幼儿园，2021年8月开工，2023年6月取得竣工备案证明，2023年9月完成招生投入使用。

二是持续推进保障性租赁住房筹措工作。以资源联动、功能融合、发展协同为中心，结合枢纽地区布局规律，按照"15分钟生活圈"要求，圈层式联动布局重点区域租赁租房，前三季度，共筹措保障性租赁住房5 549套。并结合"美丽家园"建设，加快推进老旧小区电梯加装工作。

图5-9　徐泾镇老集镇"城中村"改造项目

图 5-10　青浦片区中高端租赁社区——天空之城

（三）加快推进精细化秩序管理升级

一是加强风险隐患防范。将青浦片区工地进行分级分类管理，对联合检查出的问题明确整改时限和责任人，实现对安全生产和风险事件的实时预警。持续加强长效管理，强化施工车辆冲洗、扬尘污染、物料堆放、围挡规范等工作的监督管理。

二是提升城市空间治理能力。督促商业体完善周边非机动车停放方案，将区域内轨交站点的非机动车管理纳入中心一体化管理范围，挖掘闲置空间优化停车方案。

三是以信息化赋能城市管理。贯彻落实"数智赋能"要求，深化运行智慧管养平台，简化问题处置流程，提升处置效率，共处理各类一体化管养问题 1 287 起，工单整体完成率为 99.99%，市民投诉率下降 20%。

五、持续提升服务长三角和联通国际的能力

（一）持续优化营商环境

一是推动法制化营商环境建设。2023 年 2 月，青浦区举行提信心、优营商、强发展工作推进大会，并发布《青浦区提信心扩需求稳增长促发展行动方案》《青浦区 2023 年优化营商环境工作要点》（青浦优化营商环境 6.0 版），举办投资促进活动，加强与

RCEP联动，优势互补，深化区域经济合作，推动区域经济发展。

二是推动国际化营商环境建设。优化跨境贸易业务，分类推进解决重点外资项目和企业的困难问题及诉求，鼓励外资开放式创新平台建设，落实国家新版外商投资准入负面清单和鼓励外商投资产业目录，持续深化"放管服"改革。积极推动自由贸易账户相关工作。三是推动便利化营商环境建设。"一网通办"深入推进，帮办代办服务机制不断完善，企业专属网页功能接入"为企纾困"等8个区企业服务特色应用。企业变更登记全程网办系统正式上线，简易注销登记适用范围继续拓展。西虹桥分中心综合服务窗口正式对外受理业务，市场监管领域147个事项和人才服务领域相关的涉企事项已进驻综合服务窗口。

（二）持续推进科技人才引育

一是落实各类人才政策和服务。研究完善"青峰"人才购租房补贴中科技类人才相关判定标准，采用点面结合的方式，开展科技人才调研10余场，调研企业100余家，推荐2家园区获"海聚英才"创新创业示范基地；推荐6人申报"科技创业领军人才"、3人申报"青峰"人才计划、50位企业高管参加"青能浦卓"培训班；对接13家企业100余人申报个人所得税税负差额补贴政策，15家企业申报"上海市外国专家项目"。

二是积极组织开展培训活动。组建外国人才"大讲堂"宣讲队，开展外国人来华工作许可业务培训会，组织开展"海聚英才、共建科创"系列活动。落实工程硕博士培育改革专项试点工作，推进张江专项资金政策育才支持。三是积极推进人才平台建设。加快建设长三角（青浦）数字人力资源产业园项目，扎实建设上海青浦（长三角）留学人员创业园。

第四节　嘉定片区

2023年，北虹桥商务区立足于"开放北虹桥、创新领航地"的总体定位，全面融入和推动虹桥国际开放枢纽建设，对接商务区新定位、新目标、新要求，围绕"三年翻番""五年双倍"行动计划。发挥战略引擎牵引作用，强化增量创新和存量更新，推动生产性服务业向中高端延伸，推动生活性服务业向高品质转变，加快产业集聚，加快优质公共服务资源建设，加快推进"一区、一城、一湾"三大标杆性项目建设，全力推动北虹桥商务区早出形象、早出功能。

一、重点区域建设推进情况

（一）上虹桥·城市更新区

在10月12日"潮涌浦江　投资虹桥"——2023虹桥国际中央商务区投资促进大会上，《嘉定"上虹桥·城市更新区"规划》正式发布。

"上虹桥"是嘉定区政府与上海地产集团政企合作开发的城市更新项目。该项目遵循"以人为本、产城融合、多元包容、活力共享"的理念，对1.67平方千米左右的土地进行规划调整、整体提升、功能再造，着力打造"产城融合示范区、三生融合体验区、政企合作样板区"，为商务区打开了未来产业发展和功能提升的重要发展空间。

空间布局上，该项目立足北向拓展带"桥头堡"，结合区域实际和资源禀赋分为东西两个片区：东区规划约93.3万平方米土地、建筑面积113万平方米，整体架构为"一核、一带、两轴、多组团"，空间特色突出功能与生态的融合、活力与文化的叠加，聚焦商务研发功能，配套职住多业态开发，打造专精特新研发总部和高端商贸服务聚集区。西区规划约73.3万平方米土地、建筑面积107万平方米，整体规划为"一轴两心，五区连网"，倾力提供多元活力的生活居住功能，构筑生态韧性、智慧活力的城市基底，着力打造功能复合、绿色低碳、全龄友好的国际社区。目前，已基本实现"地平事了"，东区产业地块招商全面启动，华瑞时尚、聚升集团、圣和药业等项目锁定意向地块，另储备有中核华建、中测行等一批优质产业项目。西区住宅地块出让以及首批次市政基础设施建设有序推进。

图5-11 临港嘉定科技城规划示意图

（二）临港嘉定科技城

临港嘉定科技城，与临港集团合作，规划面积2.75平方千米，高质量打造成为"生命·科技"主题的多元产业生态园和高品质虹桥国际在线新经济生态园。首发项目已结构封顶，预计2024年二季度竣工，2024年下半年交付使用，配套"三路三桥"已开工建设。园区持续加强招商引资，首发项目建成并且成熟运营后，预计年税收超过2亿元，入驻企业300家以上，引入产业人才3 000人以上。推动"北虹之云"市级孵化器能级提升，力争到2025年建设成为国家级科技企业孵化器；二期拿地工作推进中，拟建设全球创新医疗技术产业基地。

持续推动园区存量项目改造提升，制定完善临港嘉定科技城整体转型升级方案，储备智能制造、生命健康优质客户，导入研发中心、生产基地项目，探索与镇、村集体合作模式路径，引入第三方合作伙伴，以点带面，逐步更新园区存量空间形态、业态，打造产业生态。目前，宏泰石材拟引入赛金生物项目，另有真赵、久康、鸿元展印等项目正在加快落地。力争成功申报市级特色园区（XR终端方向），打造商务区在线新经济生态园北虹桥主题承载区。

图5-12 虹桥新慧总部湾效果图

2023年,临港嘉定公司与格力新能源共同开展全领域、多方位合作。开展数字化转型,打造绿色生态应用场景,创建"零碳"示范园区。下一步将共同打造"格力钛""光储直柔"等上海研发中心,聚集行业人才,推动"光储空""零碳源"等新技术的研发和科技成果转化,推进相关产业在长三角、全国乃至国际市场的开发与拓展。

(三)虹桥新慧总部湾

虹桥新慧总部湾占地约18.67万平方米,建筑面积37万平方米,高标准打造成为嘉定"五型经济"重要承载区和总部集聚标杆地。项目分三期开发,共23个地块,一期在建项目有序建设,盈创、雅运、天瑞筠、蓝科、瀚讯5个项目已竣工,其余项目加快推进中;二期华庄模具、凯利项目和三期福隆、仪菲、凯笛芯项目均在加快推进中。

秉承"统一规划、统一建设、统一管理、统一运营"的建设理念,总部湾公共服务功能不断完善,道路等配套基础设施有序推进,园区管委会启动实质性运作,已初步拟定园区运营管理方案,杜绝随意出租、失管失控等问题,推进形成总部和研发类企业聚集的"研发总部核"。

二、产业能级不断提升

根据商务区"四高五新"产业发展规划，嘉定片区明确了以创新经济、总部经济为特色，培育数字新经济、生命新科技、低碳新能源、汽车新势力产业链创新融合生态集群，全力打造国际创新产业集聚区。

总部经济高地新格局初显。积极支持民营企业总部、贸易型总部等各类总部项目集聚发展，截至第三季度共有各类总部企业25家，初步形成总部企业集群。同时，加速推进新慧总部湾建设，储备更多优质总部项目，不断提升总部经济能级。此外，华住、连成、新东锦、江苏国泰等一批行业领军企业正加速发展建设。

创新经济引领高质量发展。充分发挥科技创新在稳增长稳市场主体中的重要作用，积极推进高新技术企业认定；加大产学研融合发展，促进重塑科技与同济大学、康德莱医械与山东大学、太太乐与上海海洋大学开展产学研合作；打造东锦"侨帮侨"特色创新创业基地，推动"北虹之云"获批市级孵化器，做好北虹桥地区创新创业载体服务，进一步提升科技创新浓度。

数字新经济凸显产业活力。吸引仪菲、华住、凯笛芯等为代表的一批数字新经济企业入驻，打造在线新经济平台，紧跟产业变革新潮流，构筑数字经济新引擎。聚焦数字经济引领作用，继续做强直播带货、跨境电商、游戏出海，加大培育仪菲旗下的淘美妆、泛娱乐等在线新经济企业，打造淘美妆商友会全球美尚峰会等一系列国际性高端平台，深化在线数字贸易新平台建设。持续打造游戏研发行业的数字作品确权服务平台，南洋国际科创中心（北虹桥泛娱乐平台）聚集触宝、乐元素、千数等150余家公司，重点项目10余个，极大地推动了泛娱乐产业发展。

加快人工智能产业布局。集聚智臻智能网络、纳瓦电子等重点人工智能企业。智臻智能已于2023年3月在纳斯达克成功上市，成为中国版ChatGPT第一股，工博士机器人的上市正在筹备中。持续完善国家智能传感器创新中心平台建设，力促与全区产业发展形成良性互动。

生命新科技营造创新生态。嘉定片区集聚了以康德莱医械、康德莱集团、太太乐等为代表的一批生命新科技企业，着力打造高端医疗器械产业平台，打造"新健康"科技创新生态圈。充分发挥康德莱医械龙头作用，依托华东地区最大的动物实验一站式服务平台——昕诺动物实验中心，赋能实验检测等技术资源支撑，吸引医械创新企业落地。截至2023年10月底，平台已集聚近20家相关企业，实现税收1.2亿元。做强太太乐、东锦等一批食品企业优势，积极把握进博会品牌效应，拓展绿色健康食品产业链，推动大健康产业创新发展。

低碳新能源激活转型动能。加强"新能源＋新材料"产业联动，依托重塑能源、惠柏新材料、蓝科环保等一批低碳新能源企业，激活低碳转型新动能，塑造绿色能源新优势。推动建设氢能产业园区或研发生产用地，提高氢能产业的竞争力和吸引力。

汽车新势力谋划特色赛道。加速打造新能源汽车总部集聚区。发挥以蔚来汽车、吉祥智驱、凯利等汽车新势力企业的引领作用，依托嘉定汽车完善的产业链优势，高起点建设新能源汽车平台，高标准打造新能源与新能源汽车特色产业链。澳康达二手车展示交易中心启动试运营，不断延伸新能源汽车产业链。

三、产城融合不断深化

强化规划引领作用。"十四五"以来，北虹桥商务区紧紧围绕"创新北虹桥，开放领航地"的目标，2023年聚焦商务区新要求、新部署，制定形成了北虹桥区域的国土空间中近期规划三年（2023—2025）行动计划、高质量推进北虹桥商务区建设三年行动计划（2023—2025），全力推动北虹桥发展宏伟蓝图细化为"施工图"、转化为"实景图"。

对标北虹桥商务区新的功能定位，进一步优化北虹桥空间结构，构建"一核聚能，一带润城，三轴联动，四区共荣"的空间格局。按需启动部分先期实施重点控详规划调整。截至目前，重塑、蔚来、康德莱等产业项目和临港嘉定科技城（金宝园区）均已完成控规调整，为北虹桥商务区的发展提供规划支撑。

综合交通网络更加完善。大力推进轨交网络建设。轨道交通嘉闵线全面开工，在北虹桥区域内设置有金园五路站和金运路站两个站点，均为换乘站，有序推进两个站点建设前期工作。积极实现三纵三横干道网络直通长三角，嘉闵线一线直连虹桥枢纽，轨道交通30分钟直达中心城区，不断强化交通区位优势。区区对接道路稳步推进。加快推进金运路—申昆路、金园一路—申长路两条区区对接道路建设，其中金运路—申昆路已进场施工，金园一路—申长路项目正推进前期土地手续办理及初设批复工作。持续完善综合交通设施。加快研究北虹桥商务区与虹桥枢纽的快速公交线（中运量）方案；制定14号线金园五路公交枢纽站规划；加快封浜地区乐秀路"P+R"

等公共停车设施项目前期手续，临港嘉定城公共停车设施项目视园区整体开发进度适时调整。

生态环境建设扎实推进。打造绿色生态空间。以外环绿带、近郊绿环、吴淞江生态间隔带为基本生态骨架，围绕吴淞江沿岸品质提升开展调研、征询设计方案，积极推进绥德公园、蝶语园等公园建设，打造优美宜居生态环境，竣工开园绥德公园，开工建设蝶语公园。推动绿色生态城区建设。封浜新镇绿色生态城区试点取得批复，积极推进控规调整，同步开展封浜新镇首发地块绿色生态建设指标调整。

四、功能融合逐渐彰显

高标准规划建设高端宜居的国际化社区。研究推进北虹之星建设，规划将北虹之星打造为多元活力的国际化社区，虹桥国际开放枢纽核心区的品质居住高地。截至第三季度，该地区控规修编已完成规划草案，并通过了市规划资源局技术审查。启动K12国际学校、迎虹湖公园、高压线下活力绿谷等功能项目落地路径研究，加速推动国际化社区建设。

切实提高公共服务满意度。坚持教育优先发展。全力推进建设一所初中、一所小学、一所幼儿园。开工建设北虹桥22-06地块幼儿园和北虹桥22-07地块九年一贯制学校，进一步完善教育资源，提升教育服务能级。多途径增加租赁住房。根据北虹桥地区实际，采取非居住存量房屋改建途径，推进V领地青年公寓项目建设，为北虹桥地区提供更多优质保障性租赁房源。推动文体多元共享。体育基础设施逐步完善，彩HONG智慧健身苑、全市唯一八连片门球场相继建成，95个社区健身器材超限改造竣工，新增5个健身苑点，全力打造全民参与的15分钟体育生活圈。文化资源供给不断增多，开设了江桥百姓公共文化"醉空间"、江桥镇文体中心龙湖分中心、金鹤图书馆等线下空间，做强了我嘉书房"轮值馆长""踩云间"建筑可阅读两大市级创新项目。

不断提升城市治理精细化水平。为贯彻落实《上海虹桥国际中央商务区城市管理精细化行动计划》整体工作，制定完成《北虹桥商务区城市管理精细化实施方案》和《重点任务分解表》，完成北虹桥商务区综合管养方案及三年行动计划，确定先行启动区范围，同步完成设施量清单梳理和管养经费测算。按照三年行动计划，2024年启动先行启动区综合养护工作，包括一体化保洁，道路、绿化和河道养护。2025年底，确定江桥全域综合养护实施计划表。

五、服务保障持续推进

　　持续优化营商环境。结合优化营商环境6.0版专项举措，从企业服务、政务服务、城市建设和人才安居等方面草拟了《北虹桥商务区2023年度持续优化营商环境行动方案》。提升人才综合服务水平方面，依托"上海·嘉定人才港"，深入打造人才港北虹桥分站，发挥人才港辐射作用，推进北虹桥分站人力资源服务机构入驻、揭牌等工作；持续强化人才服务。完成重点企业服务库搭建工作，截至第三季度，已有52家北虹桥商务区企业入库；组织开展嘉定人才新政宣传，提供人才政策咨询服务，提升人才服务水平。为企业注册提供便捷服务方面，在江桥镇社区事务受理服务中心设立"企业登记注册服务点"，将区政务服务中心开办企业专区业务延伸至北虹桥区域，负责区域内新设立内资企业的全程电子化登记，为企业登记提供受理、审批、打照、发照一条龙服务，实现企业开办当场核准、当场发照。在江桥市场监管所设立"为民工作室指导站"，将服务触角延伸，"零距离"为企业提供专业高效的注册许可服务，解决疑难复杂问题，为企业打造良好"生态圈"。深化企业服务模式方面，深化"一企一策"企业服务模式，助力企业匹配更高能级政策，研究挖掘企业税收潜力，进一步加强政策宣传推广，大力弘扬服务企业"店小二"精神，建立走访服务企业和企业帮办服务制度，强化对高新技术企业、专精特新企业、科技型企业的服务力度，提升一对一精准服务效能。

第六章 标志性CBD城市更新

第一节 制定标志性CBD建设方案

为牢牢抓住"中国国际进口博览会""长三角一体化发展""虹桥国际开放枢纽建设"等重大战略历史机遇,深入贯彻落实陈吉宁书记调研商务区指示精神,商务区结合深化战略内涵认识研究和核心区开发建设、规划实施评估情况,以城市更新为抓手,先后组织相关单位成立联合团队,协调相关单位作为统筹主体,全面推进虹桥标志性CBD建设方案研究制定和落地实施。

一、方案制定背景

商务区是虹桥国际开放枢纽核心功能承载区,其标志性CBD作为体现商务区高标准、国际化建设的标杆性区域,也是商务区核心功能的重要载体。面对新任务新要求,研究制定虹桥国际中央商务区标志性CBD建设方案,具有重要的战略意义与现实必要。

一是基于多重国家战略叠加赋能的战略需要。从进博会的永久举办地到长三角一体化发展的排头兵,再到虹桥国际开放枢纽建设的"一核",多重国家战略汇集,强势赋能标志性CBD建设。为深入贯彻落实陈吉宁书记调研商务区指示精神,立足"大交通、大商务、大会展、大科创"核心功能,持续发展国际贸易、高端服务业等传统优势行业,全力做优做强总部经济和功能性平台,将商务区标志性CBD打造成为上海统筹扩大内需与开拓外部市场的战略节点,在推动虹桥国际中央商务区"高质量、一体化、国际化"发展中做出示范。通过若干年的努力,把楼宇载体打造成为上海乃至全国甲级办公载体最为集中的区域,产业强度和经济密度基本达到国内外著名CBD的水平,集聚一批特色鲜明的产业集群和龙头企业,服务"引进来"和"走出去"的功能显著提升,标志性和显示度大幅度提升,努力建设成为更具竞争力、更加国际化、更具辨识度、更以人为本，与4个片区发展更加协调协同的标志性CBD。

二是应对系列问题瓶颈制约发展的现实需要。对标巴黎拉德芳斯、纽约曼哈顿、东京横滨、上海陆家嘴等国内外一流CBD，其共同特征包括：既具有世界一流的商务办公载体、高等级的公服配套，又具有标志性的CBD形象和街区特色；既具有高密度经济活动、高能级的主导产业，又有强大的金融服务和专业服务配套。反观原核心区3.7平方千米范围内，无论是商办楼宇载体，还是道路、绿化、水系等市政配套设施，经过10余年的倾力打造，基本形态和品质已经具备，绝大部分已建成投入运营，但离标志性CBD的差距是全方位的，提升的空间很大。研究制定标志性CBD方案将有利于进一步厘清商务区内部功能布局，建立健全协同高效的交通、会展、贸易、服务、咨询、科创等功能体系；有利于更准确锚定空间载体，聚焦标志性CBD示范引领作用发挥；有利于更大胆地探索改革创新试验平台，打破行政区壁垒，探索创新区域协调发展机制，实现地区间的全方位开放合作。

二、方案形成过程

从2023年3月开始，以主题教育"大兴调查研究"为契机，商务区结合深化战略内涵认识研究与核心区城市更新等相关专项工作，同步开展商务区标志性CBD建设研究课题调研。过程中，采取座谈交流、现场踏勘的方式，对3.7平方千米范围内功能性公司（主要是地产虹桥公司、南虹桥公司）、相关企业（包括已运营的房地产企业、历史遗留项目房地产企业、已整体或部分楼宇受让企业、公寓运营企业、部分入驻企业代表和相关物业公司）、属地街道相关意见建议作深入了解与充分征集。

经梳理汇总，标志性CBD建设将重点围绕以下6个方面作进一步深化研究：一是围绕轨道交通网络覆盖严重不足、常规公交分布不均，枢纽地区拥堵加剧以及慢性交通诱导系统不完善等问题，研究提出畅通内外交通循环的策略建议，进一步提升枢纽门户形象；二是围绕商务能级不足，500强企业较少、商办楼宇空置率偏高且品质不高等问题，研究提出推动存量空置业态升级转型和历史遗留项目解决，推进总部集聚及高端产业功能导入，建设国内顶级"走出去"专业服务平台，提升区域经济密度及总体能级；三是围绕会展活动缺乏总体布局、会展功能溢出效益不足、大会展生态圈仍需培育等问题，研究提出以国家会展中心为核心载体，建设虹桥国际会展产业生态圈，推动长三角会展业发展，提升国际影响力，做大国际会展之都的核心承载区；四是围绕住宅结构失衡、高能级公共服务设施缺乏、绿地水系等公共空间品质不高的问题，研究提出创新城市更新机制和制定专项资金政策，加快推进绿地、滨河及中轴线综合改造提升，鼓励支持商办改建租赁住房、商圈提质，聚集人气；五是围绕要素市场化配置、公共服务保障、城市精细化管理等存在的短板，研究提出逐步建设集国土空间、产业招商、建设时序、经济数据、政务服务、城市管理等于一体的"数字虹桥"，打造一流国际化营商环境；六是围绕当前体制机制在统筹推进空间规划、能级提升、财力投入、公共配套等方面的局限性，研究提出优化调整开发建设体制机制的策略建议。

三、方案主要内容

在积极借鉴深圳前海深港现代服务业合作区、北京经济技术开发区发展经验，并综合调研分析的基础上，以问题导向、目标导向、结果导向为原则，着重从选定范围和发展目标、比较优势及面临问题、重点任务和工作举措、工作建议四个方面展开，拟定《虹桥国际中央商务区标志性CBD建设方案》，其内容主要涉及：

一是比较优势和面临问题再认识。商务区经过10多年的开发建设和功能打造，原核心区3.7平方千米作为建成区，产业发展载体相对成熟，东西两侧有虹桥枢纽和国家会展中心功能加持，布局核心功能和优势产业的基础条件较好，定位和形象有一定影响力，区域标志性CBD形态开发已初具规模、初步成势。根据现状基础条件，对标国际一流CBD建设发展规律，坚持问题导向、需求导向、目标导向、效果导向，着重从比较优势和面临问题两个层面对虹桥标志性CBD建设方案作前置研究。其中，虹桥标志性CBD建设的比较优势主要包括区位优势、交通优势、载体优势、商务优势和流量优势等五大优势；面临问题则主要体现在企业和平台能级有待提升、交通系统有待改善、载体品质有待优化、城市形态有待更新等方面。

二是重点任务和工作举措再深化。围绕将虹桥标志性CBD打造成为上海统筹扩大内需与开拓外部市场的战略节点，会同市规划资源局城市更新专班，以城市更新重点项目清单为关键切口，深入摸排151平方千米尤其是核心区3.7平方千米城市更新诉求、难点和痛点问题，综合分析标志性CBD建设国土空间规划、产业规划、发展现状和未来目标。过程中，积极对接市发展改革委、规划资源局等市级部门开展多项专题研究，争取业务指导和政策支持。同时，加强与地产虹桥公司、南虹桥公司、新虹街道、楼宇工作站及社会企业的互动联系，征集更新意愿和政策诉求。方案最终拟定从产业功能提升、平台功能提升、综合交通提升、城市品质提升、辨识度和标志性打造等五个方面重点任务，全面对标商务区"高质量、一体化、国际化"要求，提出了与高质量发展要求相匹配的总部新高地、与打造活跃增长极相匹配的产业竞争力、与标志性CBD地位相称的培育孵化功能，建设中国企业"走出去"的国家级平台、打造一批国家授权赋能的功能平台，建设国际化人才引进培育共享服务平台、对外辐射能级更强的门户枢纽、毛细血管畅通的内部循环体系、智慧化人性化的静态交通管理、高品质的楼宇载体、高品质的生态空间、高品质的城市管理，打造标志性活力广场、特色消费新地标及标志性夜景灯光等15项工作举措。

三是衔接联动和部署落实再推进。在充分考虑原3.7平方千米核心功能区域已建成，充分研究151平方千米与标志性CBD建设范围关系，充分照顾四个片区未来发展定位，充分借鉴CBD建设国际经验的基础上，明确标志性CBD的目标，即持续提升核心功能，持续提升产出效益，持续提升城市品质，服务辐射能力显著增强，标志性和辨识度显著增强，最终与四个片区中心形成强劲的发展组团，实现高质量、一体化发展。同时，充分发挥东虹桥的产业优势、西虹桥的强劲势头、南虹桥的巨大潜力和北虹桥的后发优势，紧紧依托依靠四个片区，既错位竞争又合作共赢。据此，从健全工作机制、加强政策支持、制订行动计划等方面进一步细化明确方案配套实施路径，包括建立市有关部门、管委会、闵行区、市属国企平台公司联动机制，探索市场化机制。管委会会同市有关部门研究解决体制机制、历史遗留项目处置等重点难点问题，并支持标志性CBD涉及重大基础设施、制度创新、商业布局等纳入市级有关专项规划；围绕主要目标和重点任务，加强政策研究，在财政、城市更新、投资、人才等重点领域，储备和制定一系列能有效解决突出矛盾的政策体系，更好发挥政府对资源配置作用，推动形成有效的政策支持；科学制订具体行动计划，统筹安排年度重点项目计划，对涉及标志性CBD建设的重大工程、重点任务进行分解，落实牵头单位和工作责任，形成各部门之间的协调合作机制，确保方案目标按计划、高效率、高质量实施完成。

四、方案实施路径

为加快商务区核心区标志性CBD建设，管委会牵头推进存量建设用地开展城市更新活动，引导低效用地、闲置空间再开发利用，提升区域功能内涵、空间品质、综合交通和市政基础设施，通过以下手段强化建设方案的实施：

加强政策赋能。为更好地推动标志性中央商务区城市更新实施，通过加强政策赋能，最大程度激发市场参与积极性，开展以下四项工作：一是配合市规划资源局深化规划土地政策制定；二是会同市发改委、市住建委、市绿容局等相关行业主管部门，研究核心区更新项目的立项审批、公共绿地复合利用、建设运营管理流程、项目投融资等相关政策；三是对接3.7平方千米的产权主体，广泛征询城市更新的政策诉求；四是剖析项目堵点问题，补充完善政策内容。

编制更新方案。组建由责任规划师、责任建筑师、责任评估师组成的"三师联创"团队，会同商务区城市更新专班，重点聚焦标志性中央商务区近期重点更新区域和项目，细化更新方案内容，形成规划实施方案过程稿。

强化城市设计。组建设计团队参与城市设计工作，研究制定城市设计任务书，形成标志性CBD总体城市设计方案（包括功能布局、交通体系、绿化景观等）。

形成项目清单。通过开展存量资源摸排和更新潜力研究，厘清红线内各类更新项目的责任主体、资金概算等内容，加强红线外公共部分的更新项目探索（公共空间、绿化景观、道路等），提出资金渠道（市级、区级）和投资估算工作建议。同时，聚焦条件成熟的更新项目，明确更新建设实施安排，保证项目近远期内稳步推进。

第二节　建立健全标志性CBD城市更新组织框架

商务区管委会会同闵行区人民政府、地产虹桥公司，根据区域发展要求、更新活动紧迫性等综合研判，确定2023—2025年标志性CBD城市更新三年计划，细化更新目标、更新机制和路径，组建由市场参与、多方联合的城市更新综合体，建立城市更新工作专班，明确各方权力与责任义务，建立多方参与协商机制。通过组织相关专业团队，开展城市更新单元策划工作，研究功能结构、空间意向、更新路径、资金平衡测算、资金筹集配置、运营管理要求等相关内容。

一、成立城市更新工作领导小组

根据本市城市更新领导小组工作部署和《关于成立上海虹桥国际中央商务区标志性CBD城市更新工作领导小组的通知》，正式确立商务区城市更新工作体制机制相关事项。领导小组负责统筹推进商务区标志性CBD城市更新，建立健全工作机制，制订年度工作目标、主要任务和项目计划，协调推进城市更新重点项目，审议决策相关重大事项，研究制定城市更新政策和专项资金扶持办法。

领导小组下设办公室，具体负责标志性CBD城市更新日常管理工作。办公室牵头开展核心区标志性CBD城市更新工作，以核心区标志性CBD项目清单梳理、政策实施意见制定、城市更新方案与行动计划编制及重点城市更新项目推进为主要工作内容，定期召开城市更新工作例会，完成市更新办交代的各项任务，以城市更新指引为依据推进区域更新和零星更新。一是要在摸清核心区城市更新工作难点、堵点问题的基础上，加强专项政策的研究制定，实现土地、绿化、水务、道路等方面的政策突破。二是要充分排摸更新项目清单，结合企业诉求，研究项目操作路径，为资金的精准测算提供指导，梳理解决资金方案问题。三是要加快编制标志性CBD建设方案，明确核心目标和核心任务，按照目标导向、问题导向和需求导向的原则，将最具必要性、紧迫性和关键性的项目纳入方案内容。四是领导小组内部要加强统筹协作，加快推进体制机制完善、政策研究制定、项目排摸推进等方面工作落地落实。

二、建立工作专班

商务区管委会层面，成立了城市更新工作专班，由战略发展处、规划建设处、城运管理处、商务发展处等内部处室组成，与市、区相关部门加强协同，密切配合，有序推进城市更新工作。工作专班主要开展以下四项工作：一是配合市规划资源局进一步深化规划土地政策成果；二是会同市发改委、市住建委、市绿容局等相关行业主管部门，研究核心区更新项目的立项审批、公共绿地复合利用、建设运营管理流程、项目投融资等相关政策。三是牵头对接3.7平方千米的产权主体，广泛征询城市更新的政策诉求。四是剖析项目堵点问题，进一步补充完善政策内容，针对中轴线、重大市政设施、功能配套提升完善等项目推进过程中遇到的瓶颈问题，提出相应的政策建议。

闵行区委区政府于2023年10月份成立城市更新工作专班，与商务区管委会开展工作对接。闵行区城市更新工作专班围绕商务区核心区城市更新工作，积极配合完成城市设计方案编制、深入参与城市更新实施方案的研究，做好前期梳理排摸及实施阶段配合落地工作，并与管委会城市更新工作专班建立了商务区核心区城市更新工作例会机制。

三、明确统筹主体

明确了地产虹桥公司作为核心区3.7平方千米的区域更新统筹主体，加快组建由责任规划师、责任建筑师、责任评估师组成的"三师联创"团队，由统筹主体牵头会同管委会城市更新工作专班协同推进更新方案编制工作，重点聚焦标志性CBD近期重点更新区域和项目，细化更新方案具体内容，考虑整体性和更新时序，关注项目的可实施性和可操作性，形成方案成果，包括前期评估、专项研究与初步方案、规划实施方案、利益平衡方案和公共要素全生命周期管理清单等。

为强化专业技术力量，发挥全流程统筹支撑作用，城市更新工作建立了责任规划师、责任建筑师、责任评估师"三师联创"制度。通过前瞻性谋划、专业性策划、合理性评估、陪伴式服务，贯穿城市更新策划、规划、建设、管理的全周期。一是建立责任规划师制度。由责任规划师整合建筑量、公共要素、融合用地属性等空间资源，针对核心区策划规划联动、方案制定和控详规划完善、更新项目实施和运营管理、后续评估提升的更新活动全流程，全面开展规划统筹和技术保障。二是建立责任建筑师制度。以责任建筑师搭建全流程贯通的技术服务平台，整合各项专业设计，编制更新项目设计方案，破解建设领域规范标准与城市更新需要不适配、不规范等问题，统筹公共空间、公共艺术、标识系统，提升空间品质与标志性。三是建立责任评估师制度。以责任评估师评估产权归集、建设、运营各阶段土地与建筑等资产价值，综合平衡政府、市场和个人的利益诉求，协助政府和实施主体研判更新项目可行性，合理确定资产价值。探索建立用地、楼宇的绩效评估标准，协助研究低效用地、低效楼宇的退出和回购机制。

第三节 制定城市更新项目清单

基于打造国际化标志性CBD核心区的目标定位，管委会会同闵行区、地产虹桥，通过多种方式梳理排摸，分析区域基础、优势、问题和短板，并联合上规院、华东设计院、仲联量行"三师"团队，对标一流商务区标准，查问题、找差距、扬优势、补短板，形成了标志性CBD区域城市更新项目清单。

一、项目清单制订背景

经过10多年的开发建设和功能打造，虹桥CBD形态开发初具规模、初步成势，大商务、大会展、大交通、大科创功能深度融合，商务区发展能级和核心竞争力不断提升。但同时，区域也存在功能内涵有待丰富、城市品质有待提升、内外交通有待补强、经济强度有待提高、企业能级有待提升的发展挑战。

从空间形象现状看，城市形象缺乏辨识度，片区没有形成特色的IP标识、记忆点，门户位置未充分彰显；建筑立面以玻璃幕墙为主，天际线受航空净高所限缺乏变化，整体趋于均质化；绿化对于首层建筑界面遮挡较为严重，透视率不足，建筑退界距离较大，沿街店招展示性较差。

从内外交通现状看，核心区轨道交通覆盖不足，常规交通分布不均，内外交通拥堵叠加，交通管理效果不佳；慢行交通连续性和体验感不佳，二层廊桥使用率不高，地下空间通道被占用，枢纽通向国展的通道流线曲折，地下空间导视性较差；非机动车停放过饱和且混乱，外卖车、共享单车临时停放点位不足，缺乏网约车停靠点。

从品质活力现状看，公园绿地缺乏功能活力，绿化配置不符合使用需求，对人群吸引力不足；特色高能级社区公共服务设施缺乏，文体活动空间打造力度不够；办公空置率较高，南北部地区及周末时段人气活力缺乏。

二、项目清单制订意义

以区域城市更新行动方案为指引，通过实施更新项目，对标国际化标志性CBD的建设目标，从功能业态、交通系统、公共空间、城市形象等方面对商务区核心区整体焕新升级，优化功能布局，完善区域交通，提升城市生活品质，提高产业能级，扩大标志性CBD的社会影响力。

提升公共空间方面：增加文体活动场所，加强与水绿空间的联动；激活屋顶绿化花园，改善地下通道分时利用；实现公共空间功能植入、系统提升。

完善交通系统方面：统筹新增机动车、非机动车停车位，增加地面地上地下联通性，优化地面落客点设计；实现非机动车停车优化、落客区优化；加强区域交通联系，提升廊桥利用率和地下空间标识系统。

塑造城市形象方面：调整导视标识与界面形象，构建清晰的标识系统；统筹招商广告牌规划，升级主要建筑外立面，提升首层界面的视线通透；提升空间IP及辨识度，优化城市界面。

三、更新项目建设目标

从"商务辐射"到"双向服务"，提升功能内涵，打造"最国际范"的高端商务区。做强国际企业"引进来"高端贸易平台，打造中国"走出去"国家级专业服务平台；打造核心中的核心，设立虹桥海外发展中心、集聚各类顶级专业服务功能；聚焦产业发展定位、提升总部经济能级、建设更具竞争力的CBD。

从"枢纽独强"到"系统构建"，提升交通体验，打造"最便捷"的活力商务区。提升内外交通循环，适度分离枢纽交通与商务交通，缓解交通拥堵；融合多层次公共交通体系，提升轨道交通站点覆盖面；充分发挥地下连通空间的作用，提升慢行交通效率和体验。

从"宜商宜业"到"宜人宜居"，提升品质活力，打造"最标志"的品牌商务区。以人群需求为导向，增加居住类产品供给，构建多元住房体系；提供达到国际标准的高水平公共服务；打造标志性建筑、营造人流吸引目的地；构建"环形+渗透"公共活动空间体系；强化"绿环"生态活动功能，提升复合活力；"绿轴""绿心"空间赋能，打造标志性CBD魅力公园。

四、更新项目清单

项目清单聚焦核心区3.7平方千米、兼顾16平方千米范围内的核心功能提升、配套服务功能提升、公共空间提升、广告灯光提升、综合交通提升、市政设施提升等类型的城市更新项目，以近3年（2023—2025）具备实施条件的项目为主，同时储备部分远期更新项目。项目清单内容主要包括项目类型、规划设计条件和公共要素要求、更新方式、实施主体、投资方式、投资估算、实施路径、政策支撑、实施时序等内容。

（一）市场主体投资项目

包括虹桥龙湖天街项目的"天街里"改造、"认建认养"公共绿地提升、增设虹桥枢纽联动主轴线、在项目北侧打造下沉式广场，虹桥天地演艺中心的内外改造，毕马威KAMPUS办公楼绿色节能改造，梦百合大厦配置高星级标准酒店，中铁十五局建设EUP竖井智慧车库等项目。项目资金由各市场主体自行投资，管委会拟制订相关扶持政策予以支持。截至2023年10月，龙湖天街"天街里"改造项目开街，毕马威KAMPUS办公楼完成改造，梦百合地下空间改造工程已施工，中铁十五局EUP竖井智慧车库建设正征求绿化市容管理部门意见。

（二）政府投资项目

1. 常规建设项目

包括增设高架上下匝道、核心区外围道路联接、西交通广场综合提升工程配套道路交通衔接改造、口袋公园及滨河绿化建设、进博灯光亮化工程、箱杆合一整治、雨水调蓄池建设等项目。截至2023年10月，西交通广场综合提升工程配套道路交通衔接改造项目基本完工，龙联东路跨小涞港桥处于初设批复阶段，兴虹西路跨小涞港桥处于工可批复阶段，四座调蓄池项目进入工可阶段。

2. 标志性CBD更新项目

标志性CBD更新项目包括中轴线综合提升，北横泾河滨水空间改造提升，西交广场平台改造提升，四大绿地功能提升，空中连廊和地下通道标识标牌、交通引导系统建设，虹桥协信广场申长路侧和申虹路侧公共绿地改造提升等项目。截至2023年10月，中轴线综合提升、北横泾河护岸加固及滨水步道贯通工程等项目的设计方案已形成。

第四节　推进城市更新重点项目

一、龙湖虹桥天街升级改造项目

（一）项目背景

2023年以来，随着长三角一体化高质量发展、区域周边人口的聚集以及商务区核心企业的迭代进化，交通枢纽、区域展会、商旅来访的客流量持续攀升，这也促使多样化消费新需求在区域内越发凸显。龙湖虹桥天街牢牢把握商务区高频商务会展及广域年轻客群潮流娱乐生活方式需求增加的竞争机会，率先启动整体升级焕新。

龙湖虹桥天街项目位于商务区核心区一期05号地块，项目总占地面积78 751平方米，总建筑面积429 151.48平方米，其中地上建筑面积为256 755.48平方米，地下建筑面积为172 396平方米。土地性质为商办文娱酒店综合用途，项目分南北两区分期建设开发，已于2016年陆续竣工投入使用。

龙湖虹桥天街本次升级改造的定位为"城市灵感策源地"，商场于2023年7月10

图6-1　龙湖虹桥天街外景图

日起进行改造升级,9月底及明年初陆续完成特色街区及全馆第一阶段的场景和品牌焕新。内容包含户外主题街区、户外公园及全馆第一阶段的改造,不仅将重塑外街(原"一里九巷"),还将打造新主题新场景,为虹桥地区增加一处可供Citywalk、边逛边吃边玩、夜游等多元消费需求的新潮空间。

"天街里"已逐渐成为西上海代表性的户外商业街区,以餐饮业态为主力,搭配咖啡茶饮、体验娱乐、美容SPA等业态组合,构建了完整的夜生活场景。开街以来,"天街里"收获了众多消费者的喜爱,甚至晚上9点,部分门店仍需排队点单。本次"天街里"改造涉及面积达2万平方米,实际焕新面积近1/2,涉及场地出入口合并、增加落客区及下地库车道、内街车行道改人行步道、红线内外绿化升级改造、街面店铺门头及外摆改造等内容。同时,龙湖还计划中远期在"天街里"打造虹桥枢纽联动主轴线,并在北侧打造下沉广场,这也是虹桥天街与大虹桥多元化夜生活需求的深度对话。

(二)项目概况

提升基础设施及公共服务设施。为推进轨道交通场站与周边一体化,加强城市生命周期,龙湖集团计划增设1条地下连通道,增设1处下沉式庭院,用于加强虹桥天街项目与商务区核心区中轴线、地下大通道的人流互动,完善区域地下交通组织,提升区域活力。

优化功能品质,推进公共空间及设施升级。形成高参与感与活力感的绿地空间,

图6-2　天街里部分街区效果图

龙湖集团计划通过在虹桥天街项目的"天街里"打造行走的绿廊主题街区，营造尺度舒适、绿化丰富的花园感空间和结合主题商业运营的活力空间，提升环境舒适度，构建新型舒适的城市关系，建立慢行交通系统，打破"看不见、进不来"的城市结构。改造内容主要包括：一是地块红线内："天街里"车行道改为人行道，绍虹路、舟虹路位置增设2处落客区并增设人行横道标识，南侧车行道入口从5米扩宽至6米；"天街里"内部景观（铺地、绿植、增设商铺外摆、灯光调整、店招调整），并建设1处景观样板段；"天街里"与北侧绍虹路交接处增设人行天桥扶梯；沿申长路一侧调整部分绿化增加商铺外摆；商场外立面广告位边框升级。二是地块红线外：龙湖天街B馆南侧市政绿地调整；增设车行落客区。

对"边角地""夹心地""插花地"进行整体开发建设。为统筹布局整体商圈，使其成为具有国际范、"上海味"的城市社交目的地，填补商业服务覆盖盲区，项目预完善舟虹路地下通道及空中连廊商圈覆盖面积，建立完整商圈动线。

（三）项目进展情况

截至2023年第三季度，龙湖虹桥天街升级改造方案基本完成，部分改造工程已率先动工："天街里"街区改造工程自7月实施以来，已完成部分交通及绿化景观工程；商场A、B馆一层及地下B1、B2层正在进行一期调整改造，A、B馆二层至六层的改造方案亦在深化过程中。

完成全面升级改造后，龙湖虹桥天街将以崭新的面貌，成为更创新的商业空间，拥有更差异化的品牌组合、更丰富多元的商业场景。这也是龙湖对Citywalk等消费新需求的热切回应，亦是对国际中央商务区的全新解读，致力于引领大虹桥商业新趋势。

二、地下大通道hubo综合提升

从上海虹桥综合交通枢纽到国家会展中心，全线长1.2千米的地下人行通道，方便人们快速抵达目的地，同时还有四通八达的支路，能直通周边重要商务楼宇。作为许多人抵达上海的"第一站"，一直以来，这条通道并未得到有效运营，因未经雕琢的单调而显得格外冗长。

为激活城市公共空间，为游客呈现代表上海实力的"第一印象"，新虹街道将1.2千米的地下人行通道交给国内首个毗邻虹桥交通枢纽的商业综合体——虹桥天地运营。作为瑞安新天地旗下的高端商业地产项目，集购物中心、新天地、办公楼、演艺中心、地下商业街、酒店为一体的虹桥天地，近几年积极配合政府打造从交通枢纽到国家会

图6-3 hubo商业空间实景图

展中心的地下商业项目，希望通过地理优势，联通周边商业体，实现空间一体化和商业整体激活，打造365天潮流IP及商品展，成为全国潮流爱好者释放爱好、表达自我的精神乐园。2023年，开业8年的虹桥天地也将重新出发，定位全面升级，经过硬件改造、品牌升级，以"Join Shanghai，Join THE HUB"为主题，围绕"文化力、可持续力、社交力"策划全年文化展演活动，将这一面向长三角和世界的形象门户，打造成多元文化体验"第一站"——hubo，营造国际消费创新体验。

作为虹桥天地拓展客群、品牌升级的第一步，hubo已于2022年12月全新入市，位于虹桥商务区的核心板块，东至虹桥综合交通枢纽，西接国家会展中心，30分钟无缝直连长三角，是真正连接上海"第一站"的虹桥交通枢纽地下商业街。hubo商业空间整体设计上偏工业风，全新升级的白底黑字指引更为醒目，通过全新概念店、限时快闪店、策展与体验空间以及多功能活动区，以灵感无界、空间无界、圈层无界为理念，将hubo打造成一个具备自我表达、沉浸体验、值得探索、社交互动的上海潮流站点。

只二透明仓作为其主力店已于2022年12月初正式开业，相比只二的另外4家店，虹桥天地店作为只二平台的第一家"透明仓"，更具有突破意义，第一期3 000平方米的超大奢侈品仓库开启消费者自助式购物新体验，全部区域开放后将成为近万平方米的奢侈品寄卖及零售空间。

左右艺术超市华东首店也于2023年3月初正式开业，3 000多个国内外艺术家设计师、300多个全球知名的艺术及设计品牌，拥有潮流衍生品、年轻人的艺术品、艺术家神秘艺术品等2 000多种产品，通过艺术展览陈列的方式打造一个贩卖思想与艺术的精神超市，主售潮流衍生品、年轻人的艺术品、艺术家神秘艺术品等。这种基于策展型新零售的方式，打通了艺术的边界感，成为一种自由精神的消费场。另外，UNPOP STORE也于3月完成开业，这家贩卖有趣的杂货商店将进一步完善hubo的商业版图。

图6-4　左右艺术超市实景图

虹桥天地一直致力于创造具有前瞻性生活场景的理想街区，近些年更是专注长三角年轻一代，打造活力社交目的地。2023年，虹桥天地携手瑞德曼事务所——一个专注潮流艺术文化IP孵化和开发的先锋创意工作室，在hubo带来小红人家族全国首展，通过互动性极强的装置艺术，给年轻人带来"可治愈"的艺术。

hubo实现整体开业后，贯彻"与品牌共生共创、突破传统空间界限，打造多元融合空间"的理念，持续呈现惊喜不断、充满灵感的潮流创意。未来，hubo将凝聚多元潮流爱好者，促进圈层交流与灵魂碰撞，探索商业未来，成为交通枢纽商业的全新有趣范本。

三、西交通广场综合提升

虹桥综合交通枢纽连接长三角，是上海的"西大门"，是面向服务全国的窗口，也是服务保障进博览会的重要配套工程。自2010年以来已运行10多年，每年承担着春运、节假日、进博会等各类重大保障任务，日均客流量115.6万人次，已提前达到110万人次的客流峰值，枢纽面临补短板、增能效的自身提升需求。在加快虹桥国际开放枢纽建设的大背景下，为了满足新一轮的发展要求，对虹桥综合交通枢纽的功能配套和承载能力提出了更高定位的要求。项目建成后，可以更好地缓解日趋增长的客流量给枢纽带来的交通压力，进一步提升虹桥综合交通枢纽整体运行能级，更好地服务于进博会等国家级大型展览、展示活动的保障工作，进一步增强社会效应。同时，将虹桥综合交通枢纽从原来具备单一交通集散中心的功能，向综合性"城市枢纽"进行转变和提升，成为真正的商务区核心区的城市副中心，更好地服务于国家"长三角一体化"战略布局，进一步加快枢纽城区化的建设。

（一）项目建设内容

西交通广场综合提升项目位于锡虹路以南、甬虹路以北、申虹路以东、虹桥火车站以西区域，项目用地面积10.23万平方米。项目建设内容主要包括扩建虹桥综合交通枢纽西交通中心车库车位约1 000个，改建地面层2.38万平方米，新建西交通广场二层平台3.35万平方米、新增大巴车停车位69个，改建加固原P9、P10地下停车库及长途客运设施5.57万平方米，同步实施照明等附属设施工程。

该项目预计在2024年底整体完成。项目建成后地下层可实现二期车库与一期地下空间的一体化衔接，地面层的交通设施及功能得到全面提升，平台与核心区全面衔接，改善公交车、大巴车交通便利性；同时平台层将实现人行与商务区全面

图6-5　西交通广场综合提升工程建成效果图

衔接、城市功能植入、铁路竖向系统优化。届时，不仅虹桥枢纽车辆蓄泊、人车分流功能将显著提升，与周边商业综合体、酒店"看得见、走不到"的问题也将迎刃而解。

（二）项目特色亮点

进一步完善交通枢纽功能。虹桥综合交通枢纽西交通广场综合提升工程的打造将在进博会及重大会展活动期间，更好地承担起虹桥枢纽与国家会展中心之间重要的交通接驳功能。

进一步提升枢纽使用效率。利用本次改扩建，完善提升西交通广场停车库（P9、P10）的使用效率，挖掘潜力提升地面层的交通功能与流线组织。

进一步提升城市整体形象。虹桥综合交通枢纽西交通广场综合提升工程立足于由"城市枢纽"向"枢纽城市"的转变，作为打造虹桥国际开放枢纽起到连接"对内"和"对外"两个扇面的重要节点作用,以实现商务区功能定位与整体形象的全面提升。

(三)项目建设目标

立足长远:规划近、远期结合,服务进博会,辐射长三角及全国。

多元混合:打造虹桥枢纽TOD综合开发,促进区域站城融合。

交通便捷:虹桥枢纽自身补短板、增能效,同时优化提升对商务区、国家会展中心等核心区域进行全方位辐射。

环境优越:打造枢纽城市副中心区域景观新形象,实现高品质开发。

地下层:实现虹桥枢纽二期车库与一期地下空间的一体化衔接,增加小汽车停车位弥补枢纽停车的缺口;

地面层:虹桥枢纽交通设施及功能的全面改造提升,补短板、增能效,增加地面点对点大巴接驳位,增强与进博会的互联互通;

平台层:人行与商务区全面衔接、城市功能植入、铁路竖向系统优化、提升城市景观。

(四)项目建设进展

2023年7月,虹桥综合交通枢纽西交通广场综合提升工程项目迎来开工建设一周年。项目开工建设以来,建设单位地产虹桥公司努力克服结构加固施工、外部协调难度大,周边环境复杂,原地下车库顶板施工荷载等不利影响,不断完善施工组织,强化进度控制。施工方面,项目采用高大支撑模板施工技术,明显提高了施工安全性,有效降低潜在风险,为建筑主体结构稳定性提供了保证。此外,配合BIM技术的运用,进一步提升高支模设计的效率与准确性,通过合理安排工序工种进场时间,强化进度控制和成本节约。工程管理方面,项目采用SAP系统信息化技术,充分发挥SAP信息系统功能,帮助项目在实施过程中厘清工程范围、合同事项,实现项目目标成本的精细化、准确化、当前化管控,规范系统流程手势,进一步做好工程信息化管理。

10月,P9、P10停车场扩建已提前完工,新增1 000个车位已在长假来临前投入使用。配套新建的车库出入口也施工完成,有效加快了车辆进出场,提高虹桥枢纽疏散能力,缓解泊位紧张、排队拥堵的情况。

西交通广场综合提升工程进一步提升了虹桥综合交通枢纽功能,使虹桥综合交通枢纽与商务区核心区无缝衔接,提供更高水平的配套服务与保障,推动构建商务区宜

第六章 标志性CBD城市更新

第四节 推进城市更新重点项目

图6-6 西文通广场综合提升工程施工进展图

人宜商的慢行空间。同时，该工程有利于促进商务区与长三角周边区域协同发展，提升公共交通服务功能和品质，形成国际一流的枢纽示范区，助力商务区成为全球货物流、商务流、人流、资金流、信息流的交汇枢纽。

第七章 精细化管理示范区

第一节 建设和谐自然的品质城区

商务区认真贯彻落实《上海市城市管理精细化"十四五"规划》"打造人民城市管理精细化标杆示范区"工作要求，坚持"人民城市人民建、人民城市为人民"重要理念，在城市精细化管理中，秉承"人、城市、自然"相融合的建设目标，为人民群众创建良好的生产、生活、生态环境，不断提升商务区城市发展品质。其中，青浦区徐泾镇围绕城市更新布局和"两旧一村"改造，以加强蟠龙古镇历史风貌保护，形成江南文化和现代城市商业气息相融合，建设宜居、宜业、宜乐、宜游的精细化管理示范区，逐渐成为商务区人气打卡点。长宁区程家桥街道坚持"引进来"——把生境带进生活，和"走出去"——让生活回归自然，坚持打造因地制宜、寓教于乐、可持续发展的社区生境课堂，并形成全过程人民民主实践样本，建立更精准、可视化的社区成长指数监测，探索普适性的社区共建模式。

一、徐泾镇"蟠龙天地"

蟠龙镇在历史上是名镇，最早可追溯到距今1 400年前的隋朝时期。因水而兴的蟠龙镇旧时商业繁盛，是一个典型的江南富庶水乡。21世纪初，在虹桥板块高速建设的背景下，发展停滞的蟠龙古镇逐渐成为城市中的"伤疤"区域，私搭滥建严重，其"脏乱差"的形象与周边高速发展的城市环境格格不入，历史风貌破坏严重，改造紧迫性强。作为上海首批城中村改造项目之一，青浦区徐泾镇的蟠龙"城中村"，从前是小工厂、小作坊、仓库与民宅犬牙交错，古建筑、古街道衰败，河道淤塞、垃圾随处可见，通过改造，一举变身为白墙黛瓦、檐角飞翘、草木生辉，江南气息含于古韵之中，现代商铺鳞次栉比的古镇。成功的实践证明，积极稳步推进城中村改造有利于消除城

图 7-1 蟠龙天地鸟瞰图

市建设治理短板、改善城乡居民居住环境条件和扩大内需。

蟠龙"城中村"属于市级历史风貌保护区，在开发前期，项目组走访了30多位专家、学者及当地原住民，聘请多方顾问，追本溯源，寻找属于蟠龙专属的历史文化特色，将之烙印在整个规划建设中，再现蟠龙古镇风貌。在开发过程中注重延续古镇肌理、空间布局、街巷尺度、绿化、文物与历史建筑，深度挖掘古镇历史内涵，对"香花桥、十字街、程家祠堂"等一个个历史文脉场景重新打造，重新演绎蟠龙十景、九龙一凤古桥，将江南传统的水乡及古镇文化与充满现代生活方式的新形式融为一体，创造可居住、可生活、可工作、可休闲的特色小镇，成为青浦历史文化的新地标、新名片。

二、程家桥街道"生境花园"

绿色是程家桥街道生态环境的底色，其中两个生境花园则是璀璨"绿链"上的闪光点。"十四五"期间，将继续围绕"千园之城"建设目标，重点推进2个新增口袋公园，全力服务城市高质量发展、人民高品质生活。

生境花园是指将"生境"与"花园"融合在一起，围绕五大原则营造，即使用本地植物、杜绝外来入侵植物、丰富植物群落、减少农药化肥的使用以及为城市野生动物提供辅助的食物、水源或庇护所。围绕长宁区"令人向往的生态之城"目标愿景，程家桥街道积极探索政府主导、多元共治、精细管理的现代环境治理新路径，打造具有较高显示度的生态文明建设新样板，先后于2023年6月建成南龚社区"融·生境花园"和程桥二村"忆·生境花园"共两个生境花园，在"15分钟社区美好生活圈"中融入布局均衡、形态合理、特色鲜明的公园体系，缓解了辖区公园绿地布局盲点问题，受到居民称赞。

"融·生境花园"位于虹桥路2222弄无名道路内，总占地面积约为950平方米。改造后，紧密联合周边校社资源优势，立足生境科普游园特色，衍生为5个核心课堂。"共建共享的活力课堂"侧重调动各方积极性，参与志愿服务、建言献策、自治管理的全过程，共享花园建设的成果；"寓教于乐的知识课堂"侧重生境花园的科普教育意义，精心配置的本土植栽为本土野生动物提供水源、食源，让人们在轻松有趣的游园体验中学习生态知识、亲近大自然；"相伴成长的时光课堂"侧重以亲子邻里同游、家校相伴的形式，开展主题活动，同时建构起人与自然和谐共生的良好关系；"互动体验的趣味课堂"侧重互动科普设施带来的沉浸式活动体验；"生态共融的秘境课堂"侧重纯生境环境的建构对整个花园生态的作用,以片状生境带动园中块状及点状生境,形成有自净修复能力的可持续的有机生态系统。

"忆·生境花园"位于程桥二村内,是原小区绿化,在改造前环境差,生物物种较为贫瘠。改造后,占地总面积为1 000平方米,是长宁区已建成的、最大的社区生境花园。"忆·生境花园"在对阿尔兹海默疾病友好关怀的基础上,以开放式养老社区建设为契机,探索"三花",即"花香处方""花样年华""花园康养"为核心的医养结合,提升公共空间美感和居民幸福指数。同步推出"陪伴花园计划",开展以陪伴为主题的系列活动,吸引更多的老年人"走出家门"参与进来,在市民的家门口不断铺就绿色,将生境花园打造成"15分钟社区美好生活圈"的重要组成部分。

图7-2 忆·生境花园

第二节 提供高效便捷的交通服务

商务区以"建设辐射共享、内外联通的国际枢纽门户"为愿景，全面强化商务区辐射力、承载力和通达性，显著提升综合交通管理水平，加速形成联通国际国内的综合交通新门户，实现对外交通开放融合、枢纽交通集约高效、商务区交通品质卓越、会展交通保障有力、片区交通低碳活力的发展目标。

加强虹桥机场与浦东机场高效联动，实现两机场40分钟可达，强化对内对外联通，推动国内—国际航空中转，提升对虹桥国际开放枢纽的国际服务功能支撑。完善区域交通联系网络，加强轨道交通、中运量等公共交通体系建设，加强区域之间的公共交通联系。提升道路通行服务能力，营造舒适的出行体验。构建通达便捷的公交网络，完善人性化的公交设施，提高不同交通方式的可换乘性。规划共享单车等非机动车的停放设置，不断完善停车管理。遵循慢行优先的路权分配原则，倡导绿色出行，结合地下空间、二层连廊、绿道、景观河道岸线及桥梁等，打造全连通、人性化的慢行交通系统。强化无障碍环境建设，提升老年人、残疾人交通出行体验。

一、编制发布虹桥国际中央商务区综合交通专项规划

经过10余年发展，商务区对外交通和内部骨干设施日趋完善，但面对新形势新任务新要求，还存在一些瓶颈问题，主要表现在：连接国际和服务长三角的能力仍有待增强；核心区轨道服务与国际一流商务区存在差距；道路系统通达性不足，次支路网密度偏低；虹桥枢纽的过境交通和通勤交通叠加，集散压力凸显；"最后一公里"问题日益突出等。

为在更高起点、更高层次、更大范围优化完善商务区综合交通系统，历时两年调研论证的《虹桥国际中央商务区综合交通规划（2021—2035）》（简称《综合交通规划》）于2023年10月12日正式发布。《综合交通规划》指出至2035年，建成"开放畅达、立体融合、绿色便捷、智慧高效"的商务区现代化综合交通体系，依托虹桥综合交通枢纽，完善对外通道布局，实现"123"交通圈目标，即至长三角南北拓展带城镇1小时通达，至长三角城市群主要城市2小时可达，全国主要城市3小时覆盖。在内外

联系通道建设方面,在既有京沪高铁、沪宁城际、沪昆高铁等铁路接入虹桥枢纽的基础上,新增沪苏湖铁路和城际轨道交通沪苏嘉线(上海示范区线),提升商务区对外铁路通道服务功能。

(一)规划理念和主要特点

商务区面积151平方千米,是虹桥国际开放枢纽"一核两带"之"一核",也是上海"两翼齐飞"之"西翼",特殊的区域功能定位,决定了其特色鲜明的交通体系。

发展理念上,更加注重"枢纽引领、区域协同、体系完整、韧性发展"。枢纽引领,即要彰显开放优势,强化国际定位,提升枢纽功能;区域协同,即要强化与周边区域交通联动发展,引领长三角区域交通高质量一体化发展;体系完整,即强化综合交通承载力和网络功能,提升交通服务品质;韧性发展,即要求注重智能智慧与绿色创新,大幅度提升综合交通管理智慧化和交通出行绿色化低碳化水平。

发展目标上,紧扣"开放畅达、立体融合、绿色便捷、智慧高效"。通过建设商务区现代化综合交通体系,实现枢纽交通开放畅达、交通网络立体融合、交通服务绿色便捷、交通管理智慧高效的目标愿景,支撑国际化中央商务区全面形成,显著提升服务长三角和联通国际的能力。

发展策略上,坚持以"路(通道、道路)、站(轨道站、枢纽站)、网(公交网、慢行网等网络)"为交通基底,以"智慧、绿色、创新"为虹桥特色。重点从提升枢纽集聚辐射能级,完善对外通道,构筑内部交通系统网络和提高综合交通管理水平等四方面推进。

(二)规划的主要内容

根据规划目标,形成"1+5+5+1"总体规划布局。聚焦核心区功能提升,促进4片区合作共赢,实现"规划一张图,设施一张网,运营一张表,管理一把尺"发展目标。

第一个"1"代表一主四辅的枢纽体系。"一主"是虹桥综合交通枢纽,强化国际国内门户枢纽功能;"四辅"是立足4个地区中心构建4个片区级枢纽,形成"一片一枢纽"格局,疏解虹桥枢纽换乘压力,强化长三角地区城际服务。

第一个"5"为5个方向内外联系通道。根据商务区空间特点,完善中心城、浦东枢纽—临港新片区、南向拓展带、长三角一体化示范区、北向拓展带等5个方向对外通道。

第二个"5"表示5个系统的区域交通网。一是构建涵盖市域(郊)铁路、城市轨道交通市区线、局域线等多层次轨道交通系统网络,研究利用既有规划轨道交通通道,

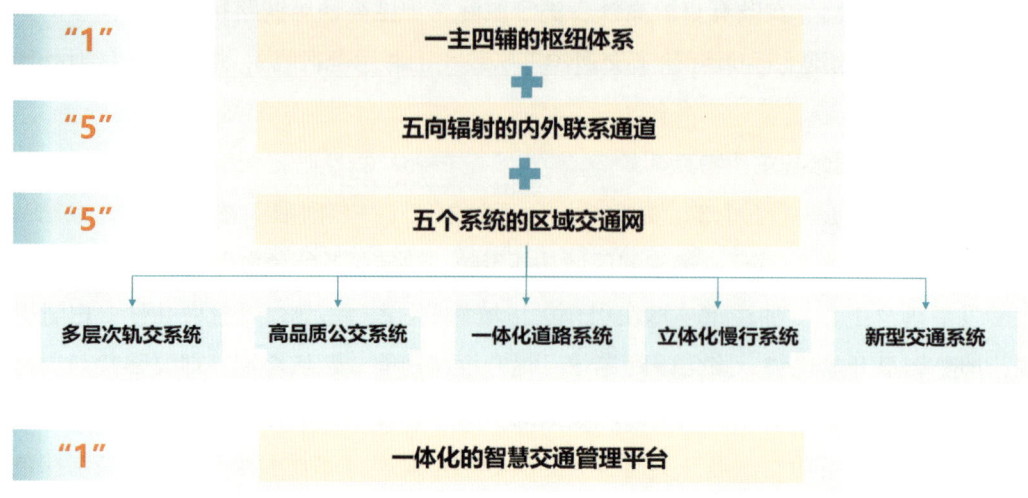

图7-3 综合交通规划"1+5+5+1"总体布局

进一步加密商务区，尤其是核心区轨道交通站点覆盖。二是构筑高品质公交系统，预控"核心放射+切向加密"的公交通道，规划若干骨干公交线路，串联服务商务核心区、轨道站点、地区枢纽等客流区域。三是建设高密度道路系统，完善高快速路网的匝道布局，适度剥离枢纽交通与地区交通。通过打通区区对接道路，结合S20和G15功能提升，贯通地面道路，构建东西贯通、南北联通的"十横十纵"地面干路网络，提高地区交通通达性。四是构建"东联枢纽、西接会展"的核心区立体慢行网络。结合地区中心、轨道车站及公交枢纽等重点区域，打造5个慢行示范区。五是鼓励发展新型交通系统，满足商务区特殊化、个性化的出行需求。

最后一个"1"即为一体化的智慧交通管理平台。推进交通设施数字化和交通管理智慧化，建设商务区综合交通信息平台，提升商务区交通综合管理水平。

二、推进上海机场联络线建设

（一）项目概况

根据《上海市城市总体规划（2017—2035）》，虹桥和浦东综合交通枢纽间规划轨道快线，枢纽之间的轨道交通出行时间缩短至40分钟以内。上海机场联络线采用时速160千米/小时，交流制式，可满足时间目标要求。

作为上海市东西主轴内的市域快速通道，上海机场联络线是上海市城市轨道交通线网的重要组成，主要承担市域内虹桥、浦东两机场间及市中心与机场间的城市客流，并兼顾浦东新区与长三角近沪地区的城际客流；是浦东衔接上海市对外主要铁路客运通道的重要联络线，是沪宁铁路通道和沪杭铁路通道向浦东地区的延伸；也是浦东二次开发的重要交通基础设施。

线路自虹桥站磁浮场引出沿沪杭客专东侧向南，穿过沪杭铁路通道后折向东沿春申塘走行，而后穿越黄浦江，沿外环线、迎宾高速南侧走行，经三林、张江、迪士尼至浦东机场，出浦东机场后接入沪通2期上海东站站西侧的机场线车场。机场联络线全线虹桥站至上海东站全长68.627千米。不含虹桥枢纽线路长度为67.29千米，其中桥梁长4.36千米、地下线长60.65千米、路基长2.28千米，桥隧比96.61%。全线设车站9座：虹桥、七宝、华泾、三林南、张江、度假区、浦东机场、规划航站楼、上海东，其中地下站6座、地面站3座，平均站间距离为8.58千米。新设下盐路车辆基地1处。

（二）建设目标

1.实现两场、三站和服务沿线地区的快速高效衔接

机场联络线是上海市域网络中东西向骨干线路，起到形成两场（虹桥机场、浦东机场）、三站（虹桥火车站、上海东站、上海南站）与主城区沿线张江、国际旅游度假区等重点地区间的快速便捷联系，进一步整合航空、高铁等对外交通资源，提高浦东机场、上海东站等地区的区域服务功能。虹桥铁路枢纽主要承担沪宁、沪昆高速通道的长途客车，长三角核心区以外的出境客流可经由本线快速通达浦东机场，是扩大浦东机场覆盖范围的捷运系统，可快速联系两场、两站客运交流。同时本线串联虹桥商务区、七宝、华泾、国际旅游度假区的内部轨道交通系统，服务市区内沿线客运需求。目前乘坐城市轨道交通浦东机场至虹桥机场大约需要2小时，而机场快线仅需要40分钟，浦东外环以外居民通过机场线出行至市中心，将节省大量的在途时间，同时有效减少换乘次数，有利于提高居民出行质量。此外，按机场线的线路走向和设站方案，机场线各站均可换乘上海市内轨道交通系统，在虹桥站可与17号线、2号线、10号线、嘉闵线等线路实现换乘，华泾站可与15号、19号线换乘，在上海南站可与15号线、1号线、22号线、金山支线、3号线等换乘，在三林南站可与19号线、奉贤线换乘，在张江站和迪士尼站可与27号、曹奉线换乘，在机场站可与2号线换乘，在上海东站可与21号线、南汇线等换乘。通过市域线与地铁网的高效融合，实现市区通达两场、三站和迪士尼以及上海市外快速通达迪士尼和浦东机场，提高居民市域出行质量的现实需要。

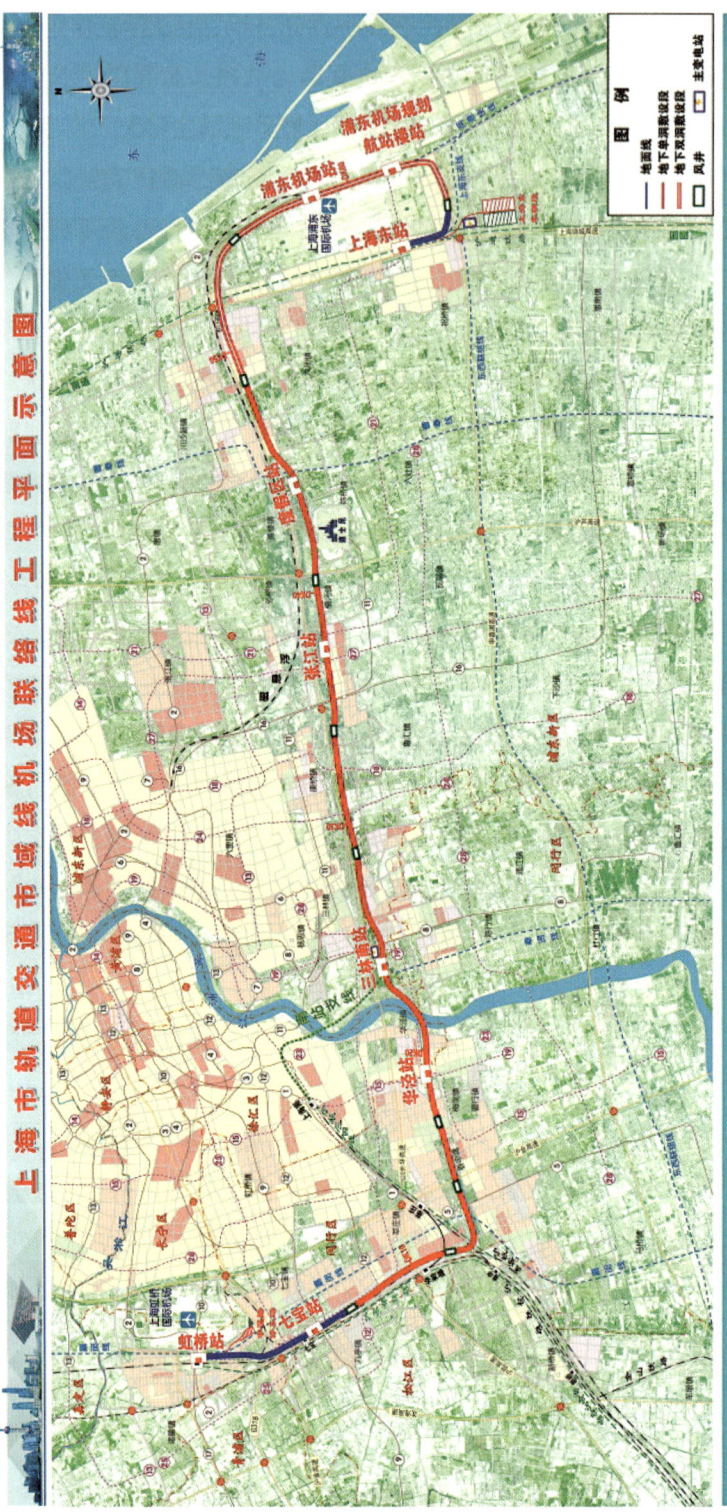

图7-4 上海市轨道交通市域线机场联络线工程平面示意图

2. 服务长三角一体化国家战略、快速直通长三角核心区

机场联络线不仅是一条市域线,与国铁网络实现互联互通后,可实现沪宁、沪杭等铁路通道向浦东地区延伸,进一步增强上海国际航空枢纽港竞争力,有利于进一步整合航空、铁路等对外交通资源,优化长三角地区交通出行选择,更高质量地服务长三角城市群,是长三角一体化在交通领域的具体落实。

第三节　推动绿色生态治理

商务区积极推进绿色生态城区建设，以绿色生态理念为指导，开展生态本底分析、定位策划、系统规划等工作，建立健全绿色生态建设保障机制，落实土地、建筑、交通、能源、水资源等绿色生态指标和技术措施。遵循"规划引领、统筹协调"原则，依据上位规划和绿色生态城区相关标准，开展现状评估和生态本底诊断，确定绿色生态定位，编制绿色生态专业规划。深化完善河长制、湖长制，充分发挥河长制平台作用，统筹协调推进生态清洁小流域建设，将区域内滨水公共空间打造成为多元功能复合化的活力空间、尺度宜人有温度的人文空间、生态效益最大化的绿色空间，建设成为更安全、更有序、更干净的滨水区和最美丽的公共活动空间。

一、小涞港水环境治理

（一）河道简介

小涞港位于青浦、闵行区界，南起淀浦河，北迄蟠龙塘，总长约8千米（其中青浦段长约7.15千米），紧邻国家会展中心东门。历史上曾以竹冈塘与蒲汇塘交汇处以北称小涞浦。小涞港经过治理重现了"水清岸绿、鱼翔浅底"的江南水韵。被评为长江经济带最美河流。核心区主要水质指标从劣Ⅴ类到Ⅳ类，水体透明度提升了4倍，稳定维持在1.5米以上。小涞港被评为"长江经济带最美河流"及"上海市三星级河道"。

小涞港（国展段）：公共活动型河段，服务于会展。2014年新开河道，新建两岸绿化；2018年周边河道环境整治，河道疏浚，两岸绿化翻建和补种，种植沉水植物等水生态修复措施；2019年河道绿化提升及雨水口改造工程。

小涞港（蟠龙港—崧泽高架段、建虹路高架—G50沪渝高速段）：生活服务型河段。2017—2018年进行了河道疏浚、水系调整、护岸绿化改建。

（二）河道治理特色

小涞港的河道治理特色归纳为6+1+1，具体是：

6道"瀑布"，即上海河道治理中首次使用的溢流堰，堰内设有可抬高和调节河道

图7-5 小涞港沿线滨水空间

水位的升降台,产生最高1.5米左右的落差,自动给河道充氧,助推水中溶解氧含量成倍增至8毫克/升。

1座水下森林,由7.2万平方米沉水植物、1万平方米挺水植物及食藻虫构成,它们在水下形成了良性活水环境:食藻虫专吃藻类、有机颗粒和悬浮物,同时产生弱酸性排泄物,抑制藻类生长,增加河水的透明度,进而让水生植物多晒太阳,并吸收水中过多的氮、磷等富营养物质,茁壮成长。

1艘自动保洁船,其两条"手臂"有30米长,可遥控开合,吸附河面漂浮垃圾、泥苔等杂物,效率相当于4艘人工清捞船和8名保洁员。

(三)河道治理措施

河道水系整治:拓宽河道,活水畅流调度,核心区设置水质净化处理站,必要时对核心区水质进行强制提升。

生态护岸改建:小涞港(国展段)通过保留原挡墙结构,在挡墙前部增加一排定植木桩,用以种植挺水及水生植物,达到对河道两侧硬质护岸进行生态化改造的目标。其他岸段尽量采用叠石护岸柔化美化、错落有致,构建可露可淹的滨河湿地。

图7-6　小涞港水下森林

图7-7　小涞港两岸植物色彩搭配

水生态修复：种植沉水植物，构建水下森林，布设曝气增氧系统。

两岸景观提升：小涞港（国展段）两岸重视植物色彩搭配，视觉层次突出。

游憩设施：居住服务段两侧可供市民垂钓，设有亲水平台。

二、华漕镇许浦港水环境治理

华漕镇许浦港为闵行区与长宁区界河，北起苏州河、南至张正浦，中心线长度约1.3千米，平均河口宽度40米。整治前河道至闵行、长宁区界位置处断头。由于河道两岸存在大量违法建筑物，逐步侵占河道水面积，造成河道调蓄能力、自净能力下降，且由于两岸农村生活污水、生活垃圾直排河道，导致水体黑臭。2017年，结合"五违四必"和"美丽乡村"建设，闵行区华漕镇重污染河道整治三期工程整治，拆除河道管理范围内违法建筑54万平方米，动迁居民及企业97户，农村生活污水收集330户。如今的许浦港河畔，碧波如镜，黑臭现象已消除，河道面貌得到根本改善，水质稳定达标在Ⅳ类水及以上标准。2021年在上海市第二届美丽河湖选树活动中，许浦港获得了"美丽河湖"称号。

图7-8 许浦港生态河道

着眼未来，打造生态"好水"。在河长的有效履职和责任担当下，以及养护单位的专业管护下，河道面貌焕然一新，水环境得以根本改善。河道水更清澈了，岸坡更绿了，不仅提升了整体的村宅面貌，更给村民提供了优美的休闲度假打卡点位，真正让河道治理成效惠及百姓。

"水清草复绿，岸美花更香"。许浦港的蝶变，为"十四五"闵行区生态清洁小流域建设项目打下了基础，也为华漕镇率先实现"都市宜居型"生态清洁小流域建设，打造"清水自流"幸福河道的目标提供有力支撑。

第四节　打造一街一景特色街道

为进一步突出区域商业体征和景观风貌特色，提升城市文化品位，商务区坚持"精细治理、品质虹桥"的工作理念，强化对街道整体景观风貌品质引导和管控，通过"特色化的街道、满活力的街道、更智慧的街道和有温度的街道"等街道景观提升理念，充分发掘不同街区独特的文化和魅力，综合打造国际商务型街道、潮流商业型街道、活力社区型街道、林荫漫步型街道、宽敞景观型街道等各类虹桥商务区的特色街道，全方面打造"一街一景"的目标。

一、新虹街道"口袋公园"

（一）基本情况

2022年，新虹街道响应国家住房和城乡建设部办公厅《关于推动"口袋公园"建设的通知》的工作指示及市、区口袋公园的建设任务，将那些散落在城市空间中的"美"打造成集健身、休闲、赏景等功能为一体的"口袋公园"。新虹街道爱博四村年轮公园于2023年3月底正式竣工，它是新虹街道特色的城市微开放空间，是新虹街道居民休息、释放压力和交流的好地方，更是一座彰显了新虹街道温度和内涵的公园。走进年轮公园，道路平坦整洁，微公园生机盎然，绿树成荫、鸟语花香。爱博四村年轮公园建设项目从设计方案，到施工过程，再到公园维护，充分及时听取群众意见建议，扩大人民有序政治参与，由"为民做主"到"让民做主"，充分践行全过程人民民主理念，"口袋公园"项目让"小口袋"彰显了"大民生"。

（二）建设理念

近年来，随着长三角区域一体化战略确立，虹桥国际开放枢纽建设迈上新台阶，如何让辖区居民和地区通过生活环境的优化和改善，建立起情感共鸣增加满意度、幸福感？如何利用城市边角地见缝植绿，既满足老百姓就近休闲健身娱乐，又提升居住环境、改善城市生态，将高速发展的城市环境建设与人民群众对生活的美好向往结合起来，也成了新虹街道新的课题。2022年，新虹街道根据上海市、闵行区口袋公园的建设要求，以"打造人人都能有序参与治理的城市"为工作理念，通过听取专题报告、开展专题视察、召开群众代表座谈会等方式，在"口袋公园"建设中充分践行全过程人民民主理念。

（三）基本做法

以"人民规划"为切入口，自上而下全过程充分酝酿。通过规划引领、科学决策，结合国家对居民出行"300米见绿，500米见园"的目标要求，通过对于区域人口密度分布、空闲场地的充分排摸，以及广泛听取相关专家意见，自上而下全过程统筹安排口袋公园选址、建设计划及后续工程推进。爱博四村口袋公园改建，充分挖掘现有的空间潜力，延展建绿空间，利用小块零星空地见缝插绿、见缝造景，将公园形态与城市空间有机融合，打造"15分钟社区美好生活圈"。

以"人民参与"为关键点，自下而上最大广度倾听民声。在爱博四村口袋公园方案的设计过程中，新虹街道深入社区调研，直达一线倾听基层"两委"班子、社工和居民百姓的"心声"。通过开展参与式的协商讨论，根据各方意见不断修改公园设计方案，以避免后期可能出现的各类冲突和社区矛盾。把公共空间营造建设作为工作撬动点，坚持让居民以"主人翁"身份参与进来，自下而上提出个体诉求，在爱博四村口袋公园改建工程过程中，逐步形成了共建、共治、共享的良好氛围。

以"人民社区"为出发点，因地制宜全过程跟踪监督问效。在满足居民、幼儿园、养老院、公交站等4类需求的基础上，合理规划3类交通动线，做到相互不扰、杜绝安全隐患。在公园使用中，还请为老服务中心对花墙认领养护，开辟苗圃草坪让幼儿园参与其中，选取各类志愿者为公园"守护者"，实现居民从公园景观"参观者"到景观营造"参与者"的转变，真正激发"口袋公园"勃勃生机。新虹街道把各类建议顾虑一一放在心上，一一"打开"进行深究、协调、确认，这不仅让街道找到了公园建设的"最大公约数"，也激发了居民参与建设美好家园的积极性，更体现了各方力量全程跟踪监督公园建设的参与度。

（四）经验启示

以党建引领、全过程民主作为打造城市微空间的根本遵循。始终坚持人民城市理念，持续走访社区，问需问计于老百姓，为居民进行城市建设答疑解惑。重点实施"公园城市"，打造口袋公园、城市微景观等，提升居民参与感、获得感和幸福感。新虹街道在社区治理、改善人居环境上下足功夫，助力打造宜居城市、海绵城市、公园城市。

以人民民主、以人为本作为推动绿色高质量发展的主要内容。坚持以人民为中心

图 7-9 新虹街道"口袋公园"

的发展思想,坚持以公园城市为建设发展理念,按照"绿化、彩化、珍贵化、效益化"的发展要求,让人民群众共享生态文明建设成果,营造"推窗见绿、出门见园"的城市生态环境。通过绣花般的细心、耐心、巧心,打造"生态、生产、生活"无界融合的生态空间。

以民主商策、民主监管作为人民城市建设满意度的重要标尺。始终坚持人民城市人民建,基层问题要用基层民主的办法来解决。共建共治共享的社会治理格局要从单向管理转向双向互动,从单纯的政府监管转向更注重社会协同治理。既需要自下而上个体诉求体现人民的参与感,也需要自上而下地治理来提升人民的幸福感和满意度。新虹街道坚持加强和创新社会治理,使每个社会细胞都健康活跃,确保社会既生机勃勃又井然有序。

二、新虹街道"申长路艺术街区"

（一）基本情况

进博会的举办为大虹桥的发展提供了绝佳的契机,但也对大虹桥的城市基础建设提出了更高要求。同时，长三角一体化成为国家战略，为大虹桥的建设带了巨大机遇和挑战。商务区艺术街区项目作为大虹桥提升城市精细化管理的深入探索，将城市有待改进的消极空间通过艺术创作的手法，全新升级城市街具和公共艺术展示，赋予其文化的精神高度，为城市空间注入活力，提升城市形象。

申长路位于商务区核心区，紧邻虹桥枢纽及虹桥机场，已成为商务区内一条重要道路，不仅承担着交通服务的重要作用，更成为对外展示的重要平台。为了打造虹桥商务艺术街区，以申长路为纽带，将以"创新城市设计、塑造特色风貌"为主题的长三角城市雕塑、街具公共艺术创意设计大赛中的作品落实，打造"一街、三区、五韵"。

（二）建设理念

商务区艺术街区项目秉持以人为本的创作理念。让人们可以感知城市空间的温度和城市文脉的传承，让公共空间的生命力得到释放，让城市和身处其中的居民，可以和城市有更紧密的情感互动。满足城市居民日益提升的精神文化需求，通过城市精细化管理，打造美好城市风貌，激发城市活力，迎接下一届进博会的到来，推进长三角城市群的发展。设计理念以"一街、三区、五韵"为主旨："一街"为商务区艺术街区示范街的打造区域，以申长路段为主，起止点为申兰路至天山西路；"三区"为商务区艺术街区，按地理位置从南至北划分为三大主题区域，即国际精品建筑美术馆、汇聚虹桥和悦览长三角；"五韵"为根据现场环境及电箱分布形式的特点打造出的五大设计主题，即山水印象、玲珑博古架、虹桥欢迎您、城市美术馆和百景园。

（三）基本做法

街区的属性在一定程度上决定了城市空间的定位，而城市街道家具是根据国家或城市的文化特征而变化的结构元素。申长路艺术街区的"悦览长三角"区域，提取"江浙沪皖"市花、水乡花窗等长三角区域的典型风貌元素，对电箱、休憩座椅等城市家具进行区域空间载体的更新改造：以"壹体树""同心花"的艺术设计形象展现携手共进、协同发展的长三角城市一体化发展理念与开拓进取的城市精神；以山水起伏与博古架为设计要素的"山水印象及玲珑博古架"系列和以园林造景中的石材形态元素打造的百景园系列，满足弱化电箱存在感，提升休憩家具美感，并与绿化区域相配适的关系美学，展现长三角区域可感知的文化融汇底蕴。

"汇聚虹桥"区域则是打造虹桥IP形象、提取国际语言文化的"虹桥，你好"街道小品、以融汇为主题的虹桥之梦艺术装置等，集聚虹桥商务与经济的特色要素，传

图 7-10 "悦览长三角"区域　　　　　图 7-11 "汇聚虹桥"区域

达商务区开放、热情好客的地域文化底蕴，打造汇聚、包容的上海虹桥品牌。这些元素在为"城市识别"添加含义及"社会生活"促进方面具有非常重要的作用。以长三角区域的城市文脉元素为主的城市聚焦性符号更具标志性和主题性，与公众建立凝聚性感知与识别，彰显城市文化"连续性"优势。以国际语言文化、城市包容理念和创意融合特性为主的城市要素建构的城市现代常规性符号，在微小空间成本范围内提升空间品质并促进城市客群行为活动的发生，达成从微观层面的城市形象活化文化资源，通过输出价值话语与生产象征空间，潜移默化地引导城市客群建立文化身份认同。

商务区申长路艺术街区在"国际精品建筑美术馆"区域，在物理空间角度将电箱表面设计转化为公共空间展台，在象征空间角度将街道构建为城市美术馆，在社会空间角度构建创意人才、技术等资源的展示共享平台。利用创新技术与技术增强手段重现各国优秀地标建筑文化精华，强调街区的可阅读性与文化交流的精神意义，使商务区的城市街道家具展现国际化、功能化的系统空间创新网络。城市美术馆作为集合创意与技术资源的特色文化公共交流载体，从人与空间环境的视觉交互层面提供视觉享受，激活街道空间的多元文化效益，引导城市居民对城市历史、文化及生活、艺术经验等意识形态的语境认同，增加流动客体的艺术性沉浸与文化情感共鸣的空间生产循环。通过以物理空间作为基础支撑，借助象征空间进行文化构筑，用社会空间进行权利增值，实现物理空间、象征空间、社会空间的"人—环境"三位一体的城市空间公共话语表达体系。

图7-12 "国际精品建筑美术馆"区域

三、新泾镇"活力仙西"美丽街区

（一）项目背景

为深入贯彻"人民城市人民建，人民城市为人民"重要理念，对标对表区第十一次党代会提出的"四力四城"奋斗目标，新泾镇聚焦虹桥国际开放枢纽重大战略的实施，坚持把打造"15分钟社区美好生活圈"作为建设"人民城市"的重要实践命题，和提升城区软实力的重要实践载体。

2021年新泾镇"15分钟社区美好生活圈"行动规划明确了构建"一轴串联，双片融合；八水交织，绿脉提升；三核引领，多心联动"的空间格局。以生活、生态、生产功能兼备的仙霞（西）路（新泾镇段）为综合发展轴，连接中心城区与机场枢纽，融合发展西部产业（临空经济示范区）与东部居住两大功能片区。2022年新泾镇将该项目列为镇党委政府重点项目，依托"活力仙西"美丽街区项目，将该路段全力打造为集生态、景观、休憩、生活为一体的健康街区、乐活走廊。

第七章 精细化管理示范区

第四节 打造一街一景特色街道

（二）项目概况

仙霞（西）路作为新泾镇核心发展轴线，沿街两侧遍布商业、养老、医疗、教育、文化等多种设置资源。东起中环路、西至外环，全长约2 600米，绿地面积约为2 371.5平方米，与镇域内曙光、林泉、淮阴、淞二、虹康、淞四、淞五等10个居民区紧密相连。

项目聚焦"健康""活力"两个关键词，依托"活力仙西"美丽街区项目，优化青溪路、林泉路、剑河路、淞虹路、福泉路、协和路等重要路口，以景观小品打造、公共空间营造、绿化美化相结合的方式，做好"一棵树、一张椅、一面墙、一平地"，形成总量适宜、步行可达、活力宜人、绿色生态的健康街区、乐活走廊，努力打造成精细化微更新示范和"15分钟美好生活圈"的更新样板。项目东西两侧共设置12节点，通过景观打造、绿化提升、空间营造等多种方式实现街区面貌的焕然一新。

（三）主要做法

"活力仙西"美丽街区项目在新泾镇党委政府的高度重视下，从以下四个维度进行推进，实现了项目整体的靓化、美化、活化和精细化。

以景观小品打造，实现健康街区、乐活走廊靓化。聚焦商户单位、居民小区等需求强烈、景观品质不高、管理困难等问题，新泾镇携手同仁医院、西郊百联、中石化、神州养老院等辖区商户单位及居民区，通过对同XIN会客厅、陆家浜生物多样性科普角、好时光枫园、协和四方等点位的格局优化、资源利用、需求解决等，形成点位亮点的串珠成链，实现街区旧颜焕新貌，变杂乱为有序，提高街区整体幸福感。

以绿化品质提升，实现健康街区、乐活走廊美化。通过前期踏勘和绿化现状，一是结合设计方案进行以"补短板和提品质"的方式进行局部复绿增绿、见缝插绿；二是灵活采用"组团种植"的方式，将乔木、灌木、爬藤、花卉、地被等结合种植，将平面绿化升级成"立体彩化"；三是构建起多彩变化的城市生态空间，打造出四季常绿、季季有花、乔灌花草搭配科学、高低错落有致的浪漫意境。

以公共空间营造，实现健康街区、乐活走廊活化。新泾镇始终坚持把全过程人民民主理念贯彻始终，顺应人民群众对美好生活的新期待，通过城市"边角料"的打造、闲置空间改造及原有休闲广场升级，营造不同主题的公共空间，涵盖老人康体健身、生物多样性科普、疗愈花园、唯美花境等功能，让不同年龄段的居民都能感知家门口的生态、家门口的科普、家门口的"小美好"，为新泾镇居民提供了积极生活、热爱自然的公共空间。

图7-13 仙霞(西)路"同XIN会客厅"

以街区治理共同体建设,实现健康街区、乐活走廊精细化。新泾镇在推进街区治理精细化管理过程中,始终坚持"共建、共治、共享"原则,探索多元主体民主参与的有效方式和实现形式。上半年,建立了新泾镇街区治理委员会,以"治理委员会—社区—单位—商户"的连接模式,新泾镇召集党建联盟、街区商户联盟、政协委员、高校专家、美丽街区志愿者等团队,实现多元主体共融,形成街区治理共同体,让精细化管理实现新街区更美丽。

第五节　推进综合养护一体化

商务区以城市管理精细化项目为基础，打破行业条块分割，积极开展综合养护试点，将区域性较强的设施打包实施综合养护和管理。2021年12月，商务区颁布实施《上海虹桥国际中央商务区市政市容综合养护导则（试行）》，提出"1+X"综合养护模式："1"表示一体化保洁；"X"表示道路、园林绿化、水务等专业的日常养护。

近年来，新虹街道结合区域特点，遵循"总体规划、局部完善"原则，先行先试开展综合养护工作，将市政、绿化、市容、环卫、排水管道养护以及环境保护、安全生产、土地管理（违法施工治理）等巡查工作进行整合，初步形成"多位一体"的综合养护管理模式，有效提升了养护管理质量和管理水平，人员、物资、资金使用率明显提升。

一、基本情况

闵行区新虹街道管辖区域19.26平方千米，处于商务区主功能区内。区域内汇集了机场、高铁、地铁、公交、快速路等多位一体的现代化交通设施。交通设施功能多、规模大、客流高。这样大的超级商务区和综合交通枢纽，必然要求城市管理能力更强、服务水平更好、应急处置更快。目前，街镇一级都面临管养设施门类多、业务杂的局面，要实现设施养护优质高效，"有问题找一家解决"乃是大势所趋。

城市养护是城市管理中的一环，其工作涉及道路、绿化、环卫等方方面面，是重要的常规性公共服务，属于基础性民生类项目，旨在提高城市市容市貌水平，建设"宜商、宜业、宜居"的城市环境。以往的城市养护工作存在条线多管理分散、资源投入大效率低、管理职责不明确等问题。为了适应商务区建设发展需要，提高城市精细化管理水平，同时在"全国文明示范区"的背景下，根据《关于进一步深化本市城市养护作业领域城市化改革工作的指导意见》精神，自2015年新虹街道主动承接了市住建委推出的"综合养护管理一体化"改革试点工作，新虹街道遵循"总体规划、逐步完善"原则，综合养护从2016年开始实施至今，通过编制综合养护管理标准、建设综合养护管理实训基地、开展综合养护管理例会、严格考核体系等措施，不断改进工作机制，初步形成"多位一体"的综合养护管理模式。

二、管理机制和成果

1. 具体做法

根据《上海虹桥商务区市政基础设施综合养护导则》，新虹街道不断明确综合养护管理养护规范和养护作业要求，对日常考核方案和应急处置预案进行了更全面的细化。如今，新虹街道综合养护工作采用"城建中心牵头，条线自管"模式，涉及城建中心、水务站、规资所、城运中心、安监所5个部门，将新虹街道分为南、中、北3个管养片区，分3个项目对外招标进行综合养护管理。南片主要负责航华地区，中片主要负责商务区核心区域，北片主要负责华美地区。

2. 工作成效

打破养护边界，整合管养资源。实施综合养护管理一体化作业之后，以块为责任区，全面覆盖辖区内各项养护管理工作，进一步整合养护管理资源，职责明确，责任到人，杜绝因界限模糊业务交错等形成养护管理相互推诿和管理盲区的问题。

落实一岗多责，节约财政资金。综合养护管理单位内部可以跨工种作业，各养护单位绿化、市政、环卫等操作一体化，有些技术含量低的业务可以一人多责，相互兼任，有利于优化人员配置，通过养护管理资源的优化配置与合理协调，实现集约化，形成人员和设施设备的综合利用。此外，得益于市场化运作的竞争性优势，促进并激励了养护和管理单位的履职责任意识，加大巡查力度，在诸如制止毁绿、占绿、公共设施维护等问题上获得了较为明显的成效，降低了后续处置环节的资金投入。

明确责任主体，提升处置效率。由于明确了责任主体，划清了职责范围，养护管理单位解决问题的主动性得以增强。养护管理单位在具体实施中作业面广，作业要求高，相关设施设备配置齐全，发现问题自己先解决，做到"不等""不靠""不推诿"，形成良性循环体系。由于权责清晰，处理单位只有一家，出现问题能够迅速确定责任单位，节省大量中间协调环节和时间成本，现场处理速度显著缩短，应急处置时间明显加快。

3. 工作措施

编制综合养护标准化管理标准。2017年12月获得市质监局"路长制街面综合养护标准化试点"项目立项（沪质技监标〔2017〕468号）。聘请标准化管理专家对项目进行指导和培训，对制度进行规范。2019年9月26日，顺利通过项目验收，识别转化29

个国家标准、2个行业标准、2个地方标准,编制了66个街道标准,为进一步提升综合养护管理水平奠定基础。

强化综合养护专业化培训工作。2018年,在华翔绿地建设了综合养护管理精细化实训基地,通过规范化作业指导手册、负面清单橱窗、现场培训等形式,对综合养护管理单位定期开展培训和演练,切实提高综合养护管理效能。

构建综合养护信息共享机制。建立了相关各方参加的"综合养护例会制度",及时研究、协调、解决综合养护工作中的相关问题;充分利用互联网信息载体,建立"综合养护微信群",在各自养护作业中发现的无法独自处置的难题,第一时间在群内发布,经由项目负责人指定对口板块及时处置,以管理集成提升综合养护的管理效率。

严格综合养护监督考核管理。坚持把监督考核工作贯穿于综合养护全过程,全面掌控服务质量,建立由第三方、网格中心(大联动)、政风行风督察员、市民巡访团(投诉)等四级参与的社会化监督的量化考评机制。分层明责、全方位、全过程监督考核,有效强化了各个实施主体自我加压的能动性,提高了城市管理的效率和效能。

加强综合养护整体执法力度。新虹街道致力于支撑综合养护管理的网格中心平台建设,将管理资源细分并配置到管理的整个流程、每个环节,全体养护人员,定人、

图7-14 综合养护现场

定点、定岗、定责"对号入座"纳入养护管理网格；网格内发生问题分工不分家，实现"一职多能"的处置。三大网格分中心，城管、公安等执法人员标配对口进驻，携手综合养护公司，形成综合管理的合力。通过网格联动，做到快速发现、快速反应、快速处置、快速反馈，实现了职责明确、相互制约的多链条、闭环式管理，有效提升城市管理中事案的处置率。针对辖区内在建工程多的特点和工地偷排泥浆、乱堆杂物等突出问题，加大执法力度，在切实维护市容环境面貌的同时，有效降低了市政设施养护和维护成本的支出。

第八章　国际一流营商环境

第一节　营商环境评估及体系构建

一、营商环境评估工作

营商环境是一项涉及经济社会改革和对外开放领域的系统性工程,是会对日常经营产生"即时"和"深远"影响的微观和宏观环境。营商环境对地区经济发展具有内在而持久的影响力,既有研究表明:营商环境的好坏直接决定了一个国家或者地区经济发展的质量和速度,只有开放、服务、创新、高效的发展环境才能吸引各类人才和企业安家落户,集聚人气,增强地方发展的活力与韧性。商务区正在努力成为国际一流营商环境的践行者,从而让市场主体获得感更强、满意度更高,全力打造市场化、法治化、国际化的一流营商环境。因此,系统评估营商环境建设、科学诊断问题已成为商务区实现高质量发展过程中亟待深入思考探究的议题。

为深入贯彻落实党中央、国务院及市委、市政府关于优化营商环境的决策部署,围绕"一体化""高质量""国际化"等3个关键,服务虹桥国际开放枢纽和国际化中央商务区建设,对标《国务院关于开展营商环境创新试点工作的意见》《上海市营商环境创新试点实施方案》《上海市加强集成创新持续优化营商环境行动方案》,在精准把握商务区特色优势、功能定位与发展战略的基础上,结合商务区实际,深入调研商务区营商环境现状,立足商务区的特殊区位优势、特色政策优势、功能定位,深入探讨营商环境的独特内涵,构建适合的评估方法和评价指标体系。结合调研和相关数据,科学评估虹桥商务区营商环境现状及存在的关键性问题。遵循"人民城市建设"和政府帮持、市场主体的理念,提出商务区营商环境优化的总体思路,从"顶层设计"入手打造市场化、法治化、国际化、便利化的一流营商环境,以期对商务区一流营商环境建设有所裨益,为服务长三角一体化和高水平对外开放创造有利条件。

二、商务区营商环境特点

以功能建设为目标。对商务区而言，营商环境建设的根本目标是实现引领长三角一体化和促进国际国内双循环的总体功能定位，在此基础上，以"大交通、大商务、大会展、大科创"为导向，确定和聚焦营商环境建设的路径与重心。

以制度建设为主线。营商环境指涉及企业等市场主体进行市场活动所涉及的体制机制性因素，而这些因素的调控主体往往指向于政府。也就是说，营商环境的服务对象为企业，而建设主体则是政府。因此，在营商环境建设过程中，政府应持续深化改革创新，完善制度建设，依托政策和制度创新寻求产业创新发展的新突破，为营商环境提供坚实的制度保障，为平台建设和功能建设保驾护航。例如，加强规则建设、立法建设、服务配套，实现重点领域改革创新试点，探索创新内外贸一体化机制，促进要素自由顺畅流动，打通制度对接通道等。

以平台建设为抓手。为实现产业生态圈构建，以及增进政企、企企的互动交流，平台建设是营商环境优化首先考虑的要点。通过构建公共服务平台、产业创新服务平台等（如设备共享平台、数据共享平台、信息共享平台、产业链协作平台等），能够最大程度消解政府与企业之间的沟通壁垒，缓解信息阻滞；并为企业间的合作交流搭建桥梁，降低企业的交易成本，提升知识溢出与转移效应。以平台建设来激发市场能动性，发挥市场的配置作用和决定性作用，从而促进企业创新和区域集群发展。

三、商务区营商环境建设成效

（一）基础设施服务持续完善

一方面，联通浦东国际机场和长三角全域的虹桥国际开放枢纽轨道交通体系进一步完善，一批跨区域交通基础设施项目开工，综合交通枢纽交通平台改造及上海轨道交通延伸等项目加快建设，区域交通服务企业水平进一步提升。另一方面，核心区中轴线绿化、虹桥前湾世界级城市滨水中央公园等综合项目持续推进，对高品质公共开放空间的打造不断加强，"职住商"结构和公共交通体系不断优化。

（二）平台建设不断拓展

大力引进国际知名会展企业总部、国际品牌重要展会与配套企业，建设虹桥国际会展产业园，国际会展之都重要承载区加快构建，通过会展刺激消费流和带动贸易流，促进"进口贸易—国内消费"的互动，以采购商变贸易商的方式链接内外部供应链，并促进中国企业海外投资贸易网络拓展。目前，已打造了多个海外贸易平台，与全球多个贸易及投资机构建立了密切联系。同时，海外贸易中心、中央法务区等有序推进，拓展了本市"一带一路"综合服务中心、知识产权保护中心、RCEP企业服务咨询站等20多个平台功能。

（三）制度建设深化创新

"产城融合发展、环境生态文明、配套优势明显、区域特色鲜明"的框架基本形成。在此框架下，商务区遵循统筹协调、先行先试的原则，不断深化体制机制改革，积极探索并形成了一批有价值的制度创新成果和经验做法。截至目前，共梳理总结出包含统筹规划、开发建设、平台功能、城市管理、综合保障等方面的制度创新经验，以及在实践中形成的综合类、业务类、服务类等多项行之有效的工作机制。党建方面，街道党工委和办事处在商务区内设立楼宇工作站，打造"枢纽党建"实践模板，凝聚商务区各方力量，区内互联互动取得新进展。街道党工委以网格为依托，借助城市运行"一网统管"，探索党建融合网格治理新架构。打造"4+29+147"网格体系，覆盖到街面、居村和每个区域单位，实现"片区网格、自治网格、微网格"三级联动的高效管理体系。

（四）政务服务优化提升

企业服务中心能级持续升级拓展，四片区服务中心、街镇分中心有序建设，提供了工商、税务等企业服务和外国人来华工作居留、许可办理、人才引进落户、居住证积分等人才服务事项，深化窗口"智能帮办"、远程"直达帮办"服务模式。政商关系方面，构建亲清政商关系、弘扬企业家精神，能设身处地解决企业急难愁盼的问题。此外，目前商务区已持续推广应用29项国家政策和20项本市支持政策落地见效，为企业提供了更多机会。

四、评估维度构建的理论基础

商务区的营商环境评价的任务是总结经验、立足当下、展望未来，需要从世界、国家、长三角、上海的战略角度回答虹桥应该建立怎样的营商环境，如何优化虹桥的营商环境。营商环境评价体系的构建不仅要回答这些问题，更要向其他优秀案例汲取经验、博采众长。当前商务区要强化全球资源配置、科技创新策源、高端产业引领、开放枢纽门户等四大功能，不断增强吸引力、创造力、竞争力，成为新发展格局下国内大循环中心节点和国内国际双循环战略链接地区，并加快向引领长三角、成为重要枢纽及发展的桥头堡目标迈进。

（一）立足商务区功能定位

商务区作为长三角区域一体化的重要枢纽，要发挥"桥头堡""极中极"作用，需要从"大商务、大交通、大科创、大会展"四个特色角度出发，营商环境的评价需要从其特殊的功能发展需求完成。此外，商务区作为国际国内双循环的重要节点，未来也将成为国际贸易货物集散地，充分发挥其枢纽功能，既作为大量外贸商品的引入地，又作为苏浙皖地区商品"走出去"的重要节点，而营商环境则需要重点关注长三角地区的总部企业，以总部企业作为支点，充分带动整个长三角地区生产要素的流动。

（二）关注中观层面，重视区域特色区位

商务区作为带动长三角区域协调发展的主体之一，其拥有对外交通发达、产业集中、国际高端人才汇集等区位优势，这些条件是否对外来资本与跨国企业或企业总部有足够的吸引力，就成为商务区开放发展的重要因素之一。因此，企业对这些区位优势的主体感受也是营商环境的重要组成部分之一。

（三）评价体系需要具有全面性、针对性和科学性

主客观数据相结合，既从企业自身的诉求和调研出发，反映企业对营商环境真实的主观感受和主观评价，也从科学性、可比性的角度出发，使评价体系更具实用性和可行性。

五、指标体系构建

在营商环境内涵界定基础上，通过对商务区产业发展规划、营商环境建设等相关文件的文本编码，构建了由便利化、市场化、法治化和国际化等4个维度构成的营商环境指标体系。

表 8-1 部分政策文本编码表

一级编码	二级编码	文 本 示 例
便利化	财政税收便利化	纳税降低与简化；智慧办税；多税合一
	政企互动便利化	简化证明事项；一窗通办；一网通办；一网统管；政务数字化改革；企业完善电子信息；便利数字开户；招标电子化
	基础设施便利化	市政公共基础设施；市内交通联动

续 表

一级编码	二级编码	文 本 示 例
便利化	商业贸易便利化	建设国际医药医械交易平台，探索医药器械贸易便利化和审评审批制度联动改革，优化各类尖端创新药及制药关键原辅料、检验检测试剂、基因技术、高端医疗器械等准入环境，畅通研制、注册、生产、销售等市场准入环节；数字贸易平台
	金融服务便利化	获取金融服务；鼓励符合条件的企业开展资本项目收入支付便利化试点；开展数字人民币应用场景研究，积极争取数字人民币在重点区域试点
	工程建设便利化	工程建设项目一站式服务；下放工程资质审批权限
市场化	商业贸易市场化	高水平建设一批面向"一带一路"国家和地区的商品直销平台、国别商品交易中心和专业贸易平台
	知识产权市场化	知识产权交易市场；知识产权治理；健全知识产权质押融资风险分担机制与质物处理机制；区域产权合作
法治化	市场监管法治化	市场公平竞争；企业信息核验；处理商业纠纷；市场主体监管链；多种服务业综合监管"一件事"改革；税收领域动态监管；市场数字化智慧监管平台
	企业服务法治化	市场准入与退出；税收免责制度；企业激励、支持、补偿、救济机制
国际化	商业贸易国际化	跨境贸易；国际互联网数据专用通道
	人才科创国际化	国际人才就业执业；国际化教育发展；数据要素交易国际化；优化科技创新支持
	会展活动国际化	进博会支撑政策常态化
	金融服务国际化	支持商务区管委会与中国出口信保合作出台针对区内企业"走出去"国际化发展的跨境保险产品。支持区内金融机构助力虹桥商务区企业赴境外上市、发行债券，不断拓宽境内外融资渠道
	企业发展国际化	支持服务贸易企业拓展海外市场
	企业服务国际化	进出口信息共享；涉外服务建设
	市场投资国际化	支持优质内外资投资类企业在商务区发展，集聚吸引创新型潜力企业落地虹桥。探索引进海外资本，打造境内外投资双向平行基金，助推企业"引进来、走出去"
	组织机构国际化	跨区域社会组织

综上，结合目前商务区营商环境相关文件，从便利化、市场化、法治化及国际化等4个维度设计一级指标体系，其中便利化、市场化、法治化作为商务区营商环境建设的基础条件，国际化作为商务区的特色条件及发展目标。

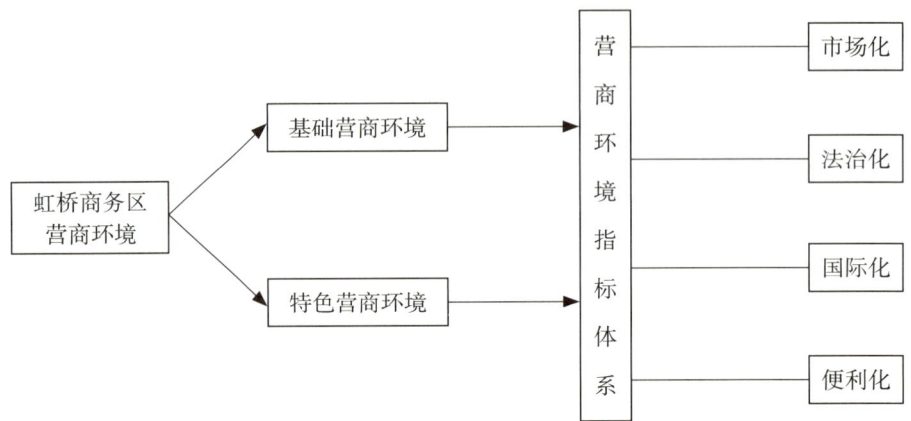

图8-1　虹桥国际中央商务区营商环境指标体系构建维度

第二节　跨区域的企业服务平台体系建设

商务区企业服务中心深入贯彻落实市委市政府深化"一网通办"改革工作要求，大力提升政务服务能力建设。在全市首家推出"政务管家"服务站、首家链接第三方资源，努力打响"全市通办、闵行快办"政务服务品牌，持续提升企业办事体验感、获得感和满意度。

一、体验优先，聚焦专业化，助力长三角一网通办

启用全新服务大厅，设置10个无差别综合服务窗口，实现企业异地注册等50个高频事项长三角通办，商事登记、人力资源等400多项政务服务无差别咨询受理。相继引入外商投资企业投诉窗口、RCEP企业服务咨询窗口，不断响应虹桥国际开放枢纽建设和长三角一体化发展的需求。

依托虹桥国际开放枢纽核心承载区叠加优势，研发超级自助终端覆盖长三角3省

图8-2　虹桥国际中央商务区企业服务中心

市8个地市所辖40个县市的全量自助服务，着力建设面向商务区、辐射长三角的一站式政务服务"加油站"。已为商务区企业提供政务服务50项、服务1万多人次。

二、深化创新，聚焦专项化，打造一站式特色专区

搭建联通国际国内"彩虹桥"，全市首家链接第三方资源，在政务大厅开辟专项服务专区，提供政策咨询、金融进博、法律公证及人才等多元的特色服务，有效呼应企业的个性化需求。

针对外籍人士来华办理居留许可、工作许可、签证续期等相关事项，设置外籍人士服务专区。针对疫情期间外国人居留业务积压的实际情况，通过开设外资企业、国际学校签证办理专区，化解重点外企、高层次外籍人才预约办证难题，推动营商环境再提升，获得了相关企业和国际学校的一致好评。已为区域内10多家企业提供特色服务，为10家企业、15家国际学校提供签证续签、停留签、工作签、团聚签等业务办理2 300人次。

三、实策惠企，聚焦个性化，推出"虹管家"帮办模式

推出全市首家"政务管家"服务站，组建"虹管家"帮办团队，落实与辖区内园区结对工作，通过建立工作微信群、定期上门走访、梳理操作流程、回答疑难问题，

图8-3 "虹管家"服务现场

采用"综合服务一对一指导、专项政策面对面咨询、项目帮办点对点服务"的管家式服务，为企业提供全生命周期的贴身服务。

为减少跑动聚集，方便企业办事，推出政务服务"云窗口"，可以视频连线区政务服务中心、区人才服务中心、街镇社区事务受理中心等，以不见面、非接触、云端批的方式，优化企业群众异地办事环境，提供"云端见、在线帮"的"零距离"服务，商事登记、股权转让等546个涉企事项可以通过"云窗口"实现零跑动办理。通过"现场虹管家帮办+远程云窗口审批"服务模式，实现全程"面对面"专属服务，已累计为近2 000家企业提供服务3 000余次。

第三节　专业服务要素资源集聚与功能平台建设

一、建设思路

虹桥国际中央法务区在"高站位谋划、高起点推动、高标准落实"的建设思路下，坚持以政府为主导，建最好的法律服务科创载体，聚最优的法律服务专业人才，创最活的法律服务辐射机制。

搭建全类型、新业态法律服务机构高效能集聚新平台。通过虹桥国际中央法务区功能平台具体实施建设，逐步在法务区内搭建一个法律服务创新集聚生态圈，制定支持法律服务业集聚发展的专项政策，快速吸引律师、公证、司法鉴定、仲裁、调解、法律科技公司、法律咨询公司、法律新媒体、法律研究和培训机构、诉讼融资等机构入驻虹桥国际中央法务区功能平台。支持本市符合条件的律师事务所等法律服务机构设立同城分支机构。支持长三角乃至全国的法律专业人才前来创业发展，法律服务机构前来设立分支机构，或者设立法律服务机构总部。在平台内打造面向长三角乃至全国法律服务机构的"虹桥会客厅"。

打造具有区域影响力的高水平虹桥国际法律服务展示引领新地标。在虹桥国际中央法务区功能平台中积极举办上海国际仲裁高峰论坛、上海仲裁周等各类高质量、高规格、国际化的法治论坛、研讨会议。鼓励互联网法律服务机构、法律咨询平台、法律科技公司、法律媒体等法律服务新业态、新模式发展，支持举办法律行业发展交流会议，为长三角乃至全国、全球法律机构提供法律科技服务和支撑。积极开展国际商事法律研究、培训和交流，形成全国乃至全球知名的国际商事法律研究、交流中心。用好"国内国际双循环"和交通枢纽区位优势，搭建开放共享、合作共赢的法律服务业交流平台。

汇聚长三角法律服务各类优势要素，建成长三角区域市场化、法治化、国际化营商环境示范区。推动长三角各地律师协会、仲裁协会、破产管理人协会、知识产权协会等加强协同合作，建立常设性议事协调机构，促进长三角法律服务市场融合发展。探索设立面向长三角的互联网法院等跨行政区域司法机构。支持上海法律服务机构拓展长三角乃至全国、国际业务。支持各类法律研究机构、培训机构发展，形成长三角法律实务人才培训交流中心。发挥虹桥国际开放枢纽企业总部集聚优势，发挥企业法务部门和公司律师的作用，加强企业合规交流和培训，提升企业依法治理水平和能力，着力打造全国法治化营商环境示范区域。鼓励各类服务创新、模式创新，建设长三角区域法律服务集聚区展示中心，使虹桥国际中央法务区功能平台建设成为引领法律服务业发展建设高地的新标杆、新亮点。

再启服务保障进博会新局面，在联动长三角的基础上，形成服务全国、辐射亚太的法治名片。充分结合5年来服务保障进博会成熟经验，聚焦闵行片区发展国际化公共服务功能和高端服务经济的主要特色，为会展经济国际化、专业化、品牌化发展提供投放精准、配套完善、机构健全、行业广泛的高水平法律服务，努力实现高端法律资源配置、基础法治宣讲、法律政策指引同步纵深推进。参与进博会区域协同服务保障机制建立健全，探索全生命周期企业法律服务保障路径。对区域内企业引进、落地、发展等全生命周期各阶段进行法律服务供给配置，逐步彰显虹桥区域内法律服务高能级配置新突破、新举措、新实践，持续放大进博会外溢带动效应，助力提升虹桥区域资源配置能力。

二、主要做法

2021年9月24日，商务区"三个一批"重大项目集中启动，虹桥国际中央法务区作为商务区功能性平台之一正式揭牌。定位于服务保障国际化中央商务区、服务长三角一体化和虹桥国际开放枢纽建设的国家战略，着力打造面向长三角、辐射全国、联通国际的法律服务"新平台"，发挥高质量、全链条、广辐射的法律服务集聚效能。

建立"三方联动"机制。成立由上海市司法局、商务区管委会和闵行区人民政府三方共同组成的（一期）建设领导小组，领导小组办公室由闵行区司法局和南虹桥集团组成，负责具体落实各项工作。

建设"一核多域"集聚区。"一核"即虹桥国际中央法务大厦暨法务区综合服务中心，面向法务区法律服务机构，提供线上线下"一站式"政务服务；面向商务区各类企业机构，搭建"家门口"法律服务平台；面向意向入驻机构，提供"全方位"政策支持渠道。"多域"即3.7平方千米虹桥商务区中的闵行片区。

提供长三角最优政策。上海市司法局制定上海市律师事务所在商务区设立同城分所政策。2023年4月，商务区管委会发布《2023年度虹桥国际中央商务区支持虹桥国际中央法务区发展政策申报指南》，确定将法务区纳入商务区政策支持范围。闵行区在

图 8-4 虹桥国际中央法务区

用足用好商务区支持政策的基础上，发布实施《闵行区支持打造虹桥国际中央法务区的政策意见》，进一步优化叠加政策顶层设计。虹桥国际中央法务区（一期）建设支持政策已全面落地实施，具体包括2项机构落户政策、3项专门奖励政策和4项服务保障措施等。

三、功能建设成效

功能平台引领带动。积极探索"功能性平台+""产业链+法律服务"模式。上海仲裁委员会虹桥中心、上海市律师协会长三角一体化行业发展研究中心/会员服务中心/联络办公室、上海东方域外法律查明服务中心虹桥联络部三大功能性平台落户虹桥国际中央法务区。法务区法务资源加速集聚，积极引进国内一流、具有国际竞争力的法律服务机构，形成多元丰富的法律服务体系。截至2023年10月31日，法务区（3.7平方千米）已入驻法律服务机构和泛法律服务机构共62家。

虹桥汇T9（法务大厦）已入驻签约法律服务机构有：上海仲裁委虹桥中心、上海市律协长三角律师行业发展中心/会员服务中心/联络办公室、上海东方域外法律查明服务中心虹桥联络部、上海市新虹桥公证处、广东广信君达（上海）律师事务所、上海大沧海新闵律师事务所、上海市建纬（虹桥国际中央商务区）律师事务所、智合全

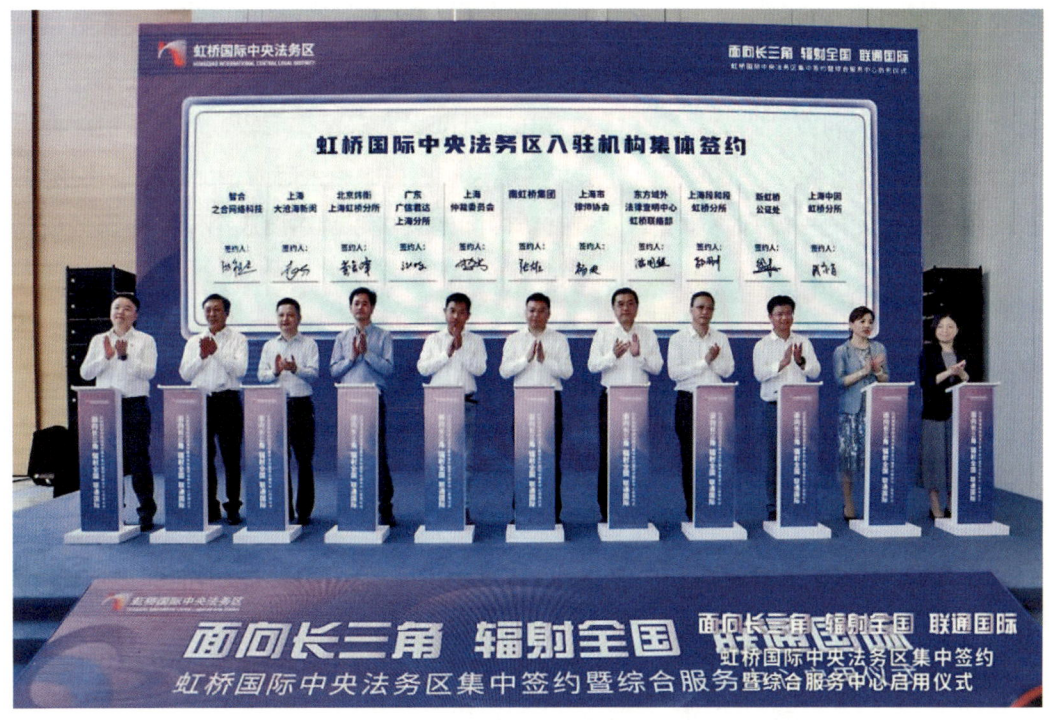

图8-5　虹桥国际中央法务区集中签约

球高质量职业发展中心、上海段和段（虹桥国际中央商务区）律师事务所、北京炜衡（上海虹桥国际中央商务区）律师事务所。入驻并办公的有：上海市律师协会长三角律师行业发展中心/会员服务中心/联络办公室、上海东方域外法律查明服务中心虹桥联络部、广东广信君达（上海）律师事务所、上海市新虹桥公证处、上海段和段（虹桥国际中央商务区）律师事务所、北京炜衡（虹桥国际中央商务区）律师事务所。

四、经典案例

确保进博会法律服务保障。2023年9月12日，为充分发挥第六届进博会驻场律师作用，切实做好进博会法律服务工作，上海市司法局和商务区管委会组织召开了第六届进博会驻场律师培训会。汇聚了来自9家律师事务所和4名进博会涉外法律服务中心的驻场律师。与会律师们就企业投资、落户等方面政策进行了深入咨询，并表示将努力做好进博会的法律服务工作，强化进博会的溢出效益，积极促进法律服务成果的实际转化，为本地区的社会经济发展贡献更多力量。

推动法律服务创新、加强知识产权等方面营商环境建设。上海国际知识产权海外维权集成服务创新论坛、第七届新兴法律服务业论坛、2023"虹桥·汇"企业数据合规与跨境监管的法律挑战论坛和虹桥外企联谊会"法律专场沙龙",都聚焦于全球法律服务业发展热点和前沿问题。这些活动旨在提升知识产权保护能级,深化法治产业发展,助力企业合规经营,形成专业要素高度集聚的法律服务生态圈,加速打造市场化、法治化、国际化的一流营商环境,为将虹桥国际中央法务区建设成全国法律服务新高地提供有力支撑。

五、意义与价值

虹桥国际中央法务区的一期首发示范阶段聚焦商务区中的闵行片区(3.7平方千米),率先在此区域内实现各项政策落地快、各类机构入驻快、各方效应见效快的创新引领目标。虹桥国际中央法务区建设二期整体跃升阶段将最大程度发挥虹桥国际开放枢纽法律服务集聚区在交通、会展、商务方面的显著优势,将建设范围推进至151平方千米全境,全面完善协同发展空间,重点保障建设高标准的国际化中央商务区三个维度内容:

全面加强法治保障。针对建设高标准的国际化中央商务区要"推动高端商务、会展、交通功能深度融合"的要求,建设虹桥国际开放枢纽法律服务集聚区有利于聚合法律支持主体多元要素,融合法律服务多能级保障举措,精准对接虹桥商务区会展经济、总部经济深层次发展中各类法治需求,推动构建接轨国际、衔接有序、高效便捷的法律服务生态圈。

持续提升营商环境。针对建设高标准的国际化中央商务区要"加快打造法治化市场化国际化营商环境"的要求,建设虹桥国际开放枢纽法律服务集聚区有利于细化制度细节,增创虹桥区域内贸易产业转型、法律服务机构升级新起点,增创法律服务人才集聚新优势,增创优化营商环境新动能。

显著优化区域协作。针对建设高标准的国际化中央商务区要"加快发展现代化服务业、持续深化长三角协同开放、引领长三角更好参与国际合作与竞争"的要求,建设虹桥国际开放枢纽法律服务集聚区有利于深化区域协同战略,形成全要素统筹、多点位联动、跨领域融合的长三角的法律服务新高地。

六、发展与展望

商务区将进一步推进上海虹桥国际中央法务区建设,发挥高质量、全链条、广辐射的法律服务集聚效能。吸引律所、公证、司法鉴定、仲裁、调解、法律科技公司、法律咨询公司、法律新媒体、法律研究和培训机构、诉讼融资等机构入驻，支持长三角乃至全国的法律专业人才前来创业发展。到2025年底，虹桥国际中央法务区一期首发示范功能平台将初步建成高集聚度、业态齐全、特色鲜明的上海法律服务"新地标"。吸引一批在长三角一体化重大战略中新业态、全类型的法律服务机构，梯次接续实现法律服务产业发展战略突破、优势合围效应。到2035年，逐步实现建设发展中远期目标，在区域内形成法律服务机构集聚度高、法律服务生态完备、民商事法律服务专业优势凸显的法律服务软实力核心生态圈。系统性打造长三角法律服务一体化示范区、法治化营商环境示范区。

第四节　企业产业链、生态圈构建及互动平台搭建

一、上海国际经贸知识产权海外维权集成服务创新论坛暨"上海国际经贸知识产权海外维权综合服务平台"

为增强本市企业国际经贸知识产权海外维权能力，服务提升上海国际贸易中心能级，助推上海对外贸易高质量发展，"2023上海国际经贸知识产权海外维权集成服务创新论坛"于2023年3月22日在沪成功举办。商务区首次发布了由市商务委指导搭建的"上海国际经贸知识产权海外维权综合服务平台"，该平台以案例化的维权服务匹配为特色，集合海外知识产权维权热点、相关国家政策法规、行业维权案例、专业维权指导站和专家库等，通过分类对接企业维权需求，有效提供海外维权服务。

图8-6　上海国际经贸知识产权海外维权集成服务创新论坛

二、"虹人汇"虹桥国际人力资源服务产业博览会

2023年3月27日，首届"虹人汇"虹桥国际人力资源服务产业博览会启动仪式暨中国上海人力资源服务产业园虹桥园区开园一周年活动在商务区举行。启动仪式现场，

全球人力资源一站式集成服务包发布，8家人力资源机构正式签约入驻园区，服务人力资源供需双方的招贤榜发布，首批优质人力资源服务机构集中亮相，上海市人力资源服务"伯乐奖"也在活动上进行了颁奖。

虹桥园位于商务区申昆路，是国家级的人力资源服务产业园，目前设置企业服务中心、创新发展中心、企业集聚中心等3个核心功能区。自2022年第一季度开园以来，虹桥园大力引进和培育优质人力资源机构，形成了集招聘、培训、人才测评、人力资源服务外包、信息软件服务等业态于一体的人力资源服务全产业链。

图8-7 "虹人汇"虹桥国际人力资源服务产业博览会

三、人力资源专场沙龙：人力资源数字化转型及共创员工体验

2023年4月24日，虹桥国际中央商务区外商投资企业联谊会（简称"虹桥外企联谊会"）在联谊会成员单位米其林中国区总部办公楼举办"人力资源专场沙龙：人力资源数字化转型及共创员工体验"活动。活动邀请上海市外商投资协会人力资源分会会长、上海外服（集团）有限公司副书记、副总裁、外服人力资源研究院院长夏海权先生分享"数据驱动的人力资源数字化转型"、米其林中国区人事副总裁李凌女士分享"'共创'员工体验，打造'幸福'工作场所"。来自上海及长三角地区的近50名外商投资企业和机构代表参加了活动。

四、企业数字化管理论坛

2023年5月19日,企业数字化管理论坛在南虹桥举行,众多国内知名企业家、顶级研究机构专家、高校教授、主要省市级行业协会领导等共聚一堂探讨分析行业与企业当下面临的机遇与挑战,助力企业人力资源数字化转型。

本次论坛按照受众与探讨方向设立了两场论坛,"企业数字化管理论坛"邀请知名高校、商学院教授与优秀企业家从组织、技术与用工模式等方面探讨企业数字化转型发展新思路。"人力资源服务行业高质量发展论坛",邀请全国各省市人才集团、人力资源服务产业园、人力资源服务机构等,通过主题演讲与圆桌讨论形式,分享新形势下人力资源服务行业的平台化转型创新实践。

图8-8 企业数字化管理论坛

五、国际贸易新形势下的外贸企业合规主题培训

2023年6月8日,由商务区管委会、上海市国际贸易促进委员会共同主办的"国际贸易新形势下的外贸企业合规主题培训"成功举行,近30家企业代表参与本次培训。本次培训活动由商务区投资促进与公共服务事务中心、上海科橘信息科技有限公司和XTransfer共同支持,旨在更好地帮助企业了解新形势下自贸协定和跨境电商发展趋势,

把握新机遇，迎接新挑战。

六、"双循环"背景下长三角·大湾区经贸与法律观察报告会

2023年7月20日上午，广信君达（上海）律师事务所在虹桥国际中央法务区法务大厦举办"法律服务联动　虹桥助力腾飞——双循环背景下长三角　大湾区经贸与法律观察报告会"，来自北京、上海和粤港澳大湾区的近百位专家学者、专业人士齐聚一堂，共襄盛举。本次活动由商务区管委会、闵行区人民政府指导，南虹桥管理委员会办公室、闵行区司法局主办，上海南虹桥投资开发（集团）有限公司、广信君达律师事务所、广信君达上海分所承办，智合、律新社提供支持。

在"双循环背景下长三角　大湾区经贸与法律观察报告会"上，演讲嘉宾从不同的视角出发，为来宾分享了其对经济与法律之间紧密关系的认识。

七、虹桥外企联谊会举办法律专场沙龙

2023年8月16日下午，虹桥外企联谊会举办了"法律专场沙龙:《外商投资法》'五年过渡期'合规倒计时、美国对华制裁措施简述及企业应对建议"，来自虹桥外企联谊会成员单位、上海市外商投资协会会员企业及相关机构30多名代表参加活动。

8月18日上午，商务区管委会联合上海外服和东虹办举办了一场企业互动平台系列活动，主题为全国社保合规化建议和讨论。活动旨在应对企业面临的"社保三统一"困境，即企业在雇佣员工时需要保持签订劳动合同主体、工资和个税扣缴主体、社保缴纳主体的一致性问题。临空及相关企业参加了此次活动，并进行了深入的交流和讨论。

8月31日下午，商务区管委会、上海律协国际贸易业务研究委员会举办了"虹桥国际中央商务区国际贸易与企业国际化经营法律问题研讨会"，会议围绕企业走出去的外部风险与合规管理、数据出境问题、海关法风险防范、数字贸易法制化路径、涉外律师服务等方面进行探讨。来自商务区管委会、上海律协国际贸易业务研究委员会及企业机构代表参加活动。

第五节　商务区人才高地核心区建设及人才服务提升

一、政策方案制定

根据市、区相关部门及商务区重点企业意见建议，结合商务区产业现状及未来规划，按照市人才办要求，初步形成商务区人才高地建设方案，并与市、四区相关部门多次征询意见。方案围绕立足虹桥国际开放枢纽建设，打造引领人才国际化创新和长三角协同的人才发展先行区的总体目标，从明确战略规划、优化空间布局、实施人才工程、创新平台载体、打造人才宜居宜业环境与创新文化等方面提出重点建设举措。

开展商务区紧缺人才目录研究工作。根据年度重点工作安排，开展区域重点产业人才现状摸底和紧缺人才目录编制工作，根据问卷调研、企业座谈等调研情况形成《虹桥国际中央商务区重点产业紧缺人才目录》（简称《目录》）。《目录》聚焦商务区功能定位和产业发展情况，覆盖商务区总部经济、服务经济、贸易经济、会展经济、科创经济和数字经济等6个重点产业领域，收录94类紧缺人才。《目录》基于市场导向及调研情况和重点产业目录，精准分析和前瞻性预判人才需求，全面构建商务区重点产业人才需求数据库。研究显示，商务区人才生态正处在增长型发展周期，发展环境持续向好；商务区总体呈现人才均衡型发展特征，逐步转向人才引领型周期；商务区人才结构升级，高学历、高活力、高收入人群比重高；国际化商务区总部经济类人才初现集聚效应，正形成富有特色的现代服务业集聚区；国际化人才氛围不断升温，外籍人才、海归人才需求旺盛。《目录》还指出商务区在人才政策、人才服务上仍有欠缺，商务区将持续推动人才高地建设，探索制定人才政策，积极推动人才服务体系发展。

二、功能平台打造

深入推进虹桥国际商务人才港建设。以平台体系为牵引，加强中国上海人力资源服务产业园虹桥园区建设，加大人力资源机构招引力度，加快引进专业性、创新型、国际化人力资源机构，发挥产业园对人才引进、服务的市场化功能。通过联合举办、协助推动等形式，举办企业数字化管理高峰论坛、人才政策宣贯、人才交流、产业沙龙等活动，不断提升园区影响力和品牌集聚效应。推动西虹桥建设青浦（长三角）数

图8-9 虹桥国际人才港

宇人力资源服务基地、北虹桥建设北虹桥人才驿站等平台。

三、重点活动策划

（一）才聚虹桥 共创未来——2023年虹桥国际中央商务区人才发展大会召开

商务区是上海"东西联动""两翼齐飞"城市新格局的重要西翼，在长三角一体化、进博会、虹桥国际开放枢纽等一系列国家战略的赋能下，逐渐成为引领长三角开放升级和国际国内双循环的关键连接点。作为国家战略的重要承载区域，商务区正加快企业集聚、产业发展、能级提升，已累计吸引和培育总部类企业500多家。"巢筑"而后"凤来"，商务区已成为国际经营、科技创新、专业服务等高端人才集聚区，为更好地支撑好、落实好国家战略要求，打出尊才爱才"组合拳"，发挥近悦远来的人才集聚"强磁场"效应，商务区将以本次活动为契机，进一步打造成为人才引领蝶变的样板之地、适宜人才大展"虹"图的筑梦之地、天下英才"桥"连相通的向往之地。

活动现场，管委会相关领导在致辞中指出，虹桥要发展，人才是根基，虹桥始终坚持广聚天下英才而用之，人才集聚"强磁场"效应初现，商务区正构建国际一

图 8-10　虹桥国际中央商务区人才发展大会

流人才发展环境，持续推进筑巢引凤，营造尊贤爱才的创新文化氛围，发展近悦远来的宜居宜业生态，也将继续会同各相关区同心协力，让天下英才奔赴虹桥、爱上虹桥、扎根虹桥！

活动现场，商务区管委会与闵行区、长宁区、青浦区、嘉定区签署协议，打造商务区人才发展共同体。商务区将统筹协同闵行区、长宁区、青浦区、嘉定区，按照"1+4"的工作格局，协调推进区域内人才互认和跨区服务共享，实现人才与政策、人才与服务的便利精准对接。

商务区管委会、闵行区、长宁区、青浦区、嘉定区在大会上进行了特色人才政策和功能平台推介，打出重才爱才"组合拳"，助力商务区发挥近悦远来的人才集聚"强磁场"效应。商务区加快国际化、专业化、创新型人才集聚的特色举措，鼓励商务区内企业总部吸引人才，并提供最高不超过200万元的人才专项补贴；针对外籍人才，积极推进国家移民政策实践基地建设，可以提供推荐商务区内的外籍高层次人才办理永久居留和3年内多次往返商贸签证等便利政策服务，符合条件的企业人才可以申请办理APEC商务旅行卡，同时外籍员工、外籍高校应届毕业生可以在商务区申请办理工作许可。商务区会同各相关区为在商务区工作的人才提供人才安居、落户等服务保障；闵行区发布《虹桥国际中央法务区支持法律专业服务业人才发展实施意见》，服务保障虹桥国际中央法务区高水平发展；长宁区发布《留学人员回国（境）过渡期内租住人才公寓专项支持政策》，打造海外人才安居最虹桥；青浦区在西虹桥建设上海青浦（长三角）留学人员创业园，打造虹桥海外人才"新高地"；嘉定区在北虹桥实行更加包容的政策制度、搭建更加广阔的时代舞台、构建更加高效的服务体系，用心用情打造宜居宜业人才生态。

会上，商务区正式发布《虹桥国际中央商务区重点产业紧缺人才目录》。《目录》基于市场导向，调研商务区内企业1 260家，覆盖从业人员约9万人，精准分析和前瞻性预判人才需求，全面构建商务区重点产业人才需求数据库。聚焦商务区总部经济、服务经济、贸易经济、会展经济、科创经济和数字经济等6个重点产业领域，收录94类紧缺人才，涵盖八大门类共计45个紧缺专业，其中：总部经济收录品牌管理、信息化管理等11类人才；服务经济收录融资业务、专利咨询等15类人才；贸易经济收录跨境电商管理、智慧供应链等14类人才；会展经济收录会展策划、涉外项目运营等12类人才；科创经济收录生物研究、能源研究等19类人才；数字经济收录人工智能研发、半导体芯片研发等23类人才。

大会现场，虹桥前湾国际人才社区建设三年行动计划发布。根据计划，三年内，前湾地区将在国际人才聚集、创新乐业示范、政策先行先试、品质宜居生态方面发力，为前湾地区国际人才社区样板建设按下"加速键"。

打造上海市"海聚英才"人才会客厅。为统筹商务区人才服务、聚焦现代服务业人才发展、加快推进上海市高水平人才高地建设，上海市"海聚英才"人才会客厅以"一个平台、三大中心"为运行基础，服务区域内的人才、企业，发挥政策宣传、政务服务、人才引进、人才培育、人才交流、项目路演、成果展示、共享空间等主要功能。

实施虹桥国际人才合作伙伴计划是商务区进一步借助各方专业资源，提升商务区人才服务能级的重要举措，纳入首批虹桥国际人才合作伙伴计划的单位共计8家，分别为华东师范大学、上海外服、万宝盛华、毕马威、帝国理工学院上海校友会、纽约大学上海校友会、法国/法语区企业中心以及新加坡中华总商会。虹桥国际人才合作伙伴计划的实施将有助于提升商务区人才发展能级、强化国际人才集聚和长三角人才交流、打造虹桥人才服务品牌。

此次大会，在外场同步举办了"聚上海 创未来"2023虹桥人才招聘会。招聘会吸引了大批求职者前来，现场人气火爆。闵行、长宁、青浦、嘉定四区共有337家企业报名参加，提供岗位1 525个，人才需求达4 279人，参加线下招聘的企业200家，提供岗位1 195个，人才需求3 294人。此次招聘会累计入场人数5 000余人，企业收到简历3 000余份，意向录用700余人，有效促进了商务区企业与全球人才的供需匹配。

（二）其他活动

与闵行区接洽策划人才品牌活动，开展"虹桥国际人才会客厅"走进进博会活动，组织虹桥园内人力资源服务贸易、出海入华企业参展进博会，借助进博会的平台，促进商务区与国内外其他地区的人才交流，引领人才国际化创新，打响虹桥人才品牌。举办商务区出入境政策宣传贯彻活动，向与会企业介绍商务区针对外籍人才的政策资源，结合商务区虹管家特色服务，介绍人才服务特色品牌，呼吁企业与政府建立紧密联系，共同做好人才工作，结合典型案例，做好面对企业的政策宣讲。

四、外籍人士服务工作

做好商务区外籍人才服务工作。与市出入境部门研究推进移民政策实践基地建设，进一步提升外籍人才服务平台功能。推进外籍高层次人才永久居留推荐工作，提供政策宣贯、申请受理、材料收集等一条龙服务，推动商务区企业服务中心"单一窗口"功能拓展，在政务服务领域为外籍人士提供便利。

第六节　打造环境友好型宜商宜业商务区

一、住房保障

商务区作为国家战略集中赋能区域，高端产业引领、龙头企业集聚，"巢筑"而后"凤来"，商务区成为国际经营、科技创新、专业服务等高端人才集聚区。人才安居是商务区人才服务体系的重要组成部分，商务区坚持以提升产城融合、职住平衡水平为导向，完善住房供给结构，推进人才安居工程、完善人才安居配套，让精英人才住有所居，居有所安。

（一）虹桥乐贤居

虹桥乐贤居是上海地产集团租赁住房战略的品牌项目，也是商务区重点打造的人才公寓。一期为市筹公共租赁住房，主要面向注册地或办公地在商务区内的企业出租；二期为虹桥乐贤居城家公寓，由上海地产集团和华住集团合作打造的保障性租赁住房项目。二期作为保障性租赁住房，只需在上海就业，且闵行区住房面积不超过15平方米即可申请。无论是否在外区有其他住房，都可以申请。水申费为民水民电，租金可以提取公积金支付。户型种类繁多，有33平方米宽敞阳台、36平方米精致一居室、66平方米和75平方米朝南两居室等多种选择。价格实惠，并且较周边市场价格更为优惠。

截至2023年10月，已有东方航空、中海油、吉祥航空、上海航空、机场集团、携程、三棵树、联合利华、红星美凯龙、合众新能源汽车和央法律所等多家知名企业与项目签约，安排员工集体入住。

（二）COZI可遇·虹桥

COZI可遇是领盛投资旗下的公寓品牌。COZI可遇秉承着"善意、循续、出圈、焕然"的品牌信条，旨在为城市青年提供一站式的租住生活新选择。这个生活社区由一座闲置商场改造而成，提供42—98平方米多样化的户型，总计589套（其中包括177套人才公寓），约七成的户型都配有开放式阳台。长租生活社区总面积约6.4万平方米，提供共享开放内容多元的社交公区、住家级功能品质以及客制化服务准则，满足各个年龄段租户居住需求。园区内设有橡胶跑道、多功能厅、会客厅、阅览室、桌球厅和健身房等公共设施。

图 8-11　COZI 可遇公寓

在繁华都市之间，COZI可遇为城市人群带来了一个安静的居所，一个宽敞舒适的创意空间，使生活和工作在这里找到平衡。交通方式方便多样，商业街区近在咫尺，生活配套设施齐全。距离上海虹桥站只需8分钟车程，距离虹桥机场只需10分钟车程。项目目前出租率已达到80%以上，主要客户来自商务区的白领人群，例如毕马威、红星美凯龙和龙湖等大型企业员工。

（三）地产城方·虹桥璟智公寓

地产城方·虹桥璟智公寓于2022年10月开业，是上海地产集团的第一个保障性租赁住房项目，也是闵行区和上海市首批市级人才公寓。社区内拥有约2 000平方米的社区服务空间，提供健身房、会客区、自习室等公共空间，还有餐厅、便利店、山姆云仓和上汽咖啡馆等社区商业设施。该项目共有318套精装公寓，配备了各种品牌家电，并提供多种户型选择，以满足不同生活场景需求的人士。

作为保障性租赁住房项目，地产城方·虹桥璟智对申请准入条件进行了限制：申请者必须在上海市合法就业且在闵行区住房不超过 15 平方米。在这里租房可以最高提取 4 500 元的公积金，在很大程度上缓解了租金压力。此外，入住该项目还可办理居住证并落户到公共户口。

二、金融服务

（一）充分发挥专项资金引导扶持作用

集中发布申报指南。按照年度工作计划安排，依据《上海市虹桥商务区专项发展资金管理办法》等有关规定，商务区于 2023 年 4 月 12 日集中发布一批专项发展资金申报指南。

表 8-3　上海市虹桥商务区 2023 年度专项发展资金申报指南一览

序号	申报指南
1	《2023 年度虹桥国际中央商务区关于支持贸易型总部企业发展的申报指南》
2	《2023 年度虹桥国际中央商务区关于支持内资总部企业发展的申报指南》
3	《2023 年度虹桥国际中央商务区支持功能性平台发展政策申报指南》
4	《2023 年度虹桥国际中央商务区支持打造虹桥进口商品集散地政策申报指南》
5	《2023 年度虹桥国际中央商务区支持虹桥国际中央法务区发展政策申报指南》
6	《2023 年度虹桥国际中央商务区支持现代服务业发展政策申报指南》

组织线上宣讲培训。为帮助商务区企业更好地开展专项资金项目申报工作，商务区于 2023 年 4 月 19 日联合闵行、长宁、青浦、嘉定四区政府成功举办 2023 年上海虹桥商务区专项发展资金项目申报培训会，有效促进了商务区相关企业对专项发展资金政策及申报指南的理解，帮助企业更好地开展专项资金项目申报工作。

项目申报。根据《上海市虹桥商务区专项发展资金管理办法》，管委会会同闵行、长宁、青浦、嘉定四区政府对 2023 年度申请虹桥商务区专项发展资金支持项目进行了评审和批复。

（二）积极推进金融政策落地

2021 年 7 月，《关于支持虹桥国际中央商务区企业开立自由贸易账户有关事项的通知》正式发布，支持商务区内通过自由贸易账户开展跨境交易本外币结算和境外融资业务。通过金融机构推荐，管委会定期向人民银行上海总部报送符合条件的企业名单的方式，已形成常态化工作机制。截至2023年10月底，已累计推荐181家企业纳入自由贸易账户白名单，累计推荐14家企业纳入离岸经贸业务白名单。

三、医疗机构

商务区致力于吸引国内外优秀的医疗服务机构和人才，以"市场化、高端化、国际化、集约化"为导向，探索医疗服务、医技保障、管理集成、产业延伸等四大体系的创新发展模式，打造立足上海、辐射长三角、服务全国的高端医疗服务集聚平台。

深入推进新虹桥国际医学中心建设。医学中心背靠虹桥综合交通枢纽，规划总面积约100万平方米。其中，一期地块建设于2010年3月正式启动，2020年基本完成开发建设，规划用地面积约42万平方米，建筑面积约70万平方米，规划总投资约100亿元。未来，园区拟在二期地块的开发建设中继续引入有品牌、上规模的国内国际医疗机构，重点发展先进专科医疗服务，打造医疗服务贸易平台，培育医疗服务产业链，进一步拓展健康金融、健康管理、旅游医疗及配套服务等业态。近年来，已吸引了复旦大学附属华山医院、上海百汇医院、上海星晨儿童医院等近10家医院、近30家医疗机构入驻。

（一）复旦大学附属华山医院（虹桥院区）

复旦大学附属华山医院（虹桥院区）位于闵行区金光路958号，是国家卫健委与上海市人民政府共同打造的医学园区内唯一的三级甲等医院。院区住院核定床位800张，拥有全球最大的NICU（神经外科监护病房）、术中核磁复合手术室等。院区定位"大专科、小综合"，致力不断推动国家神经科学临床医学中心、长三角创伤医学中心、大虹桥区域医疗中心建设。旨在立足上海，辐射长三角，服务全中国百姓。目前院区门诊开诊科室包括神经外科、神经内科、皮肤科、感染科、康复医学科、骨科、普外科、心内科、中西医结合科等国家级重点专科/重点学科。百余名专家教授坐诊，为患者提供与本部同质化的医疗资源。

（二）上海百汇医院

上海百汇医院是新虹桥国际医学园区内唯一的中外合资综合医院，是百汇班台有限公司与虹信医疗投资控股有限公司合资兴建的一所医院。百汇班台是亚洲最大的私立医疗集团之一，旗下的31家医院分布于新加坡、马来西亚、印度、中国、文莱以及

第八章　国际一流营商环境

第六节　打造环境友好型宜商宜业商务区

图8-12　复旦大学附属华山医院（虹桥院区）

图8-13　百汇医院

阿拉伯联合酋长国，总床位超过6 000张。该院设置床位450张，用地约3.33万平方米，建筑面积约7万平方米。建成后，该院将作为百汇集团开拓中国医疗服务市场的旗舰项目，为上海及长三角区域的居民提供优质的国际化医疗服务。

（三）上海星晨儿童医院

上海星晨儿童医院（复旦大学附属儿科医院新虹桥国际项目）位于上海新虹桥国际医学园区，占地面积约1.2万平方米，建筑面积约3.4万余平米，规划床位200张，定位为三级专科儿童医院。由上海复星医院投资（集团）有限公司、上海虹信医疗投资控股有限公司、上海复旦医疗产业创业投资有限公司三方共同出资建设，建成后的医院委托复旦大学附属儿科医院运营。医院主要设置儿内科、儿外科、儿童保健科等临床专业。医院将依托复旦儿科医院高素质临床团队、资本化运作优势与国际医疗资源，积极探索商业医疗保险、儿童家庭健康管理等创新商业模式，努力将医院打造为具有国际医疗标准和国际化管理服务水平的儿童医疗健康中心，为上海市及长三角地区家庭提供多元化、个性化的儿童健康管理与医疗服务。

图8-14　复旦大学附属儿科医院新虹桥分院

四、国际教育

作为境外人士在上海的主要聚居区之一,商务区集聚了上海英国外籍人员子女学校、上海李文斯顿美国外籍人员子女学校、新加坡国际学校、德国学校、法国学校、韩国学校、西华国际学校等诸多外籍人员子女学校,为在商务区居住、工作的外籍人员子女提供优质国际教育,并持续鼓励区域内符合条件的外籍人员子女学校自主面向全国招生。

(一)上海英国外籍人员子女学校

上海英国外籍人员子女学校浦西校区是诺德安达教育集团在华教育领域的旗舰校,该校将"学术成就、运动课程、科技探索、表演艺术、公民意识"作为学校的"五大支柱",激发学生的个性特长,培养充满进取心和社会责任感的学生。学校IGCSE成绩通过率达90%,远高于全球67%的平均水平,校长申安迪因此荣获上海市白玉兰奖。经过多年努力,上海英国学校已成为在沪外籍人士公认的优质学校,每年有超过2 000名外籍学生在此就读。2016年开始,学校与华东师范大学长期合作开展实习实践活动,已协助培养了近100名具有国际视野的优秀教育工作者。此外,学校还积极与属地镇政府合作,解决外籍员工子女入学问题,促进优质外资企业在华漕镇落户。

图8-15　上海英国外籍人员子女学校

（二）上海李文斯顿美国外籍人员子女学校

上海李文斯顿美国外籍人员子女学校（SLAS）是为上海改革开放招商引资配套服务而成立的一所国际学校。

自2003年开办至今20年来，学校不断整合完善教育资源，课程涵盖了幼、小、中、高等年级，为各个年龄阶段的外籍学生提供了优质的教学质量，获得了较好的口碑及赞誉，尤其是在双语教学上累积取得非常有效的经验，成为上海地区双语教学的模范。

该校是经由美国西部院校教育联盟（WASC）核准的正式成员，凡由该校转学或毕业的学生的学籍及成绩均可得到美国大、中、小学校的认可，直接申请入学并免托福TOEFL考试，并获得设立为留学生考试SAT与ACT考点的资格。

五、文体设施

为进一步优化商务区的公共文体服务环境、满足商务区企业和市民的体育运动和文化娱乐需求，大虹桥把创新拓展全民健身和文体活动空间作为构建更高水平公共文体服务体系的重要途径。未来在商务区出门进行体育锻炼和文化活动，可供选择的场地将愈发多样。

（一）虹桥体育公园

虹桥体育公园位于商务区长宁片区的绥宁路820号，项目分为地上及地下两部分，地上为市民绿化公园与凌空驿站，地下为多样化的体育空间。公园以"体育+"为导向，将实现体育空间与公园绿地、文化展览、社区服务、商业服务等功能的多重融合。公园的体育空间以航天为主题进行设计，为使用者营造身临其境般的太空科技运动体验，同时亦能获取丰富的航天知识。虹桥体育公园的体育业态包含游泳馆、篮羽运动馆、壁球馆、剑道馆、乒乓球馆、健身房、滑板馆、棋类运动馆、虚拟高尔夫馆、综合运动轰趴馆等，涵盖了10余种大众体育项目。其中篮球、羽毛球、壁球等场馆配备了赛事级专业场地，可以满足专业赛事的举办。此外，公园的地面部分储备了户外足球场、网球场的规划设计，还将配置若干亲子活动项目。公园的配套业态则包含运动康复馆、咖啡馆、中餐厅等。

公园对标市体育局颁布的"都市运动中心"建设标准，将体育运动和康体休闲功能相融合，突出各类户内外运动项目的主导功能，辅以特色化的配套服务，如专业训练、运动康复医疗、文化科普展示、城市安全（应急）疏散等。通过体育设施与公园

第八章 国际一流营商环境

第六节 打造环境友好型宜商宜业商务区

图8-16 虹桥体育公园

绿地的结合,拓展市民运动新场所。未来,体育公园还将成为企业团建的重要目的地,也通过举办一些大众喜闻乐见的篮、羽、乒等赛事成为大虹桥企业间互动的纽带。

(二)虹桥音乐公园

虹桥音乐公园位于长宁区广顺北路592号,西北走向的广顺北路将音乐公园分为东、西两个片区。东片区为临空1号公园(暂名),公园东、北两侧紧邻吴淞江(苏州河)、西至广顺北路、南至临华路。西片区为防护绿化带,东临广顺北路,西临上海S20外环高速。地上绿化面积为9万平方米,14个单体建筑面积(包含地下车库)为1.6万平方米。

音乐公园坐落于大虹桥的国家级临空经济示范区,是辐射长三角的文化交流集散地,发挥着音乐产业的孵化与聚合和文化品牌深耕的价值,定位为打造上海最潮流的音乐文化新地标。音乐公园作为临空园区的配套区域,承担着北端门户景观及弥补上海音乐特色公园空白的重任,借助虹桥交通枢纽、苏州河滨水景观带的巨大优势,打造城市的独特音乐艺术名片。

虹桥音乐公园有以下两大核心亮点。一是位于虹桥交通枢纽附近,周边可辐射上

图 8-17　虹桥音乐公园

海虹桥临空经济示范区及长风生态园区等，可辐射人群较多。二是虹桥音乐公园属于中心城区唯一的中大型音乐主题公园；项目离住宅区较远不存在噪声污染。

公园内的中央草坪区由1.6万平方米观演大草坪、370平方米演艺舞台组成，除了给游园者宽阔舒朗的露天活动空间外，也起到了核心演艺的功能。是各类音乐庆典在园内的主场地。通过白天的乐迷聚会、夜晚的辉煌舞台瞬间点亮苏州河激情。同时，利用公园的特殊属性，可举办音乐、生活节类的活动，打造一个集音乐舞台、亲子休闲、宠物爱好者、创意集市等于一体的时尚地标。除了众多音乐人的表演，还汇聚了各类创作者、个体耕耘者、设计人员、意见领袖等，从创意制品、风格呈现，到地景艺术，融合建筑、美学、艺术、人文等多元文化。

附录1　虹桥国际中央商务区大事记

2月4日　市委书记陈吉宁调研虹桥国际中央商务区并指出，商务区承载了多项国家战略任务，要深入学习贯彻党的二十大和习近平总书记考察上海重要讲话精神，进一步深化对战略内涵的认识，准确把握自身定位和比较优势，紧扣一体化、高质量和国际化，找准工作切入点和着力点，凝聚各方合力、大胆攻坚突破，更好把蓝图转化为施工图、实景画，为继续当好改革开放排头兵、创新发展先行者做出更大贡献。

3月1日　2023年虹桥国际开放枢纽建设工作现场会在国家会展中心（上海）举行。市委书记陈吉宁在会上强调，要深入学习贯彻习近平总书记关于推动长三角一体化发展的重要讲话和指示批示精神，按照党中央部署要求，齐心协力、共同奋斗，推动虹桥国际开放枢纽建设迈上新台阶，在新征程上更好服务国家现代化建设大局，为深入推动长三角一体化发展、服务构建新发展格局作出新的更大贡献。市委副书记、市长龚正主持会议。市委常委、常务副市长吴清通报虹桥国际开放枢纽建设两周年工作情况，江苏省委常委、常务副省长马欣，浙江省副省长张家胜，安徽省委常委、常务副省长费高云，国家发展改革委副秘书长欧鸿出席会议并讲话。

3月31日　"共享虹桥国际开放枢纽建设机遇"福建企业家圆桌会在福州举办。会上，管委会、青浦区人民政府、中国进出口银行上海分行等单位领导致辞。活动吸引了30余家企业参会，涵盖数字经济、国际贸易、高端制造等领域，与会企业家与商务区、闵行区、青浦区有关部门的负责人进行热切交流，为福建的企业家开启了一扇投资兴业的机会之门。

4月13日　商务区召开学习贯彻习近平新时代中国特色社会主义思想主题教育动员部署会议。管委会领导主持会议并作动员部署，市委第十四巡回指导组组长曹卫东作指导讲话，副组长李佳玉及指导组成员到会指导。会议指出，一是要深刻认识开展主题教育的重大意义，以饱满的政治热情投入主题教育；二是要严格对标中央和市委的部署要求，牢牢掌握主题教育正确方向；三是要切实加强组织领导，以更高标准、更严要求推动主题教育走深走实。

5月25日 "潮涌浦江 投资虹桥"——2023虹桥国际中央商务区投资促进大会在东虹桥1BP国际会议中心举行。本次活动积极响应"潮涌浦江 投资上海"全球分享季系列活动，通过项目发布、揭牌、签约和内资企业总部授牌等形式，全面展现虹桥国际中央商务区作为国家战略集中赋能区域的发展动能，并向海内外投资者发出盛情邀请，共享"大虹桥"发展机遇。活动现场，管委会领导作商务区发展情况报告。

5月25日 华源副市长调研商务区。分别听取管委会、市发展改革委、市规划资源局等相关单位"1+1+5"专项工作推进情况的汇报。

6月13日 市人大常委会部分组成人员围绕相关主题到商务区开展视察。市人大常委会副主任宗明一行实地视察了宝汇跨境直播项目，了解一站式直播电商解决方案、打造国际贸易生态圈开展情况；视察了虹桥海外华商会进博及贸易促进中心，了解海外华侨华人住在国企业、商引进来和中国企业出海双向服务平台打造情况；听取了市发改委、商务区管委会相关工作推进情况介绍，并与部分园区内企业代表等进行了座谈。

7月10日 经国务院同意，国家发展改革委印发了《关于推动虹桥国际开放枢纽进一步提升能级的若干政策措施》，明确围绕做强虹桥商务区这"一核"，做优做精北向拓展带、南向拓展带这"两带"，引领带动长三角全域更高质量一体化发展等3个层面，提出了24条具体措施。这是继2021年《总体方案》落地之后的一次重大政策升级。

8月24日 华源副市长调研虹桥国际中央商务区，听取商务区强化产业集聚效能、完善公共配套服务情况，优化规划和核心区城市更新政策情况，以及近期重点工作情况的汇报。

8月25日 "长三角企业家圆桌会·绍兴"成功举办，吸引了来自生物医药、电子信息、智能制造等领域的20余位优秀企业家参会。管委会领导和上海市浙江商会党委副书记、执行副会长、秘书长吴仲春致辞，管委会党组成员、副主任张斌对商务区进行主题推介，闵行区委常委、副区长赵亮和嘉定区副区长李峰分别就商务区闵行片区和嘉定片区进行投资环境介绍，到会企业家们在交流发言环节，就所在产业、营商环境、政策扶持力度、国际化发展、遇到的瓶颈问题等与政府进行了面对面交流。

9月27日 2023年虹桥国际中央商务区人才发展大会在国家会展中心（上海）召开，并同步举办了"聚上海 创未来"2023虹桥人才招聘会。活动现场，管委会与闵行区、长宁区、青浦区、嘉定区签署协议，推进打造商务区人才发展共同体。

附录1　虹桥国际中央商务区大事记

10月12日　新一期"潮涌浦江　投资虹桥"活动暨"战略赋能新机遇开放引领新高地"——2023虹桥国际中央商务区投资促进大会在国家会展中心（上海）举行。会上，通过展示前三季度投资促进成果、解读虹桥国际开放枢纽2.0升级版政策、发布《虹桥国际中央商务区综合交通规划（2021—2035）》以及授牌生产性互联网服务平台、签约重点产业项目等形式，全面展现商务区在共享高质量发展机遇、助力长三角功能提升等方面的最新成就和下一步发展预期。

10月12日　市政府召集40余家相关单位，在国家会展中心（上海）召开虹桥国际开放枢纽暨虹桥国际中央商务区建设工作会议，华源副市长出席并讲话。会上，市发展改革委介绍本市贯彻落实虹桥政策升级版重点任务分工方案；管委会介绍"高质量推进商务区建设三年行动计划"；市商务委解读《加快提升商务区服务企业"走出去"能级的若干措施》的重点内容。华源副市长在会上对商务区工作提出三点意见：要提高站位、凝聚共识，准确把握高质量推进"大虹桥"和商务区建设的战略内涵和重要意义；要抢抓机遇、攻坚克难，加快把虹桥国际开放枢纽和商务区发展的宏伟蓝图高质量转化为施工图、实景画；要明确分工、加强协作，全力推动各项工作任务落实落地。同时还重点围绕"五个着力"（着力推动虹桥政策"升级版"落地见效、着力优化商务区管理体制机制、着力推进商务区三年行动计划加快实施、着力统筹高水平"走出去"和高质量"引进来"、着力完善商务区核心CBD规划和城市更新工作机制），对商务区工作提出了新的部署和要求。

11月6日　虹桥国际开放枢纽建设分论坛暨2023虹桥HUB大会在国家会展中心（上海）举办。大会以"深化区域协同创新　赋能虹桥国际开放枢纽高质量发展"为主题，在承继前两年成功举办经验的基础上，紧扣一体化、高质量、国际化和开放创新，系统演绎了在加快推进长三角一体化发展新形势新要求下，科技创新与区域协同的双向赋能，加快建设现代化产业体系与加速推进区域产业协同的双向促进，高水平开放与深化区域协同的双向成就，深度诠释进博主旨，持续放大进博会溢出效应。会议由华源副市长主持，市委副书记、市长龚正，商务部党组成员、副部长盛秋平，国家发展改革委党组成员郭兰峰，以及中国银行行长刘金等分别致辞。2014年诺贝尔经济学奖得主、图卢兹经济学院经济学教授兼名誉院长让·梯若尔，亚洲基础设施投资银行行长兼董事会主席金立群，国务院发展研究中心副主任隆国强、香港中文大学（深圳）前海国际事务研究院院长郑永年等分别做主旨演讲。

11月25日　2023年大虹桥企业家论坛在国家会展中心（上海）召开。本次论坛由虹桥国际中央商务区管委会与长江商学院联合举办，以"'虹'扬企业家精神，迈向新商业文明"为主题，紧扣一体化、高质量、国际化，高水平推动商务区建设，汇集国际国内成就卓著的各界企业家代表和专家学者800余人齐聚虹桥，以虹桥实践实际行动书写放大进博会溢出效应，扩大投资促进规模能级，落实党中央、国务院《关于促进民营经济发展壮大的意见》文件精神。

附录2　国家发展改革委《关于推动虹桥国际开放枢纽进一步提升能级的若干政策措施》

近年来，长三角地区四省（市）和有关部门按照党中央、国务院决策部署，深入贯彻落实《虹桥国际开放枢纽建设总体方案》，"一核两带"功能布局初步形成，高端商务、会展、交通功能持续提升，科创产业融合日益深化。为深入贯彻党的二十大精神，推动虹桥国际开放枢纽进一步提升能级，增强国内国际两个市场两种资源联动效应，积极服务构建新发展格局，制定以下政策措施。

一、强化虹桥商务区核心功能

大力发展高能级总部经济、高流量贸易经济、高端化服务经济、高层次会展经济，加快打造功能复合型国际化中央商务区、国际贸易中心新平台。

（一）支持虹桥商务区打造"丝路电商"合作先行区辐射引领区，率先与相关国家合作试点国际高标准电子商务规则，探索互利共赢的合作新模式。

（二）支持虹桥商务区引进更多贸易促进机构、商会协会等国际经贸组织功能性机构落地，依托全球数字贸易港加快培育发展数字内容分发、知识产权交易等知识密集型服务贸易。

（三）支持虹桥商务区内符合条件的企业率先试点跨国公司本外币一体化资金池政策，允许主办企业在一定额度内购汇，允许跨国公司在境内办理境外成员企业本外币境外集中收付业务，赋予企业更多资金汇兑自主权。

（四）支持虹桥商务区内的社会办医疗机构依规定配置甲类大型医用设备。

（五）虹桥商务区内符合条件的医疗机构可按照《临床急需药品临时进口工作方案》相关规定申请临时进口临床急需的少量药品。

二、促进"一核两带"融合发展

尊重市场规律，强化优势对接，统筹区域空间，优化功能布局，支持以"一核"辐射带动北向、南向拓展带，以"两带"特色功能支撑服务"一核"，依托毗邻区、产业链、创新圈、交通网，支持苏州、嘉兴打造长三角城市群重要节点城市，共同打造具有全球影响力的国际开放枢纽。

（六）推动位于虹桥商务区和北向、南向拓展带的全国重点实验室协同开展基础研究和技术攻关，构建高水平区域创新网络。

（七）按照《高新技术企业认定管理办法》，落实国家高新技术企业在虹桥国际开放枢纽区域内互认，支持高新技术企业自由流动。

（八）推进虹桥国际开放枢纽区域内智能网联汽车测试牌照和测试结果互认互通，支持在虹桥—昆山—相城、嘉昆太协同创新圈等区域构建智能网联汽车道路测试区，率先开放跨省市道路测试。

（九）支持将在虹桥商务区实施的国际人才管理改革试点等政策推广到虹桥国际开放枢纽全域。

（十）对虹桥国际开放枢纽区域内纳入当地重点扶持产业目录企业聘用的外国"高精尖缺"人才，按规定提供签证、工作许可、居留许可等方面便利服务。

（十一）在不直接涉及公共安全和人民群众生命健康且风险可控的领域，探索建立虹桥国际开放枢纽国际职业资格证书认可清单制度，对部分需持证上岗的职业，允许取得境外相应职业资格或公认的国际专业组织认证的国际人才，经能力水平认定或有关部门备案后上岗。

（十二）支持上海、苏州联动开展数字人民币试点，推动创新场景开放和应用互联互通。

（十三）支持上海确有需求且符合条件时申请在虹桥商务区设立综合保税区，拓展保税研发、保税维修、加工贸易等业务。支持嘉兴综合保税区在符合条件时申请扩区，并开展综合保税区高质量发展综合改革试点。支持虹桥国际开放枢纽内综合保税区联动发展。

（十四）支持太仓持续深化中德合作，推动建设中德（太仓）产业合作发展基地，打造对德合作新高地。支持苏州工业园区推进共建中新"国际化走廊"，不断拓展科技创新、绿色发展、数字经济、双向投资、金融与服务业等领域合作。

（十五）扩容升级国际互联网数据专用通道和"服贸通"数据专线，支持有需求的企业依法依规接入专用通道，助力服务贸易和数字经济健康快速发展。

（十六）支持在虹桥国际开放枢纽区域内探索医学检查检验结果互认共享制度，建立健全以患者为主索引的医疗数据共享方式和制度。

三、引领长三角更高质量一体化发展

加强服务长三角地区的功能平台建设，推动虹桥国际开放枢纽与合肥、芜湖等长三角地区城市联动发展，逐步实现资源共享、政策共通、平台共建，以协同开放提升整体实力，以功能升级促进区域合作，合力打造强劲活跃增长极的新引擎。

（十七）支持虹桥国际机场进一步加密城际空中快线，提升公务机运营服务质量。加强浦东国际机场与虹桥国际机场联动，更好满足虹桥国际开放枢纽对中远程国际航线的需求。加快嘉兴航空联运中心建设，提升航空货运保障能力。支持依托芜湖航空货运枢纽建设，打造服务长三角面向国际的航空服务业集聚区。

（十八）推进太仓港区远洋集装箱中转通道建设，用好联动接卸业务模式，鼓励发展铁水联运、江海联运和江海直达业务，打造虹桥综合交通枢纽功能拓展区。支持合肥高质量开行中欧班列，强化与沿海港口城市协同联动，发展海铁联运新通道。

（十九）支持共建跨区域轨道交通网，推动沪乍杭铁路等项目前期工作，加快实施沪苏通铁路二期、通苏嘉甬铁路、金山至平湖市域铁路等项目，提升节点城市枢纽功能。加快推进打通高速公路未贯通路段和拓宽瓶颈路段前期工作。

（二十）支持虹桥商务区为长三角地区开展招商引资、国际人才招引，以及设立城市展示中心、研发中心、营销公司、外事联络处等功能性机构预留空间、创造条件。支持在江苏、浙江、安徽举办中国国际进口博览会招商路演、供需对接等系列活动，指导支持地方参与相关展会、论坛工作。

（二十一）集聚全球创新要素，构建覆盖科技咨询、研发测试、科技金融、成果转移转化等全链条的科研服务体系，为长三角科技协同创新提供专业化服务。

（二十二）支持合肥国际金融后台服务基地建设，鼓励跨国公司和高新技术企业在基地设立研发中心，探索金融支持科创发展新模式，满足企业多元化融资需求。

（二十三）推动长三角生态绿色一体化示范区数据中心集群、芜湖数据中心集群优化算力布局，加强与国家超级计算昆山中心联动发展，积极承接长三角中心城市实时

性算力需求，并在探索完善数据基础制度方面先行先试。

（二十四）支持设立国家海外知识产权纠纷应对指导机构，建立海外知识产权纠纷指导专家库，围绕重点产业不断完善海外业务知识产权纠纷应对机制。以技术产权、文化创意等领域为切入口建立知识产权公允市场价格评估体系。

Chapter I High Quality Economic Growth

Section One Background Situation

2023 is the beginning year of fully implementing the spirit of the 20th National Congress of the Communist Party of China. China combines the effectiveness of policies with stimulating the vitality of business entities, form a strong driving force for promoting high-quality development, and promotes the effective improvement of quality and reasonable growth of quantity in the economy. China must make good use of policy space, find the right direction for development, and solidly promote high-quality economic development.

In 2023, the China's economy showed a trend of stabilization and recovery, returning to a normal operating track, and market expectations accelerated to improve. Consumption and production activities have returned to normal, consumption potential has gradually been released, the service industry is developing well, growth momentum continues to strengthen, and the pace of high-quality development is steady and strong. Data shows that in the first three quarters of 2023, China benefited from the rapid recovery of the service industry, with strong development of the industrial sector and a faster growth rate of added value in the service industry than the overall GDP growth. Global trade bottomed out and rebounded, and the Chinese economy demonstrated super resilience. With the improvement of residents' income, coupled with policy support and a rebound in consumer willingness, the driving effect of consumption on the economy continues to strengthen. Innovation momentum continues to empower economic growth, and the accelerated pace of green transformation will inject new impetus into China's economic development. Although the external environment is becoming more complex and severe, and domestic economic development is also facing pressure, the long-term fundamentals of China's economy have not changed. The characteristics of strong resilience, great potential, and abundant vitality have not changed, and the conditions supporting high-quality development have not changed. With the accumulation of positive factors promoting development, the economy is expected to continue to recover and improve.

Since 2018, the China International Import Expo have been successfully held six times. It relies on the advantages of China's large market and the functions of international procurement, investment promotion, cultural exchange, and open cooperation platforms, makes positive contributions to accelerating the construction of a new development pattern and promotes world economic development. The CIIE will accelerate the enhancement of its window function in building a new development pattern, and provides new opportunities for the world with China's new development; Fully use the platform role of promoting high-level opening up, and make the Chinese market a shared market for the world; Better provides global shared international public goods and services, promotes the construction of an open world economy, and enables win-win cooperation to benefit the world.

The Hongqiao International Open Hub is a major strategy of the central government to promote the integrated development of the Yangtze River Delta, and is also an important component of China's opening-up strategy. As the core area of the Hongqiao International Open Hub, the Hongqiao International Central Business District has further enhanced its "big business" function since the promulgation of the "Overall Plan" two years ago. Focusing on strengthening advantageous industries and expanding economic scale, the business district gathers a group of domestic and foreign high-level enterprises, institutions, and platforms, striving to reflect high-density, high-quality, high-yield, and high efficiency economic development. The function of the "Big Exhibition" is further strengthened, fully leveraging its platform advantages and spillover effects as a permanent venue for the China International Import Expo, accelerating the gathering of high-end international and domestic exhibitions and conferences, focusing on expanding the connotation of the exhibition industry, and promoting the "Big Exhibition" to become a strategic support for domestic and foreign enterprises to seize the global trade high ground. The "big transportation" function has been further strengthened, and the transportation connections inside and outside the business district have become more smooth, with flow and factor aggregation. The main urban

Chapter I　High Quality Economic Growth

Section One　Background Situation

clusters in the Yangtze River Delta, with Hongqiao Comprehensive Transportation Hub as the core, are becoming closer to international exchanges. The integrated development of comprehensive transportation is being promoted, and the "air rail intermodal transportation" products are being opened to most cities in Jiangsu, Zhejiang, and Anhui. The function of "big science and technology innovation" has been further strengthened, and the business district is focusing on advantageous industries, accelerating the gathering of market-oriented innovation entities, continuously enhancing the ability of scientific and technological innovation policy sources, gradually forming a cross regional innovation cooperation mechanism, and coupling and symbiosis between industrial development and scientific and technological innovation.

The Hongqiao International Central Business District is closely adhering to integration, high quality, and internationalization, focusing on both "bringing in" and "going out", further opening up the development and radiation sectors, improving the overall identity and core competitiveness. Accelerate the expansion of the "import" channel, focus on leveraging the advantages of world-class traffic entry, amplify the spillover effects of the CIIE, accelerate the layout of digital trade and service trade new blue oceans, build a preferred destination for high-energy trade entities, attract more international trade functional institutions to land, and accelerate the creation of the "Silk Road E-commerce" cooperation pilot zone and the national service trade innovation and development demonstration zone, Build import and export commodity distribution centers and import trade promotion innovation demonstration zones. Establish and improve a policy and service system for "going out", and implement a number of comprehensive service platforms such as Hongqiao Overseas Trade Center, Hongqiao International Business Talent Port, and Hongqiao International Central Legal District to support the internationalization of enterprises. Accelerate the development of productive service industry, and with professional and comprehensive service support, become an important channel and base for enterprises to enter overseas markets. Strengthen the functions of large science and technology innovation, large commerce, large exhibitions, and large transportation, develop a high-energy headquarters economy, a high flow trade economy, a high-end service economy, and a high-level exhibition economy, and make every effort to create a functional composite international central business district and a new platform for the international trade center, better serve the construction of a new development pattern, lay a foundation for high-level institutional opening up, and form a joint force of departmental and municipal coordination, regional coordination, and urban coordination, Promote the early implementation of reform measures, and more headquarters based and high-energy level enterprises will settle down early to help Hongqiao achieve high-quality development.

Section Three   Investment Attraction

Deeply implement the Hongqiao International Business Partner Program, strengthen the "1+1+4+X" joint investment promotion system, continue to maintain high frequency and accuracy in going global for investment promotion, accelerate the attraction and aggregation of high-end commercial elements from various headquarters enterprises, and establish the "Investment Hongqiao" brand.

I. Continuously deepening investment promotion for going global

The business district fully leverages the role of international business partners, gathers the joint efforts of the four districts to "go out" and attract talents. It has hosted about 20 entrepreneur roundtable events in Chengdu, Shenzhen, Beijing, Xiamen, Quanzhou, Haikou, Ningbo, Yantai, Shaoxing, Guangzhou, and Wuhan, and jointly introduced excellent domestic and foreign chain owners, "anchor" enterprises, and various headquarters enterprises. More than 300 enterprises have participated in the conference. After the conference, each district has established a dedicated person coordination mechanism to continuously track and coordinate projects. Among them, nearly 50 enterprises are in the process of coordination, negotiation, or have started construction, registration, and landing. Among them:

On March 31st, the Fujian Entrepreneur Roundtable on "Sharing the Opportunities of Hongqiao International Open Hub Construction" was held in Fuzhou. At the meeting, relevant leaders gave a detailed introduction to the national strategic empowerment of Hongqiao International Open Hub, Yangtze River Delta Integration, and CIIE, and drew a blueprint for the future development of Hongqiao. The relevant functional departments of the management committee made a theme promotion of "Sharing Hongqiao Opportunities and Creating a Better Future". The event attracted more than 30 enterprises to attend, covering fields such as digital economy, international trade, and high-end manufacturing. The attending entrepreneurs had enthusiastic exchanges with relevant leaders in the business district, Minhang, and Qingpu districts, opening a door for Fujian entrepreneurs to invest and develop their businesses.

On June 15th, the "Yangtze River Delta Entrepreneur Roundtable · Ningbo" was successfully held. The business district, as well as the Changning and Jiading areas, and nearly 30 entrepreneurs from Ningbo gathered together to discuss cooperation opportunities. In the strategic layout of the national Yangtze River Delta integration, the cooperation between Hongqiao and Ningbo can "mutually strengthen and empower each other", with enormous potential. At the meeting, the government and enterprises had face-to-face communication, and representatives of the enterprises were full of confidence in future cooperation. Nine enterprises expressed intentions to negotiate or invest.

On August 25th, the "Yangtze River Delta Entrepreneur Roundtable · Shaoxing" was successfully held, attracting more than 20 outstanding entrepreneurs from fields such as biopharmaceuticals, electronic information, and intelligent manufacturing to attend. Relevant leaders of the management committee gave speeches and theme introductions, while investment environments in the Minhang and Jiading districts were introduced. During the exchange and speech session, the attending entrepreneurs discussed their industries, business environment, policy support, and international development We had face-to-face communication with the government regarding the bottleneck issues we encountered.

On September 12th, the Shenzhen Entrepreneur Roundtable was successfully held. Comrades from the management committee shared the theme of sharing the opportunity of Hongqiao. Qingpu and Minhang districts respectively introduced their investment environments. The roundtable attracted more than 30 entrepreneurs from different fields such as artificial intelligence, aviation, metaverse, fashion consumption, and life and health to attend the conference. On site, they communicated and exchanged ideas with the government on industrial development, digital economy support policies, talent policies, and more.

II. Convene a series of high-energy investment promotion activities

On March 9, in order to promote the coordinated development of various areas in the Shanghai Hongqiao International Central Business District, the first "Hongqiao Finance and Economics Summit" was grandly held in the Jiading area of the Hongqiao International Central Business District with the theme of "turning rainbows into gold and building bridges for mutual benefit". At the event, the leaders of the business district stated in their speeches that the district will overcome the impact of the epidemic and maintain good development vitality in 2022. This year has started well, and the economic development has shown strong resilience. A large number of enterprises in the Yangtze River Delta and even across the country have established international business segments and research and development centers in business districts. At the same time, the Jiading area of the business district, which focuses on the development of innovative economy, has gathered a group of leading enterprises with innovative vitality. The main body of enterprises in the region has been consolidated, the innovation ecology has been continuously optimized, and talent services have been continuously upgraded, resulting in fruitful development. The relevant leaders of the Jiading area introduced the "Four Cities Construction" in Jiading, as well as the breakthroughs and progress made in the new energy vehicle industry cluster, high-end medical chips, online new economy, and other fields. He stated that the positioning of the Jiading area of the Hongqiao International Central Business District is to "open up Beihongqiao, innovate and lead the way", and Beihongqiao will transform major opportunities into regional development momentum. Cooperation is the key to mutual benefit and development. Jiading is an open, innovative, and inclusive urban area, and Beihongqiao is a rising land for investment and entrepreneurship. In this "Hongqiao Finance and Economics Summit", experts, scholars, and institutional executives from different fields gathered to express profound insights on digital development trends, corporate financial empowerment, and regional collaboration prospects. In addition, guests from Beihong Office, Quansi Meide, Bank of China Shanghai Branch and other units also shared their views and insights.

On May 25, in order to fully showcase the development momentum of the business district as a national strategic concentrated empowerment area, and to extend a warm invitation to investors at home and abroad to share the development opportunities of "Dahongqiao", the business district held the "Chaoyong Pujiang Investment Hongqiao 2023 Hongqiao International Central Business District Investment Promotion Conference" in the Changning area. Shanghai leaders and representatives of enterprises attended the event. At the event, the main leaders of the business district delivered a report on the development of the business district. The Changning area released projects for life and health characteristic industries. Relevant leaders from Shanghai unveiled the plaque for the Hongqiao International Economic Organization Cluster and issued certificates for newly recognized domestic headquarters enterprise representatives. Key industrial projects in each area were centrally signed to further strengthen economic scale, core functions, and economic density.

On October 12, the business district held a new phase of "Chao Yong Pu Jiang · Investment Hongqiao" and strategic empowerment new opportunities at the National Convention and Exhibition Center, opening up and leading a new highland-the 2023 Hongqiao International Central Business District Investment Promotion Conference. Shanghai leaders and representatives of enterprises attended the event. The main leaders of the business district gave a work report on "strategic empowerment of new opportunities and opening up to lead new heights". Relevant departments of the municipal government interpreted and released policies on "Several Policy Measures" and "Comprehensive Transportation Plan". The Jiading area released a special plan for "Shanghongqiao". The municipal government and relevant leaders of the business district awarded licenses to the productive internet service platform of the business district, The relevant leaders of the municipal government witnessed the centralized signing of contracts for key industrial projects in each district. The event comprehensively showcases the latest achievements and future development expectations of the business district in sharing high-quality development opportunities and helping to enhance the Yangtze River Delta region.

III. Continuously strengthening international empowerment and expanding Hongqiao's "circle of friends"

In terms of strengthening the international economic organization service cluster, Hongqiao Business District has accelerated policy optimization and functional agglomeration, continuously improved its international perspective, continuously improved the level of Hongqiao Overseas Trade Center, focused on building an international exchange and cooperation work network, and created a "quasi overseas" business environment. It has attracted 37 international trade and investment promotion institutions, including the Singapore Chinese Chamber of Commerce and the Swiss Center, to settle in Hongqiao Overseas Trade Center, Contact over 150 countries and regions.

Reorganize and form the 2023 Hongqiao International Business Partner and Hongqiao Investment Promotion Partner around international professional services, international financial investment, and other fields. The main criteria for identifying Hongqiao International Business Partners are internationally renowned service organizations and national level business associations, with a focus on strengthening international empowerment and brand leadership, and enhancing the international professional service level of the business district through key cooperative institutions; The focus of investment partners is to expand investment channels, search for key target enterprises around the industrial positioning of the business district, and do a good job of docking, negotiation, and landing. In 2023, the Hongqiao Business District further improved its investment promotion and cooperation mechanism, identifying a total of 16 institutions as Hongqiao International Business Partners and 35 institutions as Hongqiao Investment Promotion Partners, building a broad, multi-level, and precise partnership ecosystem.

Chapter II   International Central Business District

Section Four   Enhance the Level of Headquarter Economy

Deeply implement the "Rainbow Gathering" plan at the headquarters, continuously improve the policy system, make good use of the policies of the trade oriented enterprise headquarters and private enterprise headquarters in the business district, support the accelerated development of various headquarters enterprises, organize special investment promotion to grasp the increment and stabilize the stock, increase the introduction of trade oriented enterprise headquarters and private headquarters, and foreign R&D centers, and promote the application of foreign headquarters or R&D centers by McKinsey Food, Dun&Bradstreet, Hendrix, and Ruishige Medical, Carry out the recognition of trade oriented headquarters in 2023, adding 2 regional headquarters of multinational corporations, 4 foreign-funded research and development centers, and 4 foreign-invested companies. Actively implementing the requirements of "accelerating the construction of the Yangtze River Delta private enterprise headquarters cluster area", policies have been successively introduced around strengthening industry leading functions, supporting the international development of headquarters enterprises, supporting the introduction of international talents, and carrying out international business cooperation. A group of headquarters enterprises with certain leadership have been gathered, and 17 private enterprise headquarters in the business district have been newly cultivated.

We have successively introduced policy measures to support the development of domestic headquarters enterprises and trade oriented headquarters enterprises, and promoted the implementation and implementation of preferential policies. The facilitation policy for investment companies has come into effect, and Asia Investment (Shanghai) Private Equity Fund Management Co., Ltd. has been successfully established. Continuously optimizing facilitation measures such as fund utilization, cross-border trade, cross-border research and development, and personnel entry and exit for multinational corporations, the global resource allocation capability of headquarters enterprises continues to improve. At the same time, we will promote the continuous smoothness of the industrial chain, supply chain, and trade chain, and the functional advantages of the business district will continue to be amplified. More than 500 headquarters enterprises have been attracted, including 51 domestic headquarters enterprises recognized, covering key industries such as new energy, new consumption, and biopharmaceuticals. The comprehensive contribution of headquarters enterprises continues to increase.

From the perspective of enterprise investment scale, the annual total tax payment of 51 domestic headquarters enterprises is nearly 3.5 billion yuan, accounting for about 8.7% of the total tax revenue of the business district. It is an important growth point for the business district to focus on strengthening regional core functions and forming new vitality for economic development. From the perspective of industrial ecological layout, more than 70% of enterprises are highly matched with the industrial orientation of the business district, including new energy represented by Trina Solar, Jingke Energy, and Reshaped Energy, biopharmaceuticals represented by Lanwei Medical, Xiansheng Pharmaceutical, Yuyue Medical, and Huitai Medical, fashion consumption represented by Anta, Midea, Baiqiu, and Bosideng, as well as Gechuang Dongzhi and Guanglian Da The productive internet service industry and digital economy represented by Yuanqing Technology. With the accelerated formation of a distinctive industrial ecosystem, the development of emerging industries in business districts is showing a trend of coupling, symbiosis, agglomeration and upgrading.

From the perspective of coordinated development in the Yangtze River Delta, industrial linkage is becoming closer. By establishing its headquarters in Hongqiao and deploying its branches and production bases in the Yangtze River Delta, we aim to achieve a leap in energy levels; Or it could be that the group authorizes, manages, and R&D headquarters to settle in Hongqiao, aligning with Shanghai's advantages, and the industrial linkage development pattern of "headquarters+base" is becoming increasingly clear, gradually becoming a new path for the development of headquarters enterprises. In July, the Dahongqiao Photovoltaic Industry Alliance was established, and high-level headquarters such as Dongjian Shuneng and GCL Group accelerated the introduction. The business district has become a hot spot for the development of the headquarters economy chain.

In an effort to build a new highland of headquarters economy, the Business District, with precise policy support and business services, continues to expand its economic scale, strengthen its core functions, and increase its economic density. It continues to increase its support for enterprises to "go global", empowers headquarters enterprises to develop internationally, and speeds up the formation of international economic organization service clusters with Hongqiao international business partners relying on functional platforms such as the "the Belt and Road Comprehensive Service Center in Shanghai", Focusing on six major service functions, including information and information, financing platforms, professional services, project investment, talent services, and risk prevention, we strive to create a one-stop service window for enterprises to go global. In addition, the business district is accelerating the research and development of a policy service system for enterprises to go global, organizing a series of policy training and preaching activities, and providing strong support for the international development of enterprises to go global.

In attracting and cultivating high-level headquarters institutions, the business district continuously innovates investment promotion models, improves investment promotion efficiency, and enhances the attractiveness and influence of Hongqiao on enterprise investment by continuously holding "going out" entrepreneur roundtable meetings and "bringing in" high-level investment promotion activities, forming a brand effect of investment promotion, consolidating the joint efforts of the four districts to attract large and strong enterprises, and establishing a dedicated person docking mechanism for each district, We will continue to do a good job in project tracking and coordination, and nearly 50 companies are currently in talks or have started construction, registered and landed.

Section Five   Empowering the Digital New Economy

Starting from its own endowment advantages, the business district leverages its unique advantages, strengthens its "big science and technology innovation" function, and promotes collaborative innovation in the Yangtze River Delta. Relying on its superior economic and geographical location, as well as the clustering advantages of headquarters research and development centers, we aim to enhance the R&D and innovation strategy functions of enterprise headquarters, form a collaborative innovation platform for the Yangtze River Delta industry, and empower the high-quality development of the regional industrial chain. Continuously gathering innovative entities and promoting the improvement of innovation concentration in business districts. Relying on the grand platform of the CIIE, international enterprises are competing to release new products, technologies, and services, and multiple global medical innovation technologies have successfully landed in China. The construction of the Shanghai International Technology Trading Market has achieved remarkable results. Through the Yangtze River Delta technology market coordination and integration mechanism, it has linked 33 domestic technology transfer sub centers, more than 300 service institutions in the Yangtze River Delta, and 11 overseas sub centers. It has hosted and introduced 12 international large-scale technology transfer exhibition forums, hosted and hosted 51 scientific and technological achievement roadshows and matchmaking meetings, and released over 10,000 demand information online. It has successfully matched and achieved nearly 135 scientific and technological innovation cooperation projects, The collaborative network directly facilitated the transaction amount of international technology transfer projects to reach 1.1 billion yuan, and introduced multiple high-tech enterprises to settle in the business district. The Shanghai International Medical Technology Transformation and Innovation Center has signed a contract to promote the transformation of cutting-edge technology achievements both domestically and internationally.

Taking the implementation of the "Hongqiao International Online New Economy Ecological Park Planning and Construction Plan" as the starting point, we will focus on cultivating online new economy, stimulating new industrial momentum, deeply cultivating the field of online new economy, and steadily developing industrial digitization and digital industrialization. As of September 30th this year, more than 3 000 enterprises with considerable scale in the online new economy have gathered, with a total registered capital of over 15 billion yuan. A group of leading enterprises and unicorn enterprises represented by Ctrip, Pinduoduo, Lianying, Huace Navigation, Cloud Exhibition, Super Competition, etc., as well as a group of platform oriented enterprises represented by Yifei, such as Guoquan, Yangzhuoyuan, Zebra Zhixing, Xinyihui, Kuka Robotics, etc. have emerged A group of emerging enterprises represented by Tingdong Film have cultivated industrial development clusters in areas such as digital trade, intelligent connected vehicles, industrial internet, and digital content. The four major areas of Changning, Minhang, Qingpu, and Jiading within the scope of the business district actively guide their development, presenting a new situation of digital economy development with different focuses, advantageous cooperation, and good momentum. The business district has gathered over 14,000 scientific research and technology service industry enterprises, accounting for 17.5%, which is 3.4 times the city's average level. It has also gathered modern innovative pharmaceutical industry clusters represented by Xinda Biotechnology and Yunnan Baiyao, which integrate research and development, clinical practice, and service. Knowledge intensive industries such as digital content distribution and intellectual property trading have begun to take shape, forming distinctive features. The existing incubators such as Beidou Xihongqiao Base and Suhehui have been upgraded to carry out vertical and deep incubation. Famous multinational corporations such as Bosch and Unilever, as well as industry leaders such as Ctrip and iQiyi, are building professional incubators around their own industrial chains. The 7th China Innovation Challenge (Shanghai) Yangtze River Delta Regional Integration Development Special Competition and Annual Sharing Conference were successfully held, promoting the formation of a good atmosphere for innovation and entrepreneurship.

We will focus on building a digital characteristic industry cluster and accelerate the construction of a global digital trade port and a national digital service export base. Strengthen

Chapter II International Central Business District

Section Five Empowering the Digital New Economy

the construction of digital infrastructure. Continuously promote the construction of 5G demonstration zones, accelerate the implementation of industrial platforms and application scenarios such as Hongji Station encryption layout and artificial intelligence, build functional hub type high-level facilities that serve global data flow convergence, actively promote indoor distribution networks in key parks and characteristic buildings, and build a data port that connects to the world, is ubiquitous at high speed, and integrates intelligence. Create a digital industry ecosystem. Efforts will be made to introduce and cultivate leading online new economy enterprises in ten major fields: digital trade, digital exhibition, digital content, digital health, industrial internet, digital travel, metaverse, quantum information, big data, and aerospace information. Focusing on key directions such as integrated circuits, new displays, communication equipment, and intelligent hardware, we will accelerate the cultivation of a group of internationally competitive large enterprises and ecological leading enterprises with industrial chain control capabilities. Establishing a digital trade brand. Accelerate the construction of a group of digital trade brands with international genes and development potential, and attract the regional headquarters, research and development centers, delivery centers, and important platforms of multinational companies in the digital field to settle down. Give full play to the role of trade promotion agencies, increase the promotion of Hongqiao Digital Trade brand through exhibitions, summits, bilateral cooperation and other means, build overseas promotion channels, and continuously expand domestic and foreign influence.

Case 1: Suhehui Global Shared Economy Digital Trade Center and Suhehui Entrepreneurship Incubation Base are located in Building A and Building B, No. 633 Jinzhong Road, Changning District, in the core area of Shanghai Hongqiao North Airport Economic Park, with an area of 6,573 square meters. The incubation enterprise uses more than two-thirds of the total area of the base, and the base provides enterprises with entrepreneurship incubation related policies, finance and taxation, laws, investment and financing, human resources, incubation operations Professional services such as marketing promotion. Since May 2021, 211 incubated enterprises have landed. Has successively won awards such as Shanghai Zhongchuang Space, Shanghai Entrepreneurship College, Shanghai Science and Technology Entrepreneurship Nursery, and Shanghai Advanced Collective in Science and Technology Innovation and Entrepreneurship Services.

Case 2: Ctrip Smart Travel Industrial Park is a digital technology park created by Ctrip Group to meet the development trends and needs of the future travel industry, which is a gathering of enterprises related to the smart travel industry chain. The park focuses on areas such as smart transportation, smart tourism, smart business travel, and smart logistics, gathering high-quality innovative industries and talents to promote the upgrading and innovative development of the smart travel industry. The leading industry in the park is online tourism. Since its establishment, the park has fully supported the development of enterprises and provided professional services and solutions in various aspects. As of the end of October, the landing rate of Ctrip Smart Park has reached 70%, and the rental rate is as high as 100%.

The future business district will continue to optimize the innovation and entrepreneurship ecosystem, focusing on advantageous industries and categories, enhancing the core competitiveness and innovation capabilities of enterprises and research and development institutions, and enhancing the strategic ability of market-oriented technological innovation forces. At the same time, we will focus on policy and institutional breakthroughs, promote the creation of a platform for configuration innovation elements, build more high-quality cooperation platforms, and promote the creation of important carrier platforms such as international talent ports, technology trading functions, intellectual property protection centers, and global digital trade ports. We will continue to promote policy innovation, provide more convenient innovation elements and other supporting support, and better transform the value of human flow, logistics, and commercial flow into economic value and innovation value, Support enterprises to accelerate technological innovation and business innovation, and promote high-quality development of business districts.

Chapter III New International Trade Center Platform

Section One Silk Road E-commerce Cooperation Pilot Zone

On October 17th, the State Council issued a reply on the establishment of a "Silk Road E-commerce Cooperation Pilot Zone" in Shanghai. According to the "Plan on Creating a Pilot Zone for Silk Road E-commerce Cooperation in Shanghai" (hereinafter referred to as the "Plan"), it is clear to create a "Silk Road E-commerce" radiation leading zone in the Hongqiao International Central Business District.

I. The main content of the plan

The Plan focuses on prioritizing institutional openness, subject cultivation, and mechanism cooperation, accelerating the integration with international high standard economic and trade rules, exploring institutional and mechanism innovation, and expanding the opening-up of the e-commerce field to the outside world. The overall goal can be summarized as "four batches", that is, by 2025, to form a group of institutional open achievements with demonstrative and leading roles, gather a group of e-commerce operators with international competitiveness, create a group of regional carriers with unique characteristics, build a group of public service platforms that promote the common development of "Silk Road e-commerce" partner countries, make e-commerce transactions and international cooperation and exchange more active, and significantly enhance comprehensive service functions, To provide achievement support and practical experience for the development of "Silk Road e-commerce". Focusing on expanding the openness of the e-commerce field, creating a pioneering and experimental environment, and vigorously promoting international and regional exchanges and cooperation, a total of 19 specific tasks.

One is to expand the openness of the e-commerce field. There are a total of 7 tasks, including expanding international data services, implementing high standard trade facilitation measures, promoting the application of international standards for electronic documents, exploring cross-border interoperability of digital identity and electronic authentication, expanding cross-border e-commerce imports, promoting innovative development of cross-border e-commerce exports, and promoting cross-border RMB settlement of "Silk Road e-commerce". Propose the construction of a data transaction registration service system and an international data trading board, and participate in international standard cooperation for data circulation; Promote international trade cooperation through a single window, share and exchange customs clearance data, and support trade facilitation measures such as "one order, two reports"; Building a cross-border electronic invoice interoperability platform to support banks in using electronic invoices as import payment vouchers and promoting their use; Promote the domestic and cross-border use of electronic transferable records such as bills of lading and warehouse receipts; Support the establishment of a digital identity cross-border interoperability platform and explore the connection of cross-border service rules; Support the establishment of an electronic authentication service interoperability platform to meet the online exchange and verification needs of digital document businesses such as electronic contracts and electronic certificates of origin; Introduce and cultivate more high-quality goods based on the export demand of partner countries; Supporting various entities such as cross-border e-commerce enterprises, traditional foreign trade enterprises, and logistics enterprises to build overseas warehouses in various forms, and building comprehensive service platforms for overseas warehouses, among other pilot measures.

The second is to create a trial and error environment. There are a total of 6 tasks, including building a central functional area in the customs special supervision area of the Free Trade Zone and Lingang New Area, building a radiation leading area in the Hongqiao International Central Business District, establishing a global distribution and distribution center for cross-border e-commerce, cultivating and strengthening "Silk Road e-commerce"

Chapter III New International Trade Center Platform

Section One Silk Road E-commerce Cooperation Pilot Zone

enterprises, improving "Silk Road e-commerce" infrastructure, and creating an international talent gathering place. Propose to promote bonded display in customs special supervision areas, expand cross-border e-commerce models, and provide one-stop import services for partner country enterprises; Gathering partner countries for trade and investment promotion in the Hongqiao International Central Business District, organizing and carrying out activities such as cultural exchanges, trade docking, and product exhibitions for the Silk Road e-commerce; Establishing a global distribution center with multiple customs supervision functions in special customs supervision areas, and researching and exploring new customs supervision models for goods entering and exiting warehouses; Promote the aggregation and development of e-commerce platforms and professional service institutions, and build independent cross-border e-commerce stations; Improve the construction of e-commerce infrastructure such as warehousing, logistics, and payment, and establish a sound cross-border e-commerce settlement system; Optimize and improve the scope of key institutions for talent introduction in the field of e-commerce, and provide preliminary measures such as facilitating the application for multi-year work permits and work-related residence permits for outstanding foreign e-commerce talents.

Thirdly, we will vigorously promote international and regional exchanges and cooperation. There are a total of 6 tasks, including conducting think tank exchanges on "Silk Road E-commerce", promoting the application of digital technology in "Silk Road E-commerce", promoting research and exchange on "Silk Road E-commerce", facilitating e-commerce exchanges and cooperation with partner countries, promoting regional cooperation on "Silk Road E-commerce", and building an international service system for "Silk Road E-commerce". Propose to initiate the establishment of the "Silk Road E-commerce" International Think Tank Alliance to conduct research on cross-border e-commerce rules, industry docking, and intellectual property protection; Build a "Silk Road E-commerce" digital technology application center, promote the application of technologies such as cloud computing, blockchain, big data, Internet of Things, and digital twins, and carry out pilot work on the traceability of imported gemstones and gemstones; Establish a "Silk Road E-commerce" cooperative training center, and build an e-commerce talent training system that is coordinated by the government, universities, society, and enterprises; Establish a national pavilion that integrates functions such as goods, tourism, and cultural exhibitions, and hold a "Silk Road Cloud Product" themed consumption promotion activity; Promote cooperation among cross-border e-commerce public service platforms in the Yangtze River Delta region in areas such as customs clearance, logistics tracking, and enterprise consulting, and encourage cooperation among cross-border e-commerce industry associations in the Yangtze River Delta region; Build cross-border service platforms and overseas investment service platforms for the Silk Road e-commerce, and implement pilot measures such as full cycle and full chain services.

II. The advantages and characteristics of building a "Silk Road E-commerce" radiation leading area in the business district

Based on national strategies such as the integrated development of the Yangtze River Delta, the China International Import Expo, and the Hongqiao International Open Hub, the business district promotes the in-depth development of the Hongqiao Import Trade Promotion Innovation Demonstration Zone. More than half of the enterprises engage in trade with "Silk Road E-commerce" countries, forming a good foundation for using "Silk Road E-commerce" to promote new development patterns and high-quality development.

Internally connected and externally connected, the spillover effect of the CIIE is significant. Relying on the "6-day+365 day" year-round exhibition and sales platform, Hongqiao Pinhui and Greenland Global Commodity Trade Port have set up 36 sub centers nationwide, especially in the Yangtze River Delta; 63 national pavilions, including 19 national pavilions of "Silk Road E-commerce" partner countries; The operation of Hongqiao International Coffee Port and International Wine Cellar is orderly; Relying on the Hongqiao Bonded Logistics Center (B-type), we have successfully assisted the "Silk Road E-commerce" partner country's characteristic exhibits to enter the Chinese market through "post exhibition cross-border e-commerce". We have a good foundation in the distribution channels of "Silk Road E-commerce", the construction of national pavilions, and category clustering.

Service first, Chinese brands and enterprises have outstanding advantages in going global. The business district has gathered over 7,000 digital trade enterprises and over 500 headquarters enterprises, especially private headquarters such as Anta, Midea, Baoxiniao, and Yagor, which have settled their international business sectors in the business district, resulting in a high demand for investment and trade with the outside world. At the same time, relying on Shanghai "the Belt and Road" Comprehensive Service Center, Hongqiao International Business Talent Port, Hongqiao International Central Legal District, Intellectual Property Protection Center, RCEP Enterprise Service Consulting Station, Enterprise Internationalization Service Workstation and other platforms, the "going out" service matrix of enterprises has been formed. In particular, Hongqiao Overseas Trade Center has gathered the Shanghai Representative Office of the Silk Road International Chamber of Commerce, China Switzerland Center, Singapore Enterprise Center 37 overseas investment and trade promotion institutions, including French and Chinese economic and trade enterprises, connect international and domestic markets.

Optimize supporting facilities and demonstrate the comprehensive node function of trade circulation. The logistics system in the business district is well-established, gathering 174 express delivery enterprises such as Three Links and One Delivery, Debon, and SF Express. 12.7% of the country's and 80.3% of the city's goods are distributed through Hongqiao, a hub of the domestic circulation, providing professional services for trade and investment exchanges in the "Silk Road E commerce" countries.

III. Measures for the Business District to Participate in the Creation of a Pilot Zone for Silk Road E-commerce Cooperation

In order to deepen the promotion of the "Several Policy Measures for Further Upgrading the Energy Level of Hongqiao International Open Hub" and the "Plan for Creating a Pilot Zone for" Silk Road E-commerce "Cooperation in Shanghai", and to promote the construction of the Hongqiao International Central Business District as a radiating leading zone for "Silk Road E-commerce" cooperation that links the Yangtze River Delta, serves the whole country, and connects the international community, and to become an important carrier of Shanghai's "Silk Road E-commerce" cooperation pilot zone, The business district has formulated a three-year action plan for the Hongqiao International Central Business District to fully promote the "Silk Road E-commerce" cooperation pilot zone. By 2025, the year-on-year growth in import and export trade of "Silk Road E-commerce" partner countries in Hongqiao International

Central Business District will be significantly higher than the city's average level; Explore a one-stop service model for high-quality characteristic products and services from partner countries of "Silk Road E-commerce" to connect with the Chinese market, and form a professional exhibition and sales center for "Silk Road E-commerce", a national pavilion for "Silk Road E-commerce", and a model room for "Silk Road E-commerce" live streaming economy; Introduce and cultivate a group of leading enterprises and platforms that lead the development of "Silk Road e-commerce" and have the ability to integrate the industrial chain; We will make every effort to build an e-commerce ecosystem driven by consumption, create a business environment with international trade characteristics conducive to the development of "Silk Road E-commerce", and become a node gateway linking the Yangtze River Delta urban agglomeration and the "the Belt and Road" countries and a new highland of Shanghai International Trade Center. Focus on the following three aspects:

Continuously amplify the comprehensive effect of the CIIE. Relying on year-round exhibition and sales platforms such as Hongqiao Pinhui, we will promote the upgrading of the "Silk Road E-commerce" National Pavilion and professional exhibition and sales platforms, and add more sub centers to lead more regions to participate in "Silk Road E-commerce" cooperation. Vigorously developing the live streaming economy of "Silk Road e-commerce", for example, supporting Russian wine, New Zealand honey, Cambodia cashews, etc. to enter the domestic market through the Hongqiao Pinhui live streaming base. By relying on platforms such as Shanghai International Friendship City Port, we regularly organize national cultural exchanges, trade exchanges, and product exhibitions. Organize a "Silk Road Cloud Product" themed consumption promotion activity to build an e-commerce ecosystem driven by consumer demand.

Strengthen the focus on building professional service capabilities. Effectively leveraging the advantages of Hongqiao Overseas Trade Center, on the basis of gathering 37 international trade institutions and organizations, we will also introduce a group of trade institutions and organizations of "Silk Road E-commerce" partner countries. Accelerate the substantive implementation of a new round of international economic and trade agreements such as RCEP in business districts, establish RCEP enterprise service consulting stations, and take the lead in business districts in areas such as import market access, convenient customs clearance,

Chapter III　New International Trade Center Platform

Section One　Silk Road E-commerce Cooperation Pilot Zone

and personnel mobility. Encourage policy oriented and market-oriented financial institutions to provide financial services for "Silk Road e-commerce" trade transactions, overseas warehouse construction, cross-border trade, warehousing and logistics, etc. For example, reducing corporate risk through cross-border e-commerce policies and overseas investment insurance policies. Vigorously developing the productive service industry and implementing the cross-border e-commerce international talent training plan; Improve professional services such as legal, talent, intellectual property, and consulting support, comprehensively promote the internationalization transformation of domestic enterprises and the deep cultivation of domestic markets by multinational corporations, promote the efficient and convenient flow of high-end commercial elements such as information flow, capital flow, trade flow, and international talents, and become an important channel for local and Yangtze River Delta enterprises to expand the overseas market of "Silk Road e-commerce".

High quality promotion of digital transformation key platform construction. We will focus on building a digital technology application center for "Silk Road E-commerce", and explore the full traceability of key products in the "Silk Road E-commerce" business through the application of technologies such as blockchain, big models, big data, and the Internet of Things. We will also do a good job in verifying transaction authenticity, and form a demonstration in cross-border trade clearance, electronic invoices, risk monitoring, and other technologies. Support the Hongqiao Trade Digital Empowerment Center to promote the digital transformation of all aspects of trade, including research and development, manufacturing, cross-border customs clearance, logistics and warehousing, and empower small and medium-sized brands of "Silk Road e-commerce" enterprises to develop in the Chinese market.

Section Four Productive Internet Service Platform

In July, the General Office of the Shanghai Municipal People's Government issued several opinions on promoting the high-quality development of productive internet service platforms in the city, clarifying the promotion of Pudong New Area, Baoshan District, Putuo District, Lingang New Area, Hongqiao International Central Business District and other regions to create a new highland for the agglomeration and development of productive internet service platforms, promote the integrated development of "platform+park", and accelerate the agglomeration of productive internet service platforms. Under the guidance of the Municipal Commission of Commerce, the business district will work together with relevant units in the four districts to carry out map battles, coordinate and promote various work.

I. Development goals and priorities

By 2025, cultivate three or more leading platform enterprises with global influence, resource allocation, and innovation drive; Gathering more than 10 high growth enterprises with the ability to integrate industrial chains, supply chains, and value chains; Cultivate several digital system solutions and products that are miniaturized, rapid, lightweight, and precise; Strive for the landing of several national and municipal platforms, build a cluster of productive Internet service platforms characterized by digital transformation demonstration and professional services, and become a new highland for the construction of Shanghai International Trade Center, which links the Yangtze River Delta urban agglomeration and important cities along the "the Belt and Road".

We will focus on cultivating a number of benchmark digital transformation and professional service platforms, with serving the real economy as the core, improving the industrial ecology as the key, and optimizing the development environment as the key. We will build a demonstration hub for productive internet service platforms that connect the world, a spillover effect transformation center for the CIIE, and a promotion center for the "going out" of productive internet service platforms in the Yangtze River Delta. Radiation drives the "four districts", that is, the Minhang area focuses on legal services, talent services, digital health and other fields, with a focus on strengthening the aggregation of specialized digital service platforms. The Changning area focuses on laying out new tracks such as digital consumption, digital travel, and big data, and expanding the brand of digital commerce service platforms. The Qingpu area focuses on exhibition and trade, industrial internet, aerospace information, digital logistics and warehousing, and other fields, optimizing the functions of logistics and warehousing service platforms; The Jiading area focuses on artificial intelligence technology innovation and solidifies the characteristics of the technology innovation service platform.

II. Key measures

Develop implementation plans to accelerate the cultivation of application scenarios. The Implementation Plan for Creating a Demonstration Hub for Productive Internet Service Platforms in Hongqiao International Central Business District has been formulated, which clarifies the three year development goals, as well as 16 key tasks in four aspects: "supplementing elements and strengthening ecology, optimizing exhibition industry integration platforms, promoting platform element interaction and docking, and promoting platform+park integration development.". Focusing on digital transformation and professional services, combined with the core functions of "big transportation, big business, big exhibition, and big science and technology innovation" in the business district, cultivating application scenarios, such as guiding Hongqiao International Coffee Port to cooperate with Yitong to create an online trade platform, supporting cloud based exhibitions to use Alibaba Cloud computing, big data, and artificial intelligence technology to promote the digital transformation of the exhibition industry chain, Support the construction of a centralized procurement platform for Shanghai Hongqiao Digital Supply Chain Cluster with logistics and warehousing as its characteristics.

Sort out the first batch of 22 cultivation lists and several investment promotion lists to form a gradient development system. The first batch of 22 key cultivation enterprises, including 3 listed in the city level key cultivation list. From the perspective of industry category, there is one enterprise in the bulk commodity trading service platform; 1 industrial product e-commerce service platform enterprise; 11 digital transformation service platforms, covering fields such as digital architecture, pan semiconductors, smart logistics, fashion consumption, and digitalization of exhibitions; There are 9 professional service platform enterprises, including service platforms in the fields of law, foreign trade services, human resources, technology transactions, etc. From the perspective of development stage, there are 7 leading enterprises, 4 high growth enterprises, 8 potential enterprises, and 3 reserve enterprises. Guanglian Da is the top brand in the domestic digital architecture field, and Guoquan is a prefabricated vegetable head brand. From the perspective of platform influence, the focus is on cultivating platforms with international resource allocation capabilities. For example, Ctrip eBooking serves 1.2 million hotel partners worldwide, Zhenkunxing focuses on building its own platforms in North America, the European Union, and Southeast Asia markets, and InnoMatch has established overseas branches in multiple countries. At the same time, the business district has formed the first batch of 7 investment promotion lists through the "Entrepreneur Roundtable" going out activities, among which the Nori Shanghai International Headquarters project has entered the land acquisition process.

The focus is on promoting work around a group of park platforms, application scenarios, and institutional policies. One is to carry out the "One District, One Special" special action. Guide the four districts to combine their own functional positioning and industrial foundation to create a digital service highland with distinctive regional characteristics. Among them, Minhang District will strengthen the gathering of professional digital service productive internet service platforms, Changning District will expand the brand of digital commerce productive internet service platforms, Qingpu District will improve the functions of logistics and warehousing productive internet service platforms, and Jiading District will implement the characteristics of technological innovation productive internet service platforms, Accelerate the introduction of high-energy entities and industrial agglomeration. The second is to implement the "park+platform" empowerment plan. Cultivate a group of characteristic buildings and parks with leading enterprises as the core to gather the upstream and downstream industrial chain, focus on guiding park operators and leading enterprises to build digital service platforms, accelerate the formation of industrial ecology through digital empowerment, and create 3-4 "park+platforms" with display and concentration. Such as China Beidou Industrial Technology Innovation Industrial Park, Kangdelai Hongqiao International Innovative Medical Device Industrial Park, Hongqiao International Coffee Port, Hongqiao International Convention and Exhibition Industrial Park, etc. At the same time, actively participate in the development of industrial maps for municipal productive internet service platforms. The third is to continuously improve the policy and institutional innovation system. On the basis of the existing urban two-level support policies on functional platforms, bulk commodities, Internet plus producer services, etc., make good use of the municipal "1+X" support policies, increase support for the platform in combination with the adjustment and optimization of the new round of special funds in Hongqiao, and guide the four districts to introduce targeted industrial policies. The fourth is to increase publicity and strengthen attraction capabilities. At the "Chaochong Pujiang Investment Hongqiao" investment promotion conference, a number of key platforms were launched, and a series of special publicity reports such as typical cases were carried out. Carry out the "Entrepreneur Roundtable" going out activities in four districts, dynamically update the recruitment list, implement "one enterprise, one policy", and increase the introduction of key platforms.

III. Typical cases

The InnoMatch Global Technology Supply and Demand Docking Platform was established in August 2022, provided by Kexun Kehui (Shanghai) Technology Services Co., Ltd. for platform construction and operation, and supported by the National Technology Transfer East Center's technology transfer ecosystem. The platform takes the integration of industrial technology demand and technological achievements as the basic model, integrates global innovation elements such as technology, talent, services, and capital, enriches various business scenarios, improves the efficiency of technology supply and demand docking, and empowers offline technology achievement transformation business with the digitization of scientific and technological resources. The aim is to build a technology trading hub platform with global influence, forming a new growth pole for the digital economy in the field of science and technology.

As a digital building platform service provider, Guanglianda Technology Co., Ltd. has been focusing on the construction information industry for more than 20 years. Focusing on the business areas of the entire lifecycle of engineering projects, it provides professional applications in the construction engineering field as the core foundation support for all parties involved in the construction industry chain, as well as urban operations, finance, education, and other fields, with industrial big data as the core foundation A digital building full lifecycle solution that provides value-added services such as industrial chain finance.

Zhenkunxing Industrial Supermarket is a leading digital one-stop industrial product procurement and management service platform in China. Realize transparency, efficiency, and cost reduction in the industrial supply chain through a digital procurement and sales collaborative network. From management tools to business intelligence, provide standardized software operations services (SaaS) to help small and medium-sized enterprises quickly complete digital transformation. By utilizing IoT technology and data intelligence, we provide online monitoring, leasing, and maintenance services for general equipment, achieving intelligent management of factory materials.

Shanghai Heihu Technology Co., Ltd. is a technology company specializing in the field of industrial internet software. It provides manufacturing enterprises with an algorithm driven, flexible and configurable cloud based manufacturing collaboration platform, enabling real-time aggregation and collaboration of key production factors such as production, quality, materials, and equipment. The manufacturing cloud is online, and the upstream and downstream of the industrial chain are interconnected and efficient, helping manufacturing enterprises improve operational efficiency, quality, and flexible manufacturing capabilities, Flexibly and quickly respond to changing market demands.

Chapter IV The Sixth China International Import Expo

Section One Basic Overview

The 6th CIIE, in accordance with the overall requirement of "getting better and better", continues the theme of "sharing the future in the new era", actively leverages the functions of international procurement, investment promotion, cultural exchange, and open cooperation platforms, and has achieved fruitful results. The opening theme of the Hongqiao Forum has become more prominent, continuously contributing wisdom to building an open world economy. About 1 500 representatives from political, business, and international organizations from 154 countries, regions, and organizations gathered at the "Four Leaf Grass" exhibition. 72 countries and international organizations made appearances at the national exhibition, and 3,486 enterprises from 128 countries and regions participated in the enterprise exhibition, showcasing 442 representative debut new products, technologies, and services.

I. Anchoring the overall requirement of getting better and better, fully showcasing the style of CIIE in all aspects

China will always be an important opportunity for world development, firmly promoting high-level opening up, and continuously promoting economic globalization towards a more open, inclusive, inclusive, balanced, and win-win direction. The CIIE can accelerate the enhancement of its window function in building a new development pattern, and provide new opportunities for the world with China's new development; Fully leverage the platform role of promoting high-level opening up, and make the Chinese market a shared market for the world; Better provide global shared international public goods and services, help promote the construction of an open world economy, and enable win-win cooperation to benefit the world. New requirements have been put forward for the "three major positioning" of the CIIE, further pointing out the direction for the "better and better" CIIE.

Premier Li Qiang attended the opening ceremony and delivered a keynote speech, sharing several specific stories of China's entry into the World Expo. He pointed out that economic globalization is a historical trend and the direction of people. Open cooperation and mutual benefit are the wisest and most natural choices. Premier Li Qiang visited the enterprise exhibition before the opening ceremony, and after the opening ceremony, he toured the museum together with foreign leaders present. Leaders from multiple countries and heads of international organizations delivered speeches on site. Vice Premier of the State Council He Lifeng presided over the opening ceremony.

The National Comprehensive Exhibition has become an important platform for showcasing comprehensive images. The national exhibition provides an important platform for countries with different levels of development to enhance exchanges, promote cooperation, and achieve mutual benefit, and has been highly appreciated by participating countries. Bahrain, Central Africa, Dominica, Gambia, Guinea Bissau, Honduras, Mali, Oman, Sierra Leone, Togo, Zimbabwe and other 11 countries participated in the exhibition for the first time. Each participating country actively promotes its investment environment, tourism resources, advantageous industries, and distinctive products, and holds nearly 200 colorful booth activities. With the theme of "New achievements of Chinese path to modernization provide new opportunities for world development", the China Pavilion focuses on the achievements of the 10th anniversary of the construction of the pilot free trade zone, highlights the latest achievements of China in promoting high-level opening up and high-quality development, and tells the world a wonderful story of "China is good, the world will be better". Honduras brings delicious coffee, cocoa, fruits, seafood, and more; Serbia uses multimedia to showcase scenes such as rivers and trees, allowing viewers to experience the beautiful scenery and unique lifestyle of the area; Finland takes the Nordic style of "Happy Home" as its theme, showcasing a unique and minimalist design with Finnish characteristics; The Fiji booth creatively recreates the beach scenery, refreshing visitors. Various exhibits and interactive

Chapter IV The Sixth China International Import Expo

Section One Basic Overview

items in the museum are widely welcomed by the audience and have become a popular check-in spot for visitors.

The enterprise's commercial exhibition features a gathering of merchants, numerous new products, and significant results. 3,486 companies from 128 countries and regions participated in the exhibition, of which 289 were from the Fortune Global 500 and industry leaders, the highest number in history. The six exhibition areas focus on high-quality development and high-quality life, with innovation leading as the common theme and technology empowerment becoming the mainstream trend. The exhibits on the booth have a strong sense of technology, novel themes, and a variety of highlights. 442 representative debut new products, technologies, and services will be showcased in a concentrated manner. The Innovation Incubation Zone has attracted over 300 innovation projects from 39 countries and regions to participate, exceeding the total of the previous two editions. Small and micro enterprises in the special zone actively participated in the selection activities, and won the "Most Market Potential Award" in four tracks including green and low-carbon, medical and health, digital economy, and innovative technology. For the first time, hold a cross-border entrepreneur tour, a special matchmaking meeting for small and medium-sized enterprises, and an on site transaction activity in the automotive exhibition area. Actively strengthening matchmaking and organizing nearly a hundred specialized matchmaking activities, and taking multiple measures to promote transactions, the "shopping cart" of buyers combines fireworks and technology. The African "sweet bread" Benin pineapple has made its debut in China, successfully signing large orders, and a large number of high-tech products have also been favored by professional audiences. It is expected to accelerate its entry into the Chinese market and help industrial upgrading. According to statistics, the intended transaction amount of this year's CIIE is 78.41 billion US dollars, an increase of 6.7% compared to the previous year.

The Hongqiao Forum continues to contribute wisdom to building an open world economy. The open theme is more prominent. Focusing on the theme of "Joining Hands to Promote Development, Opening up and Winning the Future", 22 sub forums conducted in-depth discussions around four areas: "Open Development", "Open Cooperation", "Open Innovation", and "Open Sharing"; The flagship report "World Open Report 2023" has been released, with the latest World Open Index released and a special seminar held. The lineup of speakers is strong. 8 guests at or above the vice national level, 68 at the provincial and ministerial level, 6 Nobel laureates and Turing Prize winners, 8 academicians (academic committee members) from both domestic and foreign sources, 22 well-known experts and scholars, and 118 executives from Fortune Global 500 and industry leading enterprises. There were a total of 345 speakers from various fields such as politics, business, and academia. Innovative functions promote investment in China. Organize a series of activities for the "Year of Investment in China", including a summit and Shanghai City Promotion Conference, a special investment promotion event for the Free Trade Zone, and a roundtable meeting for foreign-funded enterprises. Multiple sub forums will conduct in-depth discussions on promoting the business environment, promoting trade and investment docking, and amplifying the comprehensive effect of the forum. The participation of all parties has significantly increased, with over 8,000 attendees at the Hongqiao Forum, the highest in history. The United Nations Development Programme and other international organizations have collaborated to host sub forums, with a record high number.

Professional support and cultural exchange activities amplify the comprehensive effect of the exhibition. We will hold 122 supporting activities, including policy interpretation, contract coordination, investment promotion, research release, and product display. Among them, activities hosted by international organizations, relevant departments, local governments (trading groups), and central enterprises account for over 40%. Add supporting event group viewing services to attract more event guests to visit and negotiate at the exhibition booth, further strengthening the "exhibition promotion" function. The high-level events such as the China Time honored Brand Innovation and Development Conference, China International Petroleum Trade Conference, and the Yangtze River Delta G60 Science and Technology Innovation Corridor High Quality Development Conference have been held for multiple consecutive sessions, forming a strong brand effect. The trade and investment docking conference invited nearly 4,000 exhibitors to participate in negotiations and docking, achieving 416 cooperation intentions. Organized 96 centralized signing events and achieved over 600 cooperation intentions. 71 new product launch events were held, showcasing 142 cutting-edge technological products. 738 institutions participated in cultural exchange exhibitions, and Chinese and foreign performance groups brought over 200 booth activities and public welfare performances, all of which exceeded the level of previous years.

On site services highlight technological elements and green concepts. The convenience of personnel entering and dining has been greatly improved. Add 4 security verification points directly to the museum, and increase the number of electronic document verification channels by 45%. Multiple temporary dining areas have been added outside the original commercial plaza dining area for exhibitors and attendees to choose from nearby, alleviating the pressure of large passenger flow and improving dining satisfaction. Strengthening the application of artificial intelligence technology, adding robot inquiry and navigation services, integrating online inquiry and offline navigation, the novel and interesting "Digital Treasure" robot has become the "portable assistant" of exhibition guests, achieving a better navigation experience. The online procurement hall plays an important role, providing full process services such as information dissemination, trade matching, and itinerary arrangement. Professional visitors have posted procurement needs over 10,000 times, intelligently matching more than 220,000 exhibitors and more than 1.37 million exhibits. Carry out the "Zero Carbon Expo and Zero Plastic Expo 2.0" campaign, purchase 8 million kilowatt hours of green electricity through inter provincial green electricity trading, and achieve 100% green electricity exhibition for the first time. Encourage all parties to record their carbon footprint and lead the trend of "carbon neutrality" era. Develop relevant cultural and creative products based on hot topics such as low-carbon and environmental protection, and create a new carrier for the dissemination of green exhibition concepts.

II. Taking the CIIE as an opportunity to play the strongest tone of openness again

One is to promote the signing and landing of exhibits, creating greater market opportunities. At this year's CIIE, the Shanghai trading team strengthened precise docking and negotiation, and held 25 supporting activities including centralized signing, policy interpretation, and new product launch. The Shanghai trading group reached an intention purchase order of 9.5 billion US dollars, a year-on-year increase of 5.3%, ranking first among trading groups in various regions of the country for six consecutive years. The intended orders come from 35 countries and regions, and the procurement scope is further expanded. Shanghai continuously strengthens the "6 day+365 day" trading service platform function and promotes more CIIE exhibits to enter the Chinese market. For example, leveraging the role of a global commodity trading port platform, more than 6,000 products from China International Import Expo have been promoted to enter the circulation markets of 25 provinces and cities in China. For example, the Hongqiao International Central Business District Bonded Logistics Center (B-type) promotes the "exhibition transfer guarantee, exhibition transfer cross" business model, supporting participating enterprises to participate in the CIIE through bonded exhibition and sales models.

The second is to contribute the wisdom of Hongqiao and better connect with international high standard economic and trade rules. Premier Li Qiang emphasized in his keynote speech the need to "promote high-level institutional opening up of the Shanghai Pilot Free Trade Zone.". The Ministry of Commerce and the Shanghai Municipal Government jointly held the "Investment in China Year" Summit and Shanghai City Promotion Event. Guests such as Secretary General of the United Nations Conference on Trade and Development Greenspan and Executive Director of the United Nations International Trade Center Hamilton delivered speeches, providing insightful insights for Shanghai's high-level opening up. Shanghai held two sub forums in Pudong and Hongqiao, with Nobel laureate in economics Jean Thiel and Asian Infrastructure Investment Bank President and Chairman of the Board of Directors Jin Liqun, as well as academic experts and entrepreneurs, gathered together to provide suggestions for the future development of Pudong and Hongqiao. Pudong will take the lead in building an institutional system and regulatory model that is in line with international economic and trade rules. Hongqiao will continue to enhance the radiation of institutional innovation, the attractiveness of technology clusters, and the leading force of industrial upgrading.

The third is to strengthen technological integration and focus on gathering innovation momentum. This year's CIIE has 442 new products, technologies, and services showcased, with outstanding innovative features. The Innovation Incubation Zone has over 300 projects from 39 countries and regions participating in the exhibition. Among them, Shanghai actively supports three platform enterprises, including the Nordic Innovation Center, National

Technology Transfer Eastern Center, and Qidi Star, and has brought more than 80 high-quality projects from Nordic countries and regions such as Brazil and Australia to the stage. At the "Gathering Frontiers and Creating the Future" innovation incubation special event, the "Shanghai Science and Technology Innovation Policy Service Guide" was released to assist the incubation and development of innovative enterprises. While the National Convention and Exhibition Center gathers global products and technologies, Shanghai Lingang has gathered the world's "strongest brain" and conducted a "brainstorming" at the 6th World Top Scientists Forum. Also in the sixth edition, the two are connected by open cooperation and collaborative innovation.

The fourth is to expand practical cooperation and assist in a more inclusive and shared open world economy. Premier Li Qiang proposed in his keynote speech to "build a 'Silk Road E-commerce' cooperation pilot zone in Shanghai.". Shanghai is accelerating the docking of international high standard economic and trade rules, exploring institutional innovation, expanding the opening up of e-commerce, making every effort to build a new highland of international cooperation in the digital economy, and serving the high-quality development of the "the Belt and Road". At this year's CIIE, there were 120 foreign guest groups and over a hundred executives from Fortune Global 500 and industry leading enterprises, experiencing the popularity of CIIE and the temperature of Shanghai. Shanghai leaders met with foreign dignitaries and corporate executives who came to Shanghai to participate in the CIIE, actively promoting enterprises to make good use of the CIIE as an international public good and further promoting exchanges and cooperation in fields such as economy, trade, science and technology innovation, and education. In addition, the Shanghai Cultural Exchange Museum made its debut at the CIIE, showcasing the stories of 90 local and overseas high-quality products in 7 exhibition areas under the theme of "showcasing spillover effects through the debut of CIIE".

III. With the goal of striving for excellence, service guarantee takes a new step forward

From the perspective of exhibitors, focusing on intelligence, green and convenience, and ensuring high-quality services, we have achieved a safe and orderly exhibition and convenient and comfortable viewing. It can be summarized as "six firsts" and "six optimizations".

The "six firsts" mainly include: firstly, the establishment of a space computing platform for the CIIE, which accurately calculates and traces the real-time digital dynamics of the exhibition hall. It has been applied to real-time perception of pedestrian flow trends and abnormal crowd gathering alarms, providing new ideas and methods for emergency response. The second is the first introduction of convenient measures for franchising and approving animal and plant products and food products for exhibition. A total of 43 franchising approvals were processed at the 6th CIIE, with exhibits from 8 countries including Kiribati and Malta, covering a variety of food and agricultural products such as aquatic products and pineapples. Thirdly, for the first time, an all green electricity exhibition was held, and 8 million kilowatt hours of green electricity were purchased through inter provincial green electricity trading. In addition to achieving full green electricity exhibitions, during the 6th China International Import Expo, carbon emission data such as building operation and catering supply will also be accounted for. The purchase of carbon quotas will be adopted to neutralize greenhouse gas emissions from exhibitions and achieve zero carbon exhibition goals. The fourth is the establishment of a legal service guarantee group for the first time. Set up four on-site service points, including a foreign-related legal service center, mediation center, intellectual property comprehensive service center, and a one-stop service window for the Xihongqiao People's Court, and form a legal service volunteer team to provide legal consultation and other services more than 500 times. The fifth is the first time that the theme event of "Debut Night of CIIE" has been held in the exhibition hall, enriching the consumption scenes of CIIE and allowing exhibitors to fully enjoy the high-quality products of CIIE. The "Silk Road Cloud Products" e-commerce festival was launched online synchronously, and an exclusive live broadcast room for the "Silk Road Cloud Products" was opened. Activities such as check-in for the CIIE and cloud browsing exhibitions were also launched. Six is the first time that non reserved social vehicle designated drop off points have been set up in the parking lots around the National Convention and Exhibition Center, further tapping into parking resources and optimizing parking lot functions. Exhibitors who have not booked a vehicle can get off here and walk for 10 minutes to reach the exhibition hall.

The six optimizations mainly include: firstly, optimizing the process of document processing. This year, the certification process has been changed from series to parallel, and the processing time has been further compressed. Emergency certification can be completed within 24 hours at the earliest. At the same time, the scope and time of using electronic documents have been expanded, and exhibitors who have lost or forgotten their documents can easily apply online and quickly enter the museum. The second is to optimize transportation measures. Rail transit, chartered passenger transportation, ground buses, and taxis provide comprehensive support for the travel needs of exhibitors, with over 70% of intensive modes of transportation, of which rail transit accounts for about 45% and chartered passenger transportation accounts for about 30%. In addition, nearly 3,000 parking spaces are subject to flexible reservation, and large parking spaces are promptly adjusted to be open to small cars when remaining. The third is to optimize the guarantee of food supply. 53 fixed dining options, 7 temporary dining options, and 12 mobile dining cars provide exhibitors with a wide range of dining options. Promote moderate ordering and "small portions", and carry out self-discipline commitments

Chapter V   Collaborative Development of Four Sub Regions

Section One   Minhang District

I. The level of headquarters economy continues to improve

Focusing on the headquarters economy, taking proactive measures and precise investment attraction, further amplifying the policy empowerment effect of the upgraded version of Hongqiao International Open Hub, and doing a good job in supplementing, extending, upgrading, and building chains. We have innovatively established four specialized industry investment promotion business units, namely International Trade, Biomedical, Central Legal District, and New Track, all of which adopt a dual team leader responsibility system. One team leader is appointed by Nanhongqiao Group and relevant district committees and bureaus, relying on a professional and capable investment promotion team to carry out precise investment promotion and industrial cluster research, completing the transformation from industry wide investment promotion to industry chain investment promotion, and promoting the rapid improvement of investment promotion efficiency. Intensify investment promotion efforts for going global, visit enterprises, seek cooperation, and discuss development in key cities such as Beijing, Guangzhou, Shenzhen, Xiamen, Fuzhou, and Hefei, and promote the accelerated landing of key enterprises. Give full play to the advantages of grid services provided by six building workstations, establish a regular enterprise visit mechanism, demand resolution mechanism, and enterprise executives and talent care mechanism, and actively build a first-class business environment. Focusing on investment reception, transaction group guarantee, and urban environment guarantee, we have sorted

Chapter V Collaborative Development of Four Sub Regions

Section One Minhang District

out 12 key tasks to ensure the smooth hosting of the 6th CIIE, benchmarking and actively implementing them. Successfully held major events such as the "Core of Hongqiao, Future Comes" 2023 Hongqiao International Central Business District (Minhang Part) Enterprise Commendation Conference, and the "Minhang District Chaochong Pujiang Investment Shanghai Global Sharing Season -" Investment Minhang Monthly Sign "Investment Attraction Project Centralized Signing Ceremony, further stimulating regional development vitality.

II. More optimized industrial cluster layout

Give full play to the coordinated promotion mechanism of industrial project tackling, closely monitor key project nodes, proactively connect and provide cross disciplinary services, promote the rapid layout and landing of high-energy and leading headquarters projects, and basically form a good trend of accelerated agglomeration of key industries and vigorous construction. One is to further consolidate the biopharmaceutical industry cluster. Four ongoing projects, namely Weigao, Yunnan Baiyao, Xinda, and Neusoft, are urgently advancing their construction. Among them, Xinda, Weigao, and Yunnan Baiyao have achieved phased engineering results and successfully achieved structural topping out, which is of symbolic significance for the construction of the biopharmaceutical industry cluster. Three projects, namely Zhengda Tianqing, Xiansheng Diagnosis, and Xiansheng Pharmaceutical, have started construction. The preparatory work for the construction of the biopharmaceutical industry has been accelerated, and major projects such as Meide Na and Qianmai Medical have successfully signed and landed. The adjustment of the intended land use control regulations of Shiyao Group has been initiated, and the biopharmaceutical industry cluster has fully entered the "acceleration run". The second is to accelerate the layout of green and low-carbon new tracks such as photovoltaics. Iconic and leading leading enterprises such as Trina Solar, Jingke Energy, GCL Group, Sunshine Power, and Runyang New Energy have all rushed to land. Among them, Trina Solar has started construction and is focusing on building a new highland for the new energy industry with its headquarters economy. Thirdly, a group of major industrial projects represented by the digital economy industry should be promoted as soon as possible. Saiyi and Xinyiteng are accelerating the preliminary work of land transfer,

Nori Group has completed the equity transfer, and Mingzhi Electric has completed the land transfer. The commercial commercial land plot of the esports center and the first phase of Impression City have successfully achieved structural topping out, while the second phases of Zhuoran and Impression City have started construction. The Huishang Yangtze River Delta Headquarters Center has completed the signing, and the Qianwan Yuntai project has started smoothly, creating a research and development headquarters park for the Yangtze River Delta region.

III. Continuous deepening and expansion of trade functions

Further undertake and amplify the spillover effects of the CIIE, continuously strengthen the construction and operation of the Hongqiao Import Commodity Exhibition and Trading Center, and introduce nearly 100 new trading enterprises such as Jinshenbao and Macon, totaling 877. Successfully held events such as the Shanghai Silk Road E-commerce Cloud Shopping, Shanghai Coffee Industry Summit Forum, "Charming Cuba" Promotion Week, China Vietnam Enterprise Exchange Conference, and Japanese Liquor B2B Trade Fair, built a display and exchange platform, and expanded the influence of the trading center. Relying on the bonded logistics center (B-type), we aim to optimize and strengthen the international trade industry, actively explore customs facilitation measures and innovative policies, expand service radius through off zone bonded display and trading business, and establish a supervision model for off zone bonded display of Anman art. The Hongqiao Overseas Trade Center continues to promote the establishment of international "friend circles" for trade promotion institutions. In the first three quarters, a total of 13 trade and service institutions have been introduced, including the Russia China Business Center, the China Switzerland Center, the China Europe Cooperation Promotion Association, and the Singapore Center.

IV. High starting point planning to create the Hongqiao Qianwan area

The Qianwan area is located in the center of the Hongqiao International Central Business District, covering an area of 30 square kilometers. 10 square kilometers north of the Beiqing Highway is a key construction area in the near future, and it is the largest and most complete

Chapter V Collaborative Development of Four Sub Regions

Section One Minhang District

area of development in the Hongqiao International Central Business District. The plan is to build the Qianwan area into a core functional carrier area of the Hongqiao International Open Hub, facing world-class "reception halls" both domestically and internationally, leading a high-quality living model area for the people's city, serving the strong and active growth pole of the Yangtze River Delta and national development, forming a "10+10+10" regional development framework, and constructing a composite urban structure of "one bay, one core, four centers, and four axes". "Yiwan" refers to the C-shaped Qianwan Park formed by "Yiwan Yinsu River"; Build a 2 square kilometer Central Activity Zone (CAZ) vitality core around Qianwan Park; "Four Hearts" is a TOD development cluster formed around four rail transit stations; Extending outward from the central activity area, forming four urban axes connecting the surrounding areas.

Qianwan aims to create a charming urban image with the vision of "Infinite City, Future Qianwan". Qianwan will use five design strategies, including "infinite infiltration of water green space, infinite charm of urban image, infinite connectivity of three-dimensional transportation network, infinite vitality of public service facilities system, and infinite intelligence of digital city system," to depict a "city friendly, highly suitable, dense road network, transparent buildings, clear colors, and simple lines" urban blueprint, and create a new landmark with iconic regional significance in the west wing of Shanghai, Coordinate the six major functions of commerce, industry, ecology, public services, housing, and transportation, and combine urban renewal and refined management to enhance regional quality, including industrial level, transportation advantages, and urban quality. In terms of urban spatial quality, the ecological and public supporting infrastructure is good, and the 10 kilometer Wusong River Ecological Corridor has been basically completed. Multiple international schools highlight the advantages of international supporting services. Relying on Qianwan Park, we aim to create a landscape pattern of "one bay, two lakes, three zones, and eighteen scenic spots", connecting major public cultural and sports facilities such as Hongqiao International Cultural and Art Center, Hongqiao International Conference Center, and Hongqiao International Urban Cultural Exhibition Center. The park seamlessly integrates with the surrounding cities, fully constructing an ecological pattern of "five parts water, green, and five parts city" in the Qianwan area.

V. Accelerated improvement of professional service level

Relying on key functional platforms, we will accelerate the gathering and development of professional service industries that match the internationalization of the central business district, continuously improve the professional service system of the entire industry chain, and provide professional service support for various enterprises to go global. The Hongqiao International Central Legal District Legal Building has been launched, and special support policies have been introduced. 18 leading legal service institutions, including Beijing Weiheng, Guangxin Junda, Duan Heduan, and Zhongxia, have been introduced, bringing the total number to 58. Activate the Legal Building and Comprehensive Service Center, fully providing a "one-stop" government service and a "doorstep" legal service platform. Successfully held more than 20 events, including the 7th Emerging Legal Services Summit Forum, and the platform's attractiveness continues to increase. Develop special support policies to provide support in various aspects such as establishment fees, rental subsidies, talent protection, and opening local branches. Hongqiao Park, a human resources service industry park in Shanghai, China, has been recognized as a demonstration zone for innovative development in the city's service industry. It has introduced 56 new human resources enterprises, including Borje, and has achieved a cumulative tax revenue of 350 million yuan since its opening 18 months ago. Recognized as a demonstration zone for innovative development of the city's service industry, empowering enterprises to improve their human resources system. Holding events such as the first anniversary of the opening of Hongqiao Garden, and launching the "Hongqiao International Talent Reception Hall" during the 6th CIIE, we organized 8 leading human resources enterprises to participate in the CIIE, showcasing the advantages of Nanhongqiao International Talent Service. For the first time, we proposed the concept of international talent service and international talent pool at the CIIE, promoting international talent exchange.

Holding the first anniversary event of the opening of Hongqiao Park, we launched a list of 56 services in 6 categories and a "1+3 upgrade package" service, forming a comprehensive human resources service industry chain that integrates recruitment, training, talent evaluation, and human resources service outsourcing, accelerating the improvement of talent levels in

Chapter V   Collaborative Development of Four Sub Regions

Section One   Minhang District

the service area. The Enterprise Service Center of Hongqiao International Central Business District has expanded the scope of entry and exit processing based on regional positioning. The scope of foreign personnel's work visa processing has been expanded from Class A to Class B, helping to attract and gather talents. Actively promoting entry and exit policies to key enterprises and high-end foreign talents, opening up green channels for expert talents, formulating one person one plan, and successfully accepting permanent residency services for executives from enterprises such as Baihui Hospital and CDP. The construction of the "Global Technology Supply and Demand Docking Platform" in the Shanghai International Technology Trading Market has been awarded by the Municipal Productive Internet Service Platform, forming a global technology exhibition center and trading market with international leading role, promoting the gathering of technological elements for the development of high-end industries in Minhang, and accelerating industry incubation.

VI. Continuous deepening of planning optimization

To benchmark against the highest international standards and the best level, continuously and deeply plan high-quality planning schemes, and form a batch of excellent planning achievements. Basic construction of planning and implementation control system. The implementation platform for the overall control of the Qianwan area has achieved results in the formation of nine special topics, and efforts are being made to promote the submission, approval, and release of results. Through nine major systems including urban landscape, public service facilities, and underground space, construction standards and control requirements are determined to guide the work of the Qianwan area from development and construction to operation and maintenance, achieving comprehensive management throughout the entire lifecycle of "planning, construction, management, investment, operation, and maintenance". A batch of special plans have formed results. The green ecological professional plan has been approved by the district government, serving as the basis for the implementation of the plan in the creation of a green ecological urban area. Expert evaluation has been completed for special plans such as communication and gas, and results have been formed for special plans such as underground space, comprehensive transportation, water supply, water conservancy, sewage, and rainwater. The international plan collection for ecological space planning on both sides of the Wusong River has been orderly promoted, providing planning support for regional development and construction. Closely follow up on the evaluation and optimization of the urban rail transit network planning, and promote the rapid determination of the planning for the rail transit Line 25 and its branch lines. Steadily promoting urban landscape design and achievement display. Optimize the urban landscape plan. The third phase plan of Qianwan Park is basically stable, depicting the long history of the park from classical to future, laying the foundation for the park's urban atmosphere with intertwined urban and water in the Qianwan area, and creating an ecological green quality benchmark; Comparison and selection of bridge schemes for Qianwan Park to create a systematic and iconic bridge landscape; The green space plan for the Qianwan biopharmaceutical sector has achieved phased results, comprehensively shaping the urban expression and creating a green development and charming public space.

VII. The urban quality is steadily improving

Adhere to the integration of industry and city development, leverage the special bonds of Hongqiao International Open Hub to empower, promote the acceleration and quality of project construction, accelerate the layout of a number of urban supporting projects, and build a high-quality livable and business friendly environment. The construction of comprehensive transportation projects continues to advance. Key rail transit projects such as the western extension of Line 13 and the demonstration zone line are accelerating their construction. Xinghong West Road, Jiyou Road and other roads have been completed, and backbone roads such as Minbei Road have started construction smoothly. The surrounding road network structure of the region has been continuously improved, and the development of surrounding land parcels has been promoted simultaneously. The green water system project is accelerating its progress. According to the landscape pattern of "one bay, two lakes, three zones, and eighteen scenic spots", the ecological landmark Qianwan Park Phase I and Phase II will be constructed in an orderly and high standard manner, and the Phase III plan will form results. Accelerate the construction of projects such as Xinhong Small Watershed and Xiongwei River, and deepen research on design schemes for key quality improvement projects such as the Four Green Spaces and Beihengjing Ring Road. The supporting facilities

Chapter V Collaborative Development of Four Sub Regions

Section One Minhang District

for public services are being promoted in an orderly manner. 10-07 Kindergarten and Xinhong Police Station have started construction, 07-04 Primary School and 06-02 Kindergarten are accelerating their pre construction preparation work, and the research on the project plan for Huashi Normal University Junior High School is accelerating. The Beautiful Home project is being promoted as soon as possible. The main body of the comprehensive renovation project for beautiful homes such as Aibo Liuqi Village has been completed by the end of the year.

Chapter VI Landmark CBD Urban Renewal

Section One Develop a Landmark CBD Construction Plan

In order to firmly seize major strategic and historical opportunities such as the China International Import Expo, the integrated development of the Yangtze River Delta, and the construction of the Hongqiao International Open Hub, and to deeply implement the spirit of Secretary Chen Jining's research on the Hongqiao International Central Business District, the Business District has organized relevant units to establish joint teams based on the deepening of strategic understanding research, core area development and construction, and planning implementation evaluation, with urban renewal as the focus, Coordinate relevant units as the main coordinating body to comprehensively promote the research, formulation, and implementation of the iconic CBD construction plan for Hongqiao.

I. Background of plan development

The business district is the core functional carrier of the Hongqiao International Open Hub, and its iconic CBD serves as a benchmark area reflecting the high standards and international construction of the business district, as well as an important carrier of the core functions of the business district. Facing new tasks and requirements, it is of great strategic significance and practical necessity to study and formulate a landmark CBD construction plan for Hongqiao International Central Business District.

One is the strategic need based on the superposition and empowerment of multiple

Chapter VI Landmark CBD Urban Renewal

Section One Develop a Landmark CBD Construction Plan

national strategies. From the permanent host of the China International Import Expo to the vanguard of the integrated development of the Yangtze River Delta, and then to the "one core" of the Hongqiao International Open Hub construction, multiple national strategies gather to strongly empower the iconic CBD construction. In order to deeply implement the spirit of Secretary Chen Jining's research on the Hongqiao International Central Business District, based on the core functions of "big transportation, big business, big exhibition, and big science and technology innovation", and continuously develop traditional advantageous industries such as international trade and high-end service industry, we will make every effort to optimize and strengthen the headquarters economy and functional platform, and make the iconic CBD of Hongqiao International Central Business District a strategic node for Shanghai to coordinate and expand domestic demand and explore external markets, Make a demonstration in promoting the high-quality, integrated, and internationalized development of the Hongqiao International Central Business District. Through several years of efforts, building carriers have been developed into the most concentrated area of Grade A office carriers in Shanghai and even across the country. The industrial intensity and economic density have basically reached the level of famous CBDs at home and abroad. A group of distinctive industrial clusters and leading enterprises have been gathered, and the functions of serving "bringing in" and "going out" have been significantly improved. The iconic and display level has been greatly improved, and efforts have been made to build a more competitive and internationalized area A landmark CBD that is more recognizable, people-oriented, and more coordinated with the development of the four areas.

The second is to address the practical needs of addressing a series of bottlenecks that constrain development. Benchmarking against top domestic and international CBDs such as Paris LaCrosse, Manhattan in New York, Yokohama in Tokyo, and Lujiazui in Shanghai, their common features include: having world-class business and office carriers, high-level public service facilities, and iconic CBD images and block characteristics; It has both high-density economic activities, high-energy leading industries, and strong financial and professional service support. On the other hand, within the 3.7 square kilometers of the original core area, whether it is a commercial building carrier, or municipal supporting facilities such as roads, greenery, and water systems, after more than 10 years of hard work, the basic form and quality have been established, and the vast majority have been completed and put into operation. However, the gap from the iconic CBD is comprehensive, and there is a lot of room for improvement. Studying and formulating a landmark CBD plan will help to further clarify the functional layout within the business district, establish a sound and efficient functional system for transportation, exhibition, trade, service, consulting, science and technology innovation, etc; Beneficial for more accurate anchoring of spatial carriers and focusing on the leading role of iconic CBD demonstrations; It is conducive to boldly exploring reform and innovation experimental platforms, breaking down administrative barriers, exploring innovative regional coordinated development mechanisms, and achieving all-round open cooperation between regions.

II. Plan formation process

Starting from March 2023, taking the theme education of "Daxing Investigation and Research" as an opportunity, the business district will carry out research on the iconic CBD construction of Hongqiao International Central Business District in conjunction with relevant special work such as deepening strategic understanding research and core area urban renewal. During the process, functional companies (mainly Real Estate Hongqiao Company and South Hongqiao Company) and related enterprises (including operating real estate enterprises, historical legacy project real estate enterprises, enterprises that have acquired or partially acquired buildings, apartment operating enterprises, representatives of some settled enterprises, and related property management companies) within a 3.7 square kilometer area were discussed and exchanged, and on-site inspections were conducted Deeply understand and fully solicit opinions and suggestions related to the local street.

After sorting and summarizing, the iconic CBD construction will focus on further deepening research in the following six aspects: firstly, focusing on the serious lack of coverage of the rail transit network, uneven distribution of conventional public transportation, intensified congestion in hub areas, and imperfect chronic traffic guidance systems, research will propose strategic suggestions for smooth internal and external traffic circulation, further enhancing the image of hub portals; Secondly, focusing on the issues of insufficient business capabilities, fewer Fortune 500 companies, high vacancy rates and low quality

Chapter VI   Landmark CBD Urban Renewal

Section One   Develop a Landmark CBD Construction Plan

in commercial and office buildings, research proposes to promote the upgrading and transformation of existing vacancy formats and the resolution of historical legacy projects, promote headquarters aggregation and the introduction of high-end industrial functions, build top domestic "going out" professional service platforms, and enhance regional economic density and overall level; Thirdly, focusing on the lack of overall layout of exhibition activities, insufficient spillover benefits of exhibition functions, and the need to cultivate the exhibition ecosystem, the study proposes to use the National Convention and Exhibition Center as the core carrier to build the Hongqiao International Convention and Exhibition Industry Ecosystem, promote the development of the exhibition industry in the Yangtze River Delta, enhance international influence, and expand the core carrying area of the International Convention and Exhibition Capital; Fourthly, focusing on the problems of imbalanced residential structure, lack of high-energy public service facilities, and low quality of public spaces such as green water systems, research and propose innovative urban renewal mechanisms and formulate special funding policies to accelerate the comprehensive renovation and upgrading of green spaces, riverbanks, and central axes, encourage support for commercial and commercial renovation of rental housing, improve the quality of commercial districts, and gather popularity; The fifth is to focus on the shortcomings of market-oriented allocation of factors, public service guarantee, and refined urban management. It is proposed to gradually build a "digital rainbow bridge" that integrates national land space, industrial investment, construction timing, economic data, government services, and urban management, and create a first-class international business environment; Sixth, focusing on the limitations of the current institutional mechanisms in coordinating spatial planning, upgrading energy levels, financial investment, and public support, research and propose strategic suggestions for optimizing and adjusting the development and construction institutional mechanisms.

III. Main content of the plan

On the basis of actively drawing on the development experience of Shenzhen Qianhai Shenzhen Hong Kong Modern Service Industry Cooperation Zone and Beijing Economic and Technological Development Zone, and conducting comprehensive research and analysis, the "Hongqiao International Central Business District Iconic CBD Construction Plan" is formulated from four aspects: problem oriented, goal oriented, and result oriented, with a focus on selecting scope and development goals, comparative advantages and facing problems, key tasks and work measures, and work suggestions.

The content of the plan mainly involves: first, a re understanding of comparative advantages and facing problems. After more than ten years of development, construction, and functional building, the original core area of 3.7 square kilometers has been used as a built-up area. The industrial development carrier is relatively mature, with the support of the Hongqiao hub and the National Convention and Exhibition Center on the east and west sides. The basic conditions for the layout of core functions and advantageous industries are good, and the positioning and image have a certain influence. The development of the regional landmark CBD form has begun to take shape and is preliminarily taking shape. Based on the current basic conditions, benchmarking the development laws of international first-class CBD construction, adhering to problem orientation, demand orientation, goal orientation, and effect orientation, focusing on conducting preliminary research on the iconic CBD construction plan of Hongqiao from the perspectives of comparative advantages and facing problems. Among them, the comparative advantages of the iconic CBD construction in Hongqiao mainly include five major advantages: location advantage, transportation advantage, carrier advantage, business advantage, and flow advantage; The main challenges faced are the need to improve the level of enterprises and platforms, improve the transportation system, optimize the quality of carriers, and update the urban form.

The second is to further deepen the key tasks and work measures. Focusing on building the iconic CBD of Hongqiao into a strategic node for Shanghai to coordinate the expansion of domestic demand and the development of external markets, in conjunction with the Urban Renewal Special Team of the Municipal Planning and Resources Bureau, we will use the list of key urban renewal projects as a key incision to deeply explore the demands, difficulties, and pain points of urban renewal for 151 square kilometers, especially 3.7 square kilometers in the core area. We will comprehensively analyze the national spatial planning, industrial planning, development status, and future goals of the iconic CBD construction. During the process, actively liaise with municipal level departments such as the Municipal Development and Reform Commission and the Planning and Resources Bureau to carry out

Chapter VI   Landmark CBD Urban Renewal

Section One   Develop a Landmark CBD Construction Plan

multiple thematic studies, and strive for business guidance and policy support. At the same time, strengthen interaction and contact with real estate Hongqiao Company, Nanhongqiao Company, Xinhong Street, building workstations, and social enterprises, and solicit updates and policy demands. The final plan is formulated with five key tasks, including improving industrial functions, platform functions, comprehensive transportation, urban quality, recognition, and iconic construction. It comprehensively benchmarks the "high-quality, integrated, and internationalized" requirements of Hongqiao International Central Business District, proposes a new headquarters highland that matches the requirements of high-quality development, and an industrial competitiveness that matches the creation of active growth poles The cultivation and incubation functions that are commensurate with the iconic CBD status, the construction of a national level platform for Chinese enterprises to "go global", the creation of a number of nationally authorized and empowered functional platforms, the construction of an international talent introduction and cultivation sharing service platform, a portal hub with stronger external radiation capabilities, an internal circulation system with smooth capillaries, intelligent and humanized static traffic management, high-quality building carriers, and high-quality ecological spaces 15 work measures include high-quality urban management, creating iconic and vibrant squares, creating new distinctive consumer landmarks, and creating iconic night scene lighting.

The third is to promote linkage and deployment implementation. After fully considering the completion of the original 3.7 square kilometer core functional area, fully studying the relationship between 151 square kilometers and the construction scope of the iconic CBD, taking into account the future development positioning of the four areas, and drawing on international experience in CBD construction, the goal of the iconic CBD is to continuously improve core functions, output efficiency, urban quality, significantly enhance service radiation ability, and significantly enhance its iconic and recognizable features, Ultimately, a strong development cluster was formed with the four regional centers, achieving high-quality and integrated development. At the same time, fully leverage the industrial advantages of Donghongqiao, the strong momentum of Xihongqiao, the huge potential of Nanhongqiao, and the latecomer advantage of Beihongqiao, relying closely on the four areas, to achieve both staggered competition and win-win cooperation. Based on this, we will further refine and clarify the implementation path of supporting plans from the aspects of improving work mechanisms, strengthening policy support, and formulating action plans, including establishing a linkage mechanism between relevant departments, management committees, Minhang District, and municipal state-owned enterprise platform companies, and exploring market-oriented mechanisms. The management committee, in conjunction with relevant departments of the city, will study and solve key and difficult issues such as institutional mechanisms and the disposal of historical legacy projects, and support the inclusion of landmark CBD related to major infrastructure, institutional innovation, commercial layout, etc. in relevant special plans at the city level; Strengthen policy research around the main goals and key tasks, reserve and formulate a series of policy systems that can effectively solve prominent contradictions in key areas such as finance, urban renewal, investment, and talent, better play the role of the government in resource allocation, and promote the formation of effective policy support; Scientifically formulate specific action plans, coordinate and arrange annual key project plans, decompose major projects and key tasks related to iconic CBD construction, implement leading units and work responsibilities, form coordination and cooperation mechanisms among departments, and ensure that the program objectives are implemented as planned, efficiently, and with high quality.

Ⅳ. Implementation path of the plan

In order to accelerate the iconic CBD construction in the core area of Hongqiao International Central Business District, the management committee takes the lead in promoting urban renewal activities on existing construction land, guiding the redevelopment and utilization of inefficient land and idle space, enhancing regional functional connotation, spatial quality, comprehensive transportation, and municipal infrastructure, and strengthening the implementation of construction plans through the following five means:

Strengthen policy empowerment. To better promote the implementation of urban renewal in the iconic Central Business District, by strengthening policy empowerment and maximizing market participation, the following four tasks will be carried out: firstly, to cooperate with the Municipal Planning and Resources Bureau to deepen the formulation of planning land policies; The second is to collaborate with relevant industry regulatory departments such as

Chapter VI Landmark CBD Urban Renewal

Section One Develop a Landmark CBD Construction Plan

the Municipal Development and Reform Commission, Municipal Housing and Urban Rural Development Commission, and Municipal Green Environment Bureau to study the policies related to project approval, public green space compound utilization, construction and operation management process, and project investment and financing for core area renewal projects; Thirdly, connect with the property rights holders of 3.7 square kilometers and extensively solicit policy demands for urban renewal; The fourth is to analyze the problem of project bottlenecks and supplement and improve policy content.

Develop an update plan. Establish a "three teacher collaborative creation" team consisting of responsible planners, responsible architects, and responsible assessors. Led by the coordinating body, the team will work together with the urban renewal team in the business district to jointly promote the preparation of renewal plans. The focus will be on the recent key renewal areas and projects in the iconic central business district, and the content of the renewal plan will be refined, Formulate specific implementation plans (including pre evaluation, special research and preliminary plans, planning and implementation plans, interest balance plans, and a full lifecycle management list of public elements, etc.).

Strengthen urban design. Form a design team to participate in urban design work, study and develop urban design task books, and form a landmark CBD overall urban design plan (including functional layout, transportation system, green landscape, etc.).

Create a project list. By conducting research on stock resource allocation and renewal potential, clarifying the responsible parties and funding estimates of various renewal projects within the red line, strengthening the exploration of renewal projects for public areas outside the red line (public spaces, green landscapes, roads, etc.), subdividing project levels (city level, district level), and conducting investment estimates. At the same time, focus on mature renewal projects, clarify the implementation arrangements for renewal construction, and ensure steady progress of the projects in the near and long term.

Strengthen financial security. To ensure the implementation of urban renewal projects in the business district, based on the list of projects, corresponding funding support plans will be sorted out for different project types, clarifying the fundraising methods for various municipal and district level projects (public service facilities, infrastructure, etc.), and forming an overall investment and financing plan for urban renewal in the core area.

Chapter VII Refinement Management Demonstration Zone

Section One Building a First-class Urban Evironment

Building a first-class urban environment mainly includes street style, outdoor advertising, landscape lighting, comprehensive maintenance, public cultural services, residential communities, international communities, and diverse governance. The business district adheres to the main goals of health, comfort, and convenient living, with the basic principles of maintaining cleanliness, standardization, and coordination, establishing a good production, living, and ecological environment, and improving the quality of urban development. On the premise of meeting the basic living guarantee of residential communities, we will strengthen comprehensive governance and environmental construction, comprehensively improve the quality of living environment, further promote the innovation and upgrading of the "three beauties", create a batch of "one street, one scenery" in all aspects, shape urban expressions with all elements, and create readable, dynamic, technological, and warm urban public spaces. Implement the guidelines for the planning and construction of park cities in this city, improve the ecological system of green parks, enrich the connotation of "park+" and "+park" construction, and combine the characteristics of the business district to build and upgrade street gardens and pocket public parks with garden landscapes, recreational services, and cultural heritage, creating a park city surrounded by forests and interwoven greenways. Improve international education, healthcare, culture, and community commercial facilities, add characteristic supporting facilities such as international government affairs, international

Chapter VII Refinement Management Demonstration Zone

Section One Building a First-class Urban Evironment

business, and international life services, improve the level of international services, meet the needs of international talents, build consumption scenarios with international standards, and further enhance the sense of gain and happiness of the people.

I. "Panlong Tiandi" in Xujing Town

Panlong Town is a famous town in history, and it can be traced back to the Sui Dynasty 1,400 years ago. Panlong, which flourished due to water, was a typical prosperous water town in Jiangnan in the old days. At the beginning of the 21st century, against the backdrop of the high-speed construction of the Hongqiao area, the stagnant ancient town of Panlong gradually became a "scar" area in the city. Private construction and overuse were severe, and its "dirty, messy, and poor" image was incompatible with the surrounding rapidly developing urban environment. The historical landscape was severely damaged, and the urgency of renovation was strong. As one of the first urban village renovation projects in Shanghai, Panlong "Urban Village" in Xujing Town, Qingpu District, has been intertwined with small factories, workshops, warehouses, and residential buildings since then. Ancient buildings and streets have declined, and rivers are silted up and garbage can be seen everywhere. Through renovation, it has transformed into an ancient town with white walls and black tiles, soaring eaves and corners, and shining plants and trees. The atmosphere of Jiangnan is imbued with ancient charm, and modern shops are arranged in a row. Successful practice has proven that actively and steadily promoting the transformation of urban villages is conducive to eliminating the shortcomings of urban construction governance, improving the living environment conditions of urban and rural residents, and expanding domestic demand.

The "City Village" of Panlong is a municipal level historical and cultural protection area. In the early stage of project development, more than 30 experts, scholars, and local indigenous people were visited, and multiple consultants were hired to trace the origin and find the unique historical and cultural characteristics of Panlong, imprinting them in the entire planning and construction, and reproducing the style of Panlong Ancient Town. In the project development process, emphasis is placed on continuing the texture, spatial layout, street and alley scale, greening, cultural relics, and historical architecture of the ancient town. The historical connotation of the ancient town is deeply explored, and historical context scenes such as "Xianghua Bridge, Cross Street, and Cheng Family Ancestral Hall" are rebuilt. The ten scenic spots of the Panlong and the one phoenix ancient bridge in Jiulong are reinterpreted, integrating the traditional water town and ancient town culture of Jiangnan with new forms full of modern lifestyles, creating livable The characteristic town of living, working, and leisure has become a new landmark and business card of Qingpu's historical and cultural heritage.

II. "Habitat Garden" in Chengjiaqiao Street

Green is the background color of the ecological environment in Chengjiaqiao Street, and two habitat gardens are shining points on the brilliant "green chain". During the 14th Five Year Plan period, we will continue to focus on the construction goal of "a city with a thousand gardens", with a focus on promoting two new pocket parks, fully serving the high-quality development of the city and the high-quality life of the people.

Habitat garden refers to the integration of "habitat" and "garden", built around five principles: using local plants, eliminating invasive plants, enriching plant communities, reducing the use of pesticides and fertilizers, and providing auxiliary food, water sources, or shelters for urban wildlife. Centered around the vision of the "desirable ecological city" in Changning District, Chengjiaqiao Street actively explores a new path of modern environmental governance led by the government, diversified governance, and refined management, creating a new model of ecological civilization construction with high visibility. In June, two habitat gardens, "Rong Habitat Garden" in Nangong Community and "Yi Habitat Garden" in Chengqiao Second Village, were built, Integrating a park system with balanced layout, reasonable form, and distinctive features into the "fifteen minute community beautiful life circle" has alleviated the blind spots in the layout of park green spaces in the jurisdiction, and has been praised by residents.

Rong Habitat Garden is located on unnamed road 2222 Hongqiao Road, with a total area of approximately 950 square meters. After the renovation, closely combining the advantages of surrounding school and community resources, based on the characteristics of the habitat science popularization park, five core classrooms have been derived. "Co building and sharing a vibrant classroom" focuses on mobilizing the enthusiasm of all parties, participating in the

Chapter VII   Refinement Management Demonstration Zone

Section One   Building a First-class Urban Evironment

entire process of volunteer service, providing suggestions, and autonomous management, and sharing the achievements of garden construction; The "knowledge classroom that combines education and entertainment" focuses on the educational significance of habitat gardens, with carefully configured local plants providing water and food sources for local wildlife, allowing people to learn ecological knowledge and get close to nature in a relaxed and interesting park experience; The "Time Classroom for Growing Together" focuses on carrying out themed activities in the form of parent-child neighborhood visits and home school companionship, while also building a good relationship of harmonious coexistence between humans and nature; "The fun classroom of interactive experience" focuses on the immersive activity experience brought by interactive science popularization facilities; The "Secret Environment Classroom of Ecological Integration" focuses on the role of constructing a pure habitat environment in the entire garden ecology, driving block and point shaped habitats in the garden with sheet-like habitats, forming a sustainable organic ecosystem with self purification and restoration capabilities.

Yi Habitat Garden is located in Chengqiao Second Village and was originally a green area in the residential area. Before the renovation, the environment was poor and the biological species were relatively barren. After renovation, it covers a total area of 1,000 square meters and is the largest community habitat garden built in Changning District. On the basis of friendly care in Alzheimer's, "Yi Habitat Garden" takes the construction of an open elderly care community as an opportunity to explore the "three flowers", namely "flower fragrance prescription", "flower like youth", and "garden health care" as the core of medical and elderly care, to enhance the beauty of public spaces and the happiness index of residents. Simultaneously launching the "Companion Garden Plan" and carrying out a series of activities with the theme of companionship, attracting more elderly people to "step out of their homes" to participate, continuously paving the way for greenery at the doorstep of citizens, and turning the habitat garden into an important component of the 15 minute living circle.

Adhere to "bringing in" − bringing habitats into life, and "going out" − returning life to nature, adhere to building community habitat classrooms that are tailored to local conditions, incorporating education and entertainment, and sustainable development, and form samples of people's democratic practice throughout the process. Establish more accurate and visual community growth index monitoring, and explore universal community co construction models. Improve the multi-party strategic cooperation system. Focusing on carrier construction, coordinating the co construction of habitat gardens to form a joint force, continuously contributing to the improvement of community public space quality and the construction of a beautiful green home.

Chapter VIII First-Class International Business Environment

Section Two Construction of Cross-regional Enterprise Service Platform System

The Business District Enterprise Service Center has deeply implemented the requirements of the Municipal Party Committee and Municipal Government's deepening of the "One Network Service" reform, and vigorously improved the construction of government service capabilities. We are the first in the city to launch the "Government Butler" service station and link third-party resources, striving to establish the "City wide Office, Minhang Quick Office" government service brand, and continuously improve the experience, sense of achievement, and satisfaction of enterprise services.

I. Experience first, focus on specialization, and assist in one-stop service in the Yangtze River Delta region

Activate a new service hall, set up 10 undifferentiated comprehensive service windows, achieve 50 high-frequency matters such as enterprise registration in different regions through the Yangtze River Delta, and provide over 400 government services such as business registration and human resources with undifferentiated consultation and acceptance. We have successively introduced complaint windows for foreign-invested enterprises and RCEP enterprise service consulting windows, continuously responding to the needs of the construction of Hongqiao International Open Hub and the integrated development of the Yangtze River Delta.

Relying on the advantages of the core carrying area of the Hongqiao International Open Hub, we have developed a super self-service terminal that covers 40 counties and cities under the jurisdiction of eight cities in three provinces of the Yangtze River Delta. We are committed to building a one-stop government service "gas station" for the Hongqiao Business District and radiating to the Yangtze River Delta. We have provided 50 government services and served over 10,000 people to enterprises in the business district.

II. Deepen innovation, focus on specialization, and create a one-stop characteristic zone

Building a "Rainbow Bridge" to connect international and domestic resources, becoming the first in the city to link third-party resources, and opening a special service area in the government affairs hall to provide diverse characteristic services such as policy consultation, financial research and development, legal notarization, and talent, effectively responding to the personalized needs of enterprises.

Set up a dedicated service area for foreign nationals to apply for residence permits, work permits, visa renewals, and other related matters in China. In response to the actual situation of the backlog of foreign residence business during the epidemic lockdown period, the establishment of visa application zones for foreign-funded enterprises and international schools has resolved the problem of appointment and certificate application for key foreign enterprises and high-level foreign talents, promoted the further improvement of the business environment, and received unanimous praise from relevant enterprises and international schools. We have provided characteristic services to more than 10 enterprises in the region, and processed 2300 visa renewals, stay visas, work visas, reunion visas, and other services for 10 enterprises and 15 international schools.

III. Implementing practical policies to benefit enterprises, focusing on personalization, and launching the "Rainbow Steward" assistance model

Launch the first "Government Steward" service station in the city, establish a "Rainbow Steward" assistance team, implement pairing work with parks within the jurisdiction, establish work WeChat groups, regularly visit, streamline operational processes, answer difficult questions, and adopt a butler style service of "comprehensive one-on-one guidance, special policy face-to-face consultation, and project assistance point-to-point service" to provide enterprises with personalized services throughout their entire life cycle.

In order to reduce running gatherings and facilitate enterprise affairs, a "cloud window" for government services has been launched, which can be connected via video to the district government service center, district talent service center, street and town community affairs acceptance center, etc. In a non face-to-face, non-contact, and cloud based manner, the environment for enterprises and the public to work in different places is optimized, providing "zero distance" services of "cloud based meeting and online assistance", business registration 546 enterprise related matters such as equity transfer can be handled with zero movement through the "cloud window". Through the "on-site Rainbow Steward assistance+remote cloud window approval" service model, we have achieved exclusive "face-to-face" services throughout the entire process, and have provided services to nearly 2,000 enterprises more than 3,000 times.

Section Five   Construction of the Business District Talent Highland Core Area and Improvement of Talent Services

I. Policy formulation

Based on the opinions and suggestions of relevant departments of the city and district, as well as key enterprises in the business district, combined with the current situation and future planning of the business district industry, and in accordance with the requirements of the Municipal Talent Office, a preliminary plan for the construction of a talent highland in Hongqiao International Central Business District has been formed, and opinions have been solicited multiple times from relevant departments of the city and four districts. The plan revolves around the overall goal of building a leading talent development zone that leads international innovation and synergy in the Yangtze River Delta, based on the construction of the Hongqiao International Open Hub. Key construction measures are proposed from the aspects of clear strategic planning, optimization of spatial layout, implementation of talent projects, innovation platform carriers, creating a livable and business friendly environment for talents, and innovative culture.

Carry out research on the directory of scarce talents in business districts. According to the annual key work arrangement, we will carry out a survey of the current situation of key industry talents in the region and prepare a list of scarce talents. Based on questionnaire surveys, enterprise discussions, and other research results, we will form the "Catalogue of Key Industry Scarce Talents in Hongqiao International Central Business District" (hereinafter referred to as the "Catalogue"). The "Catalogue" will focus on the functional positioning and industrial development of the business district, covering the headquarters economy, service economy, trade economy, exhibition economy, etc Six key industries, including science and technology innovation economy and digital economy, have included 94 categories of scarce talents. Based on market orientation and research, the Catalogue accurately analyzes

Chapter VIII First-Class International Business Environment

Section Five Construction of the Business District Talent Highland Core Area and Improvement of Talent Services

and anticipates talent demand for key industries based on the Catalogue of Key Industries, and comprehensively constructs a talent demand database for key industries in the Business District. Research shows that the talent ecosystem in business districts is in a growth oriented development cycle, and the development environment is continuously improving; The overall development of the business district is characterized by a balanced talent development, gradually shifting towards a talent led cycle; Upgrade the talent structure in the business district, with a high proportion of highly educated, energetic, and high-income individuals; The gathering effect of economic talents in the headquarters of international business districts is emerging, forming a distinctive modern service industry gathering area; The international talent atmosphere is constantly heating up, and there is a strong demand for foreign talents and overseas returnees. The Catalogue also points out that there are still shortcomings in talent policies and services in the business district. The business district will continue to promote the construction of a talent highland, explore the formulation of talent policies, and actively promote the development of the talent service system.

II. Building functional platforms

Deepen the construction of Hongqiao International Business Talent Port. Guided by the platform system, we will strengthen the construction of the Hongqiao Industrial Park in Shanghai, China's Human Resources Service Industry Park, increase the attractiveness of human resources institutions, accelerate the introduction of professional, innovative, and international human resources institutions, and leverage the market-oriented function of the industrial park in talent introduction and services. By jointly organizing and assisting in promotion, we will hold events such as the Enterprise Digital Management Summit, Talent Policy Promotion, Talent Exchange, and Industrial Salon to continuously enhance the influence and brand agglomeration effect of the park. Promote the construction of Qingpu (Yangtze River Delta) digital human resources service base in Xihongqiao, and the construction of Beihongqiao talent station and other platforms in Beihongqiao.

III. Key event planning

(1) Gathering at Hongqiao, Creating the Future Together-The 2023 Hongqiao

International Central Business District Talent Development Conference was held

The Hongqiao International Central Business District is an important western wing of the new urban pattern of "East West Linkage" and "Two Wings Flying Together" in Shanghai. With the empowerment of a series of national strategies such as the integration of the Yangtze River Delta, the Import Expo, and the Hongqiao International Open Hub, it has gradually become a key link point leading the upgrading of the Yangtze River Delta and the international and domestic dual circulation. As an important carrier of national strategy, the business district is accelerating enterprise agglomeration, industrial development, and level upgrading, and has attracted and cultivated more than 500 headquarters type enterprises. "Nest building" followed by "Fenglai", the business district has become a gathering area for high-end talents in international operations, technological innovation, professional services, and other fields. In order to better support and implement national strategic requirements, play the "combination fist" of respecting and loving talents, and leverage the "strong magnetic field" effect of talent gathering from afar, the business district will take this event as an opportunity to further build itself into a model place for talents to lead the butterfly transformation A dream building place suitable for talent exhibitions, and a yearning place for connecting talents across the world through bridges.

At the event, the leaders of the business district pointed out in their speeches that Hongqiao needs to develop, and talent is the foundation. Hongqiao has always adhered to the principle of gathering talents from all over the world and utilizing them. The "strong magnetic field" effect of talent gathering has begun to emerge. The business district is building an international first-class talent development environment, continuously promoting the construction of nests to attract talents, creating an innovative cultural atmosphere of respecting talents and loving talents, developing a livable and business friendly ecology that is close to and pleasant to the far, and will continue to work together with relevant districts, Let the world's talents rush to Hongqiao, fall in love with Hongqiao, and take root in Hongqiao.

At the event, the Hongqiao International Central Business District Management Committee signed agreements with Minhang District, Changning District, Qingpu District, and Jiading District to create a community for talent development in the business district. The Hongqiao International Central Business District will coordinate and collaborate with

Chapter VIII First-Class International Business Environment

Section Five Construction of the Business District Talent Highland Core Area and Improvement of Talent Services

Minhang District, Changning District, Qingpu District, and Jiading District, in accordance with the "1+4" work pattern, to promote mutual recognition of talents and cross regional service sharing within the region, and achieve convenient and accurate connection between talents and policies, talents and services.

The Hongqiao International Central Business District Management Committee, Minhang District, Changning District, Qingpu District, and Jiading District promoted their characteristic talent policies and functional platforms at the conference, showcasing the combination of valuing and loving talents, and helping the business district to leverage the "strong magnetic field" effect of talent gathering that is close and far away. The characteristic measures of accelerating the internationalization, specialization, and innovative talent gathering in the business district encourage the headquarters of enterprises in the business district to attract talents, and provide special subsidies for talents up to 2 million yuan; For foreign talents, we actively promote the construction of national immigration policy practice bases, which can provide convenient policy services such as recommending foreign high-level talents in the business district to apply for permanent residency and multiple round trip commercial visas within three years. Qualified enterprise talents can apply for APEC business travel cards. At the same time, foreign employees and recent graduates from foreign universities can apply for work permits in the business district. The business district, in conjunction with relevant districts, provides service guarantees such as talent housing and household registration for talents working in the business district; Minhang District has issued the "Implementation Opinions on Supporting the Development of Legal Professional Service Industry Talents in Hongqiao International Central Legal Affairs Zone" to serve and ensure the high-level development of Hongqiao International Central Legal Affairs Zone; Changning District has released the "Special Support Policy for Renting Talent Apartments during the Transition Period for Overseas Chinese Returning to China", creating the most secure bridge for overseas talents to live in; Qingpu District is constructing the Shanghai Qingpu (Yangtze River Delta) Overseas Students Entrepreneurship Park in Xihongqiao, creating a new highland for overseas talents in Hongqiao; Jiading District implements a more inclusive policy system, builds a broader stage of the times, and constructs a more efficient service system in Beihongqiao, striving to create a livable and business friendly talent ecosystem with dedication and emotion.

At the meeting, the business district officially released the "Hongqiao International Central Business District Key Industry Shortage Talent Catalog". Based on a market-oriented approach, the Catalogue conducts research on 1,260 enterprises in the business district, covering approximately 90,000 employees. It accurately analyzes and predicts talent demand in a forward-looking manner, and comprehensively constructs a talent demand database for key industries in the business district. Focusing on six key industrial sectors including headquarters economy, service economy, trade economy, exhibition economy, science and technology innovation economy, and digital economy in the business district, 94 categories of scarce talents are included, covering a total of 45 scarce majors in 8 categories. Among them, the headquarters economy includes 11 types of talents in brand management, information management, etc; 15 types of talents in service economy, including financing business and patent consulting; Trade economy includes 14 types of talents in cross-border e-commerce management, smart supply chain, etc; Exhibition economy includes 12 types of talents in exhibition planning, foreign-related project operation, etc; Science and technology innovation economy includes 19 types of talents in biological research, energy research, etc; The digital economy includes 23 types of talents in artificial intelligence research and development, semiconductor chip research and development, etc.

At the conference, the three-year action plan for the construction of the Hongqiao Qianwan International Talent Community was released. According to the plan, within three years, the Qianwan region will make efforts in international talent gathering, innovation and industry demonstration, policy experimentation, and quality livable ecology, pressing the "acceleration key" for the model construction of the Qianwan international talent community.

Create a talent reception hall for Shanghai's "Gathering Talents from the Sea". In order to coordinate talent services in the Hongqiao International Central Business District, focus on the development of modern service industry talents, and accelerate the construction of a high-level talent highland in Shanghai, the Shanghai "Gathering Talents by Sea" Talent Reception Hall operates on the basis of "one platform and three centers", serving talents and enterprises in the area, and playing a role in policy promotion, government services, talent introduction, talent cultivation, talent exchange, project roadshows, and achievement exhibitions Main

Chapter VIII First-Class International Business Environment

Section Five   Construction of the Business District Talent Highland Core Area and Improvement of Talent Services

functions such as shared space.

The implementation of the Hongqiao International Talent Partner Program is an important measure for the business district to further leverage various professional resources and improve the talent service level of the business district. A total of 8 units were included in the first batch of the Hongqiao International Talent Partner Program, including East China Normal University, Shanghai Foreign Service, Wanbao Shenghua, KPMG, Imperial College Shanghai Alumni Association, and New York University Shanghai Alumni Association French/French speaking corporate center and Singapore Chinese Chamber of Commerce. The implementation of the Hongqiao International Talent Partner Program will help to enhance the talent development level of the Hongqiao International Central Business District, strengthen international talent aggregation and exchange in the Yangtze River Delta, and build the Hongqiao talent service brand.

At this conference, the 2023 Hongqiao Talent Recruitment Fair of "Gathering in Shanghai to Create the Future" was held simultaneously on the field. The job fair attracted a large number of job seekers and the scene was very popular. A total of 337 enterprises in Minhang, Changning, Qingpu, and Jiading districts have applied to participate, providing 1,525 positions and a talent demand of 4,279 people. 200 enterprises have participated in offline recruitment, providing 1,195 positions and a talent demand of 3,294 people. More than 5,000 people have participated in this job fair, and companies have received over 3,000 resumes. They are interested in hiring more than 700 people, effectively promoting the supply and demand matching between business district enterprises and global talents.

(2) Other activities

Contacting and planning talent brand activities with Minhang District, launching the "Hongqiao International Talent Reception Hall" into the CIIE, organizing human resources service trade and overseas enterprises to participate in the CIIE in Hongqiao Park, leveraging the platform of the CIIE to promote talent exchange between the business district and other regions at home and abroad, leading international innovation of talents, and establishing the Hongqiao talent brand. Organize the Hongqiao International Central Business District Exit and Entry Policy Promotion Event, introduce the policy resources of the business district for foreign talents to participating enterprises, combine with the characteristic services of the business district's Rainbow Steward, introduce the talent service characteristic brands, call on enterprises and the government to establish close contacts, jointly do a good job in talent work, and combine typical cases to do a good job in policy promotion for enterprises.

IV. Service work for foreign nationals

Provide excellent services for foreign talents in the business district. Research and promote the construction of an immigration policy practice base with the city's entry and exit department, and further enhance the functionality of the foreign talent service platform. Promote the recommendation of permanent residency for high-level foreign talents, provide a one-stop service of policy promotion, application acceptance, and material collection, and promote the expansion of the "single window" function of the Hongqiao International Central Business District Enterprise Service Center, providing convenience for foreign nationals in the field of government services.

图书在版编目(CIP)数据

2023上海虹桥国际中央商务区发展报告 / 上海虹桥国际中央商务区管理委员会编 .— 上海 ：上海社会科学院出版社，2024
ISBN 978-7-5520-4339-6

Ⅰ.①2… Ⅱ.①上… Ⅲ.①中央商业区—经济发展—研究报告—上海—2023 Ⅳ.①F727.51

中国国家版本馆CIP数据核字(2024)第051429号

2023上海虹桥国际中央商务区发展报告

编　　者：	上海虹桥国际中央商务区管理委员会
责任编辑：	熊　艳
封面设计：	黄婧昉
出版发行：	上海社会科学院出版社
	上海顺昌路622号　邮编200025
	电话总机021-63315947　销售热线021-53063735
	https://cbs.sass.org.cn　E-mail：sassp@sassp.cn
排　　版：	南京展望文化发展有限公司
印　　刷：	上海盛通时代印刷有限公司
开　　本：	787毫米×1092毫米　1/16
印　　张：	18.25
字　　数：	328千
版　　次：	2024年6月第1版　2024年6月第1次印刷

ISBN 978-7-5520-4339-6/F・760　　　　　　定价：158.00元

版权所有　翻印必究